AF608303

REVOLUTIONARY VISIONS

Jewish Life and Politics in Latin American Film

REVOLUTIONARY VISIONS

Jewish Life and Politics in Latin American Film

STEPHANIE PRIDGEON

UNIVERSITY OF TORONTO PRESS
Toronto Buffalo London

Toronto Buffalo London
utorontopress.com

ISBN 978-1-4875-0814-2 (cloth)
ISBN 978-1-4875-3765-4 (EPUB)
ISBN 978-1-4875-3764-7 (PDF)

Latinoamericana

Library and Archives Canada Cataloguing in Publication

Title: Revolutionary visions : Jewish life and politics in Latin American film / Stephanie Pridgeon.
Names: Pridgeon, Stephanie, 1986–, author.
Description: Series statement: Latinoamericana | Includes bibliographical references and index.
Identifiers: Canadiana (print) 20200308521 | Canadiana (ebook) 20200308661 | ISBN 9781487508142 (hardcover) | ISBN 9781487537654 (EPUB) | ISBN 9781487537647 (PDF)
Subjects: LCSH: Motion pictures – Latin America – History. | LCSH: Jews in motion pictures. | LCSH: Jews – Latin America – History – 20th century. | LCSH: Revolutions – Latin America – History – 20th century. | LCSH: Latin America – History – 20th century.
Classification: LCC PN1995.9.J46 2021 | DDC 791.43/65299240809046 – dc23

This book has been published with the assistance of Bates College, including Bates Faculty Development Funds.

University of Toronto Press acknowledges the financial assistance to its publishing program of the Canada Council for the Arts and the Ontario Arts Council, an agency of the Government of Ontario.

Canada Council for the Arts
Conseil des Arts du Canada

Funded by the Government of Canada
Financé par le gouvernement du Canada
Canada

Contents

Illustrations

Acknowledgments

This book would not have been possible without the support and inspiration of many people at various points in my personal and professional life. My fellow graduate students from my years at Emory and at Virginia continue to be some of my closest friends and interlocutors. One of my fondest memories from graduate school is watching Santiago Álvarez's short *Now!* in a seminar and seeing the very beginnings of Anne Garland Mahler's now robust, brilliant project on the Tricontinental and the Global South. My discussion of *El tigre saltó y mató pero morirá, morirá* in chapter 1 is indebted to her ideas on Álvarez, just as I owe a great deal to our friendship. Similarly, Nanci Buiza, in addition to her friendship and support, is a model scholar and teacher – a font of both knowledge and fun. Michelle Hulme-Lippert has been a delightful collaborator and interlocutor. Sandra Navarro's generosity, thoughtfulness, and insights into creepy children in film have enriched the way I approach film (chapter 4 in particular owes a great deal to listening to her ideas). The better half of my cohort of two, Sergio Gutiérrez Negrón, has inspired me through his creative and scholarly work. Fernando Esquivel Suárez and Ángel Díaz made graduate seminars fun and insightful. Nick Jones's work has been a constant source of inspiration, as have Erin Roark's thoughtfulness and intellectual boldness. Dominick Rolle always brings fun and stimulating conversation to the table. Tony Cella's friendship, from our time as undergraduates at College of Charleston to the University of Virginia to our brief overlap in Arizona, has been enriching and delightful. Stephen Silverstein is wonderful and has generously lent feedback and support to my work at various stages. I am thankful for Margaret Boyle's brilliance and thoughtfulness. Anne Stachura's intellectual exchange, loyalty, and sense of humour have made me feel at home in the academic world at moments during which I wouldn't have otherwise. David Francis has always made me belly laugh at witty (and often raunchy) things. Sarah Bogard has indulged me in everything from frivolous musings to difficult soul-searching conversations. Molly Angevine's friendship and creativity have been integral to this journey.

My colleagues at Bates College are to be thanked as constant sources of inspiration, guidance, and fun. For the intellectual community I have found in the Department of Spanish, I am especially grateful to María Gil Poisa who has always, always challenged me to think about films differently. I am grateful for Paqui López's support – from giving advice on teaching to reading article drafts – as well as the hospitality and generosity that she and Chris Eaton have offered me. Claudia Aburto Guzmán inspires me to innovate in both my research and teaching in ways I didn't think possible. David George and Elena Cueto Asín have been wonderful mentors throughout my time at Bates. On my very first day of new faculty orientation at Bates, Carolina González Valencia and I bonded over our shared love of Albertina Carri's filmmaking. Since that first conversation and in each one since then, she has made me appreciate film, art, and life in new ways. Jake Longaker and Renan Oliveira have always made sure that I rejoice in feriados. Nina Hagel's thoughts on identity politics have been a guiding inspiration to me. Anelise Shrout's wit and grit make working days brighter, as do Tiffany Salter's puns. I am thankful for Justine Wiesinger's helpful exchanges – in particular, her comments on the introduction to this book. Conversations with Jon Cavallero on film also strengthened the introductory chapter. Erica Rand's feedback helped me to broaden the scope and to raise the stakes of the questions I'm asking in this book. In Latin American Studies, Jacqueline Lyon, Baltasar Fra-Molinero, Sonja Pieck, Clarisa Pérez-Armendáriz, and Karen Melvin have been invaluable interlocutors for this project. I am grateful to Alice Doughty for organizing a weekly writing group, alongside Geneva Laurita, Geneviéve Robert, and Francis Eanes. From this group, heartfelt thanks are owed to José Villagrana for commenting on multiple drafts with both generosity and honesty. I am grateful for the mentorship and camaraderie of colleagues throughout campus, including Paul Schofield, Jonny Kurzfeld, See Won Byun, Mia Liu, Kristen Barnett, Lynn Mandeltort, Andrew Kennedy, Hamish Cameron, Myron Beasley, Colleen O'Loughlin, Leila Ben-Nasr, Myronn Hardy, Myra Wright, Therí Pickens, Elena Gambino, Áslaug Ásgeirsdóttir, Carla Abdo-Katsipis, Cody Eldredge, Laura Balladur, Kirk Read, Mary Rice-DeFosse, Raluca Cernahosci, Jakub Kazecki, Elizabeth Eames, Darby Ray, Josh Rubin, Alison Melnick Dyer, Logan Puck, Will d'Ambruoso, Dan Sanford, Melinda Plastas, Eric Dyer, Michael Sargent, Margaret Imber, and Nathan Faries. Hamza Abdi's and

Georgette Dumais's support have made working at Bates pleasant and easy. I would also like to thank the Language Associates with whom I have worked in the Spanish Department at Bates: Nicolás Correa, Saray Torrado Boada, Daniel Guarín, and Juan Poveda.

I owe the world to all of the people who have been my teachers and mentors over the years. Ever since Lola Colomina told me to read Liliana Heker in 2006 for my bachelor's essay, my mind has been consumed by stories of conflicted political, personal, and religious identifications. Before I started graduate school, Sarah Owens told me that she loved the profession because "you never stop learning," a maxim I recall frequently and with much joy. Much of my thinking about gender in literature owes greatly also to Nadia Avendaño and Alison Weber. Gustavo Pellón's guidance as my M.A. advisor and his course in literary theory were instrumental in my approach to scholarly writing. Conversations with Hazel Gold on memory, literary theory, and Jewish culture, along with her feedback on my writing, have made an indelible contribution to the scholar I am. It was Hazel who taught me that scholarly writing is a creative endeavour, and I continue to grow in my creativity as a result. Karen Stolley is the greatest academic cheerleader anyone could ask for; I aspire to provide students the kind of mentoring she has always offered me. Katherine Ostrom, my lovely co-author, panel co-organizer, generous editor, and friend, has indulged me in countless conversations that make it clearer to me why it matters to talk about how people tell their stories.

In the words of Jorge Luis Borges, "I've always imagined paradise would be a kind of library." Libraries are the best places and the people who work in them are my favourite kind of people. In particular, Phil MacLeod facilitated a great deal of my research at Emory and has continued to support me since then (especially in tracking down obscure DVDs). A "Jews in the Americas" visiting fellowship from the University of Florida's Price Judaica Libraries supported much of the research for this book; Kati Rac and Rebecca Jefferson made my time there enjoyable. Paul Losch was very helpful during both of my research trips to the University of Florida's Latin American Collection. At Bates, Christina Bell and Chris Schiff have been creative in scouring for resources. I am grateful to Perrin Lumbert for his efficiency and forgiveness with interlibrary loan books.

I have been fortunate to engage with colleagues from a variety of institutions. Like most junior scholars in Latin American cultural studies, I am indebted to Ignacio Sánchez Prado for his knowledge and generosity. Rebecca Janzen has been a wonderful interlocutor on this project – and I aspire to her level of productivity! Emily Hind has been a supportive voice, and I always delight in hearing her provocative ideas. I always look forward to hearing Inela Semilovic's interpretations of film. Ilana Dann Luna's work on gender in Mexican film is insightful, and I am so pleased to be able to cite her in the very first lines of this book. I am grateful to Erin Graff Zivin for her contributions to the field (and for the gatherings she organizes for femme/non-binary scholars at LASA). Cole Rizki's innovative work on memory and identity is both exemplary and inspirational. Exchanges with Dara Goldman, Marilyn Miller, Gina Malagold, and Daniela Goldfine have been invaluable to this project. I am grateful to Adriana Brodsky and Dalia Wassner for their leadership in Latin American Jewish Gender Studies.

I wish to thank the University of Toronto Press and Mark Thompson for ensuring that the review process was efficient and thorough. The anonymous reviewers' rigorous, thoughtful suggestions have helped this project enormously.

An earlier version of a portion of chapter 4 was previously published in *Revista de Estudios Hispánicos* 51.1 (2017), as "'Yo creo que terminé todas mis guerras': Friendship and Politics Between Jews and Non-Jews in Jeanine Meerapfel's *El amigo alemán*." A small portion of chapter 2 was published as a documentary review essay in *Latin American Research Review* 53.3 (2018), as "Here We Are to Build a Nation: Recent Jewish Latin American Documentaries."

My students in my short-term course and senior seminar on Jewish Latin American Film have all contributed substantively to my thinking about the subject. From these courses, I am especially grateful for the sustained conversations on the topic with Maya Seshan, Arianna Fano, and Helene Sudac. Beginning in my Spanish 202 course during my first semester at Bates, Nick Holmes, Madison Liistro, Carlie Gellert, Gee Torres, Olivia Fried, Cassidy Martin, Simone Messer, Lila Patinkin, Lily Patterson, Abby Decter, Meg Robinson, Holly Doyle, Jon Sheehan, and Tyler Fuller were part of a tight-knit group of students whom I taught over multiple semesters. Seeing the work that they are all doing now gives greater meaning to my teaching. My capstone advisees – Kevin Tejada, Claudia Krasnow, Marisol Hernández, Noah Lobozzo, Almira Akyatan, and Lexie Jamieson – have taught me as much as I have taught them. Working with Priscilla Guillén on gender and religion has been enriching, as have conversations with Abel Ramírez on film and immigration. I am thankful to my major and minor advisees: Alex Salazar, Claire MacKay, Hunter Quigg, Emma Bouchey, Joan Buse, Alex Cullen, Emily Pardi, Hannah Fitts, Elise Grossfeld, Lauren Hernández, Kati Cabral, Cameron Johnson, Alexa Jurgeleit, Mary Corcoran, Alex Cullen, Georgia Moses, Megan Seymour, Jordan Camarillo, Paige Rabb,

Ursula Rall, Bijou Kanyambo, Meghan Lapar, Rosie Crawford, and Julien Williamson. I am grateful for conversations with Carl Deakins, Oriana LoCicero, and Anna Setzer about their respective intellectual interests as well as for their contributions to courses they have taken with me. Madison Rozells's exemplary, painstaking work copyediting the manuscript was invaluable.

My family has been exceedingly patient with me as I have worked on this project over the years. I share some of the wit and the passionate nature of my father, Herb Pridgeon, and those shape my approach to scholarship and teaching. The irony is not lost on me that this book would never have been possible if I had heeded the rule always repeated to me by my mother, Jannell Martin, never to discuss religion and politics. I deeply appreciate her support of me and her constant willingness to talk about movies with me. On my mother's side, I am fortunate to be part of a small gaggle of socially minded, strong-willed women: my sister Jennifer, my cousins, and I grew up outspoken and curious. Having a twin sister means having an automatic best friend, and Jennifer has been a particularly great best friend. Beth Cavalier has been a fun thought partner for gender in a social science framework in addition to adding baby Grady to our family! My grandma, Janice McMahan, has always seemed very excited that I am writing a book. My aunt and uncle, Jo and Jim Stewart, have been wonderfully supportive. I am grateful for the love and support of my second family: Jane, Roland, Hunter, Ashley, and Grayson Robinson, and Debbie Liebowitz. I've thought quite often of my grandmother, Mary Lena Pridgeon, and her faith as I have reflected more on Christianity in working through this project. My aunt Jannyne was an artist and admirer of Edgar Degas. After she passed away, I came across a quote from Degas: "Art is not what you see but what you make others see." Jannyne made me see things I never would have seen otherwise; my life and my work owe greatly to her.

Joshua Robinson – in addition to being a brilliant scholar and talented professor who inspires me to be those things as well – is patient, supportive, compassionate, thoughtful, and generous. This book would not exist without him, Lucy, and Sancho.

Finally, I am grateful to the filmmakers and authors who have shared their stories with the world.

REVOLUTIONARY VISIONS

Jewish Life and Politics in Latin American Film

"A Place in the Economy of Being": Revolutionary Visions

In an interview about her 1993 film *Novia que te vea,* Jewish Costa Rican–Mexican filmmaker Guita Schyfter recalls saying to herself, "I'm going to set it in the 1960s when there is that great effervescence, right? In Mexico and in many other Latin American countries ... so that they can see that within the same Jewish community there are all the political positions possible" (Luna 131). Schyfter explains that with her film she wanted to demystify commonly held misconceptions in the early 1990s that Jews were homogeneously conservative and staunchly aligned with the State of Israel. "That great effervescence" refers to the myriad revolutionary and liberation movements across Latin America in the 1960s and early 1970s. The filmmaker's words draw attention to the absence of visible Jewish solidarity with these groups, a shortcoming she set out to correct. *Novia que te vea* ushered in a wave of Latin American films that revisit this historical period to portray the experiences of Jews with revolutionary politics in the countries and communities in which they were living. Throughout the twentieth century, as Schyfter declares here, "in Mexico and in many other Latin American countries" both national and regional politics were integral to Jewish life.

Schyfter's attempt to combat pervasive misconceptions about Jewish political affinities is by no means isolated. Jews have long sought to disentangle their identities from ascribed political identifications, and among Latin America's Jewish communities the struggle for accurate self-representation has a long history. In 1956 the Jewish Chilean historian Moisés Senderey – in what is considered to be "the first instance of a concerted effort to establish an official Jewish narrative" (Navarro-Rosenblatt 133) – takes to task the ubiquity with which in the 1920s non-Jews in Latin America referred to Jews as "*rusos*" (Russians). Senderey explains that this term, which is still in use today, attributes a Bolshevik political identification to all immigrant Jews: "The name 'ruso' – as people in many Latin American countries used to call Jews – took on a connotation of Bolshevism and that meant that Jews began to refer to themselves increasingly more as 'Hebrew,' 'Jewish,' 'Israeli' so as not to be associated with the dangerous name of 'ruso'" (72).[1] For many Latin American Jewish immigrants, the Russian Revolution was indeed an integral aspect of their political identifications. The historian Raanan Rein points out that in the 1930s Jews in Argentina were suspected of being Bolsheviks alongside the influx of leftist anarchist immigrants from Francoist Spain ("Los muchachos peronistas judíos" 40).[2] But many Jews had no desire to be identified in a way that presupposed Bolshevik political affinities, whether because they were not, in fact, Bolsheviks or because allegiance to Bolshevism could compromise their ability to go unnoticed in the countries to which they had immigrated. Yet, the conflation of "Jewish" with "Russian" has had the effect of connoting a Bolshevik tendency and speaks to how political allegiances are often misconstrued with no regard for the self-identifications of individual Jews themselves. Moreover, the slippage between the terms Senderey presents evokes the elasticity of the terms "Jew," "Judaism," and "Jewishness." One observes a similar elasticity of terms in the case of the representations that I analyse here, raising the question of what it means to be Jewish. In other words, Jewishness is often conflated with Judaism, and consequent assumptions about political beliefs stem from a monolithic understanding of any of these terms.

Revolutionary Visions disrupts this type of conflation as it closely examines how Jewishness is constructed and how political identifications orient individuals' negotiations of Jewishness. Recent, from 1993 to the present, Jewish cinematic production from throughout Latin America is rich with evidence of the many ways in which Jews affiliate and identify with disparate political organizations and movements. By "Jewish cinema" or "Jewish film" I am referring to films that depict Jewish identities and experiences. These films contest prevailing misconceptions about Jewish political beliefs and show that Jews have long been participants in the political spheres of their respective countries. Although scholars have examined the role of Jews in Latin American political history, so far Latin American cultural studies have not undertaken a careful reading of the filmic representations of Jewish experiences with revolutionary movements in this region.

To date, analyses of Latin American Jewish films focus overwhelmingly on narratives of identity and of cultural practices, almost entirely eschewing political beliefs and actions. Most such work either considers Jewish film production in Latin America as an analogue for the mainstream white middle-class experience in the age of neoliberalism and globalization, or emphasizes such issues as memory of the Holocaust, anti-Semitism, and stereotypes of Judaism (see Sheinin and Barr; Foster, "Latin American Jewish Cultural Production"; Rein and Tal). Nora Glickman and Ariana Huberman write that over the course of the twentieth century Jews "eventually became fully recognized" in Latin American film (1). Expanding on such accounts of Jewish Latin American cinema, I foreground the complexities of Jewish political identifications to argue that participation in revolutionary politics was an essential component of Jewish experiences in twentieth-century Latin America. In doing so, I am disrupting, first, understandings of Jewish life that do not take into account political action and, second, conceptions of Latin American politics that do not consider the importance of Jewish ethno-religious differences.

The participation of Jews in political action in Latin America was an important element of revolutionary culture, and it continues to be underrepresented or misrepresented within both Jewish communities and the broader cultural imaginary. With the rise and fall of Latin America's "Pink Tide" – or return of the left – in the years from 1998 to 2015, the revolutionary groups of the 1960s and 1970s have come to the fore of cultural production and political thought. These groups are often thought of as coming together through shared ideological investments. But the motivations for these shared investments have, for the most part, not taken into account the various interactions with Jewish migration and Jewish cultural avowal and disavowal. Put another way, existing critical analyses do not consider the following questions: To what extent was it possible to affiliate with revolutionary politics in Latin America *as a Jew*? What does it mean to do so *as a Jew*? And to what extent *did* Jews do so? Revising views of how these revolutionary groups coalesced and did or did not allow for Jewish self-identification recalibrates critical understandings of what it means to be Jewish in Latin America and of what it means to belong in revolutionary politics.

Film serves as a site of negotiation for Jewishness. In *The Wandering Signifier*, Erin Graff Zivin posits "Jew" as a signifier that takes on different valences according to changing circumstances. She explores "Jewishness" as a rhetorical construct deployed predominantly by non-Jews. In contrast, I use the term "Jewishness" to refer to self-identification as Jewish and/or a condition in which one recognizes Jewish beliefs and/or ethnicity as a category that bears on one's family or community identification. Thus, my usage of "Jewish film" refers to films that explicitly grapple with Jewish identities and experiences.

Revolutionary Visions argues that film often represents Jewish participation in 1960s and 1970s revolutionary movements in Latin America as an incomplete process of coming to belong, incomplete because of the complexities of both Jewish and revolutionary identifications. In this book I consider numerous examples from across Latin America, with a detailed focus on the following eight films released between 1993 and 2013: Guita Schyfter's *Novia que te vea* (*Like a Bride*, Mexico, 1993), Daniel Burman's *El abrazo partido* (*Lost Embrace*, Argentina, 2004), Cao Hamburger's *O ano em que meus pais saíram de férias* (*The Year My Parents Went on Vacation*, Brazil, 2006), David Blaustein's *Hacer patria* (*To Build a Homeland*, Argentina, 2007), Gonzalo Rodríguez Fábregas's *El barrio de los judíos* (*The Jewish Neighbourhood*, Uruguay, 2011), Jeanine Meerapfel's *El amigo alemán/Der deutsche Freund* (*My German Friend*, Argentina and Germany, 2012), Alejandro Jodorowsky's *La danza de la realidad* (*The Dance of Reality*, Chile, 2013), and Cintia Chamecki's *Danken got/Estamos aqui/Here We Are* (Brazil, 2013). These films explore the ways in which Jews came into contact with the political spheres of the Latin American countries to which their families immigrated. Further, their directors have engaged in self-representation as they grapple with these issues and project visions of their own diasporic histories in twentieth-century Latin America for a wide range of audiences, both Jewish and non-Jewish, around the world. The eight films examined here in detail are by filmmakers who either explicitly self-identify as Jewish or are from families that identified as such, with the possible exception of Gonzalo Rodríguez Fábregas (whose wife is Jewish although he himself is not). My attention is on the ways in which film directors who avow a Jewish identity depict their own communities and their own experiences.

Many of the films discussed here are available online via such platforms as Amazon, Vimeo, and YouTube. Over the past few decades, Jewish film festivals have gained popularity in places such as New York City, Copenhagen, Fairbanks, Alaska, and Charleston, West Virginia. According to the website jewishfilmfestivals.org, in 2016 there were 128 such events held worldwide, most of them in the United States. Films focused on Jewish topics from the Latin American region are often featured at these festivals. They tend to be popular attractions because stories of the Jewish condition – including cultural practices, rites of passage, narratives of exile and belonging – have points of resonance with Jewish communities everywhere. These films are also of wide interest because they recount uniquely local experiences, including the particularities of politics in this region, especially revolutionary politics.

My approach to Jewish Latin America on a regional scale rather than at the level of individual countries is in keeping with the critical model and premises that Walter Mignolo lays out in *The Idea of Latin America*.[3] These same premises also explain the very reasons why revolutionary and decolonization movements took hold of this entire region in the 1960s and 1970s, the period these films revisit. A significant corpus of recent work has directly sought to explore questions about points of contact between Latin American, Jewish, and national identities. *Revolutionary Visions* takes a regional approach to Latin American Jewish film especially because, first, there are experiences common to Jews in all of the countries throughout the region, and second, revolutionary politics at the time swept all of these countries. This book decentres the locations that have traditionally received the lion's share of scholarly attention on Latin American Jews and film scholarship, the most often studied city being Buenos Aires.[4] Consideration of a number of different cities and their Jewish neighbourhoods enables a broad analysis of Jewish life that examines ethnic, racial, and economic issues. Studying Jewish life on a regional scale acknowledges salient differences among Jewish communities, while at the same time working through common tensions and debates affecting Jews in the region as a whole in their differing processes of ideological and political self-identifications. To this end, I explore Latin American film with a watchful eye towards both comparing and contrasting countries, cities, and neighbourhoods in which Jews lived in the twentieth century. Although both the edited volume *Latin American Jewish Cultural Production* by Foster and colleagues and Glickman and Huberman's *Evolving Images* focus on Jewish Latin American culture throughout the region, *Revolutionary Visions* is the first monograph to discuss Jewish Latin American film on a regional scale.

Engagement with pan–Latin American revolutionary political movements pervades the films examined here, despite specificities between individual countries. As Graff Zivin points out, "Within the context of Latin America, not only do Jews possess distinct histories relative to their European and North American counterparts, but they also come to occupy new spaces within the cultural landscape on a symbolic level" (*The Wandering Signifier* 2). One can thus speak of a particular *collective* Latin American Jewish experience – one that nevertheless varies from country to country and individual to individual. Moreover, as Graff Zivin posits, Latin American Jews occupy specific symbolic spaces in the cultural landscape, and here I map out the space that Latin American Jews occupy through filmic self-representation. With attention to the specificities of their experiences, I draw from global theories on Jewishness to situate the particular experiences of Latin American Jews in their engagement with leftist politics throughout the twentieth century.[5]

Revolutionary movements defined political life in Latin America in the 1960s and 1970s. Jewish involvement in these movements was, in a sense, a natural progression from the ideological affinities shared between anarchist and socialist movements, in which many Jews were involved in the early part of the twentieth century, and later revolutionary and decolonization movements that gained traction in the 1960s and 1970s. At the same time, involvement in revolutionary politics upset the status quo of Jewish communities and Jewish political affinities. Particularly upsetting were the following three issues: the extreme nature of revolutionary practices such as guerrilla warfare, support for Palestine, and the assimilation into non-Jewish culture that revolutionary involvement often necessitated, most especially because of the heavy influence of Catholicism in these movements. Jewish involvement in revolutionary movements raises complicated issues relating to identity politics, a term for which there are various definitions. By "identity politics" I mean the idea that specific groups – here, Jews – share an organizing logic of political identifications on the basis of a shared practical identity. To this day, contradictions between Jewish self-identification and revolutionary activity continue to confound cultural understandings of the points of contact between identities and political affinities.

Participation in revolutionary politics in Latin America has meaning for individual identities, affecting non-Jews and Jews alike. In studying how Jewish identities inform political categories and vice versa in the films examined here, this book enters into dialogue with ongoing debates in cultural studies regarding identities and politics. The intersecting categories of Jewish and Latin American, or Latin American and Jewish, complicate the points of contact between identities and politics.[6] The observations articulated by Schyfter and Senderey remind us of a lingering problem: many non-Jews continue to subscribe to the prevalent stereotypes about the political affinities of Latin American Jews. Filmic stories of individual experiences upset these popular cultural understandings (or misconceptions) of Jews' beliefs and practices based on their identifications as Jewish. These identity politics gained traction with the advent of the New Left in the 1960s and 1970s, which was concurrent and, by many estimations, closely related to Latin America's revolutionary movements. As Deborah Dash Moore notes, "With the rise of identity politics ... the possibility now arose that a Jew could lose her Jewish identity if she adopted the wrong politics" (9). Moore is referring here to US identity politics specifically, yet the mechanisms of participation within New Left politics were largely similar in this regard to revolutionary politics in Latin America. For the New Left, as Moore shows, not subscribing to leftist politics was tantamount to disavowing one's Jewishness. Yet, while Jewishness most certainly informs political subjectivities, there is no single definitive correlation between Jewishness and one's politics.

To begin my consideration of local Jewish experiences, I offer here a very brief overview of the history of Jewish communities in Latin America, specifically as they have related to political activity. The histories of these communities date back to immigration in the sixteenth century after the expulsion of Jews and Moriscos (former Muslims and their descendants who were ordered by the Roman Catholic Church and the Spanish Crown to convert to Christianity) from Spain in 1492. Sephardic Jews immigrated not only to North Africa and Egypt, but also to Brazil, Santo Domingo, Colombia, Cuba, Puerto Rico, Mexico, and Peru. Since Jewish immigration to the New World was officially prohibited, many Jews avowed conversion to Catholicism, yet privately maintained their observance of Judaism within their homes as so-called Crypto-Jews. Others did convert to Catholicism, but their families retained artefacts, family stories, and cultural practices that strongly suggest Sephardic origins. Jewish immigration to Latin America continued discreetly and sporadically into the eighteenth and nineteenth centuries, while in Eastern Europe Judaism and Jewish culture continued to grow and change. A much larger wave of Jewish immigrants arrived in Latin America between 1880 and 1930, escaping the pogroms of Eastern Europe and, later, the Nazi terror that engulfed the continent. These were predominantly Ashkenazi Jews, although during this time some Sephardic immigration continued from both Turkey and North Africa. With the passage of time, Jewish communities in Latin America largely assimilated; for example, Yiddish is becoming increasingly scarce among these countries' Ashkenazi communities. Jews often worked first as peddlers, later establishing brick-and-mortar businesses and community organizations. Today, there are thriving Jewish communities in many parts of Latin America, with the largest ones centred in the bigger cities of Argentina, Brazil, and Mexico.[7] Engaging with the intricacies of this history, recent Latin American Jewish films portray self-representations of identities in which Jewishness and revolutionary politics are intimately connected.

In the following pages, I build a new praxis of Jewish Latin American film studies to provide the framework for this book as a whole. I posit a theoretical consideration of twentieth-century Jewish political participation and cinematic self-representation among the region's Jewish communities and articulate a critical overview of how to think of filmic portrayals of Jewish involvement in Latin America's revolutionary movements. To begin, I direct attention to the 1947 essay "Être juif" (in English, "being Jewish"), by Emmanuel Levinas, for its central idea that being Jewish necessarily means to forge a sense of belonging in the political sphere of the country to which one immigrates. I then move to theoretical understandings of assimilation and hegemony to consider perceptions of how Jews have assimilated into the national projects of their countries of refuge. Taking hegemony as a point of departure, I introduce Jon Beasley-Murray's concept of "posthegemony" – understood as self-aware engagement in ideological practices – and go on to discuss the Zionist debate as a paradigmatic example of such posthegemony. I then turn my focus to critical works on memory studies, which are helpful in interpreting how film is engaging with paradigms of memory and recent history. Within this new praxis of Jewish Latin American film studies, I offer a summary of recent Jewish involvement in filmmaking throughout Latin America, theorize how the filmmakers have engaged in a variety of cinematic modes and genres, and postulate how in doing so they have revised the twentieth-century history of their respective countries as well as representations of Jewish encounters with revolutionary politics there. Finally, I conclude this introduction with a brief overview of the chapters that follow.

The experiences of Jewish communities and individual Jews with the political climates of the countries in which they live show how the religious and the secular realms bear on one another. As they become part of the public sphere, Jewish Latin Americans find their place in the shifting interstices between religion and politics. For Jewish communities in the second half of the twentieth century, politics were often inflected by post-Holocaust categories of friendship and enmity. Assimilation and hegemony inform Jewish political affinities. Cinematic depictions of Jewish life illustrate Levinas's point that "to be Jewish is not only to seek a refuge in the world but to feel for oneself a place in the economy of being" (205). For Levinas, as for these filmmakers, being Jewish necessarily entails coming to understand oneself as part of the broader social sphere of the country in which one establishes oneself.[8] The "feeling" of which Levinas speaks was never monolithic: Jews positioned themselves in many ways with respect to the public spheres of the Latin American countries in which they were living.[9]

Jewish Latin American life was permeated with political preoccupations that ranged from the global to the local, as the films discussed in this book show. Many Jewish immigrants to Latin America (and their children and grandchildren) became central figures in the political spheres of their cities, countries, and Latin America as a whole. Among these, to name but a few, are Abraham Fabio Grobart, born in Poland in 1905 and co-founder in 1926 of Cuba's Communist Party; Eva Alterman Blay, born in 1937 and the first woman to sit in Brazil's Senate, beginning in 1992; and more recently, Jorge Telerman, born in 1956 and the mayor of Buenos Aires in 2006–2007. These and many other historical and contemporary examples from throughout Latin America evoke "a place in the economy of being" that, to Levinas, is central to the Jewish condition. In his essay, Levinas asks: "The modern world is an infinitely vast and infinitely varied notion. Is it Christian? Is it liberal? Is it set in motion by an economy, a politics or a religion? Are these not vastly differing notions separated by an abyss? And yet there is a sort of affinity among all these non-religious manifestations of this world" (206). According to Levinas, there is, then, "a sort of affinity" among economy, politics, and religion, these three spheres overlap, and being Jewish has implications for an individual's political and economic activity. Directors use film as a space in which to explore this "sort of affinity." Cinematic representation comes to occupy the space between the religious and non-religious "manifestations of the world." Much existing critical analysis focuses on the cultural practices and religious identities of Jews: film criticism must now also take into account the ways in which politics figure in stories of Jewish life.

Jewish experiences with assimilation make interpellation into the national project a central theme in cultural depictions of Jewish life throughout twentieth-century Latin America. Hegemony and citizenship – both central to assimilation processes – simultaneously bridge and divide individuals' political and religious identifications. Jewish Latin American cinema rearticulates what it means to be a citizen of a Latin American country and Jewish, demonstrating, in particular, that for Jewish populations identification with revolutionary politics and activism is complicated. Young Jews – many of them children and grandchildren of immigrants who, as such, had only recently been interpellated into the national projects of their respective Latin American countries – were drawn to revolutionary politics in the 1960s and 1970s. In this moment, they often found themselves pitted between conflicting narratives: the cultural and historical weight of their Jewish families' pasts, on the one hand, and the zeitgeist of protest and revolution within Latin American youth culture, on the other.

Processes of assimilating into the respective national projects evoke Antonio Gramsci's definition of hegemony: "The 'spontaneous' consent given by the great masses of the population to the general direction imposed on social life by the dominant fundamental group; this consent is 'historically' caused by the prestige (and consequent confidence) which the dominant group enjoys because of its position and function in the world of production" (12). Latin American Jews are shown to reckon explicitly with the hegemonic, or mainstream culture, language, and religion of the various countries in which they live. In keeping with Gramsci, the spontaneous consent afforded to the dominant culture comes into sharp relief when encountered by Jewish immigrants whose social life varies from hegemonic practices.

From their earliest days, many of Latin America's Jewish communities became active in their respective countries' political spheres. Many Jews continued to participate in socialist, Zionist, and anarchist groups to which they had belonged as labourers in the Eastern European countries from which they emigrated. Hashomer Hatzair (Young Guard) was established in 1913 in Galicia (some of which is now part of Poland). This is a socialist Zionist group for Jewish youth that went on to become popular in cities throughout Latin America; today it is the oldest Zionist youth group still in existence. "Shomer" figures into the narratives of several of the films discussed here, as over the course of the twentieth century it had a significant role in the history of Jewish political participation: often contact between Jewish youths and secular revolutionary groups was mediated through affiliation with this organization. As Elkana Margalit explains regarding the group's inception in Galicia, "The capacity of organized Jewish society to ensure continuity, to inculcate its spiritual, cultural, and religious values among the younger generation was gradually being eroded following the economic impoverishment which accompanied their economic and social extrusion from and rejection by Polish society" (147). The circumstances in which Hashomer Hatzair emerged speak to the "sort of affinity" between the religious and non-religious "manifestations of the world" that Levinas theorizes, mobilizing Judaism and Jewishness to contest economic and social extrusion.

Assimilation necessarily entails grappling with the national project of the new country and identification with local politics. Within this process, the nation, affect, and ideology converge to inform individual and group motivations. Beasley-Murray's *Posthegemony: Political Theory and Latin America* offers new ways to think through these issues. Specifically, Beasley-Murray examines the relationship between hegemony and populism. I build on that here by adding an explicit discussion of the roles of Judaism and Jewishness as they relate to assimilation into hegemony and national politics. Religion often appears tacitly in Beasley-Murray's work, but in his writings on hegemony it is never fully fleshed out. Beasley-Murray does discuss the effects of subjects' interpellation as exemplified through attendance at Mass. Of course, attending Mass has a markedly different relationship to hegemony in a predominantly Catholic country for non-Jews than it does for Jews. Nonetheless, a focus on how religion interacts with overtly political aspects of life guides Beasley-Murray's analysis and thus informs critical considerations of how, for example, Jews reconcile Jewishness with politics. I take Beasley-Murray's "posthegemony" not to suggest that people have stopped participating in hegemonic practices, but rather, as with the "post" in postmodernism or in postmemory, to denote that individuals interact with hegemony in self-aware ways. In concluding his analysis of the significance of attending Mass, Beasley-Murray writes, "When it becomes apparent that subjects 'know very well what they are doing,' but are still doing it, we have entered posthegemonic times" (182). Jewish participation in the political sphere, I argue, is a process not necessarily of setting aside one's Jewishness – although this has been the case for some – but rather of grappling with one's own Jewish customs and beliefs to reconcile them with national and local politics in a self-aware way.

For purposes of my analysis, I understand "posthegemonic practices" to be self-aware engagement with religious and political practices as informed by minority cultures and their relations to hegemony. In the case of Jewish communities, the Israeli-Palestinian debate often takes on a particular relationship to hegemony. Debates surrounding Zionism, both for and against, are central to the political subjectivities portrayed in many of the films I explore here. Some of their protagonists espouse a Zionist stance, often as a way of responding to the hostilities they have faced in an anti-Semitic world.[10] Other Jewish characters adopt a staunch opposition to Zionism. Cultural representations of both supporting and opposing Zionism speak to the pervasiveness of the Zionist question for Jewish negotiations of political beliefs. Recognizing the complexity of the Zionist debate, I introduce the conversation on Zionism here, and in later chapters I offer a reading of how those questions are represented in various Latin American films.

Abundant conversations situate Zionism within understandings of Jewish political subjectivities both in specific Latin American contexts and more globally. Judith Butler discusses ways of thinking through what it means to be Jewish outside the confines of what she considers to be the hegemonizing force of Zionism. Similar to Levinas's points of contact between politics, religion, and economics, Butler submits that "clearly, Zionism is one way that religion has entered public life, although there are ways of thinking about Zionism that are obviously antireligious" (114).[11] Butler's position that Zionism facilitates the enmeshing of religion and public life underscores the importance of this debate for thinking through the connections between Judaism, Jewishness, and secular life. According to the Argentine philosopher Tomás Abraham, one can be pro-Israel and support a Jewish homeland without being Zionist and, he adds, while supporting Palestine. Support of Palestine becomes a crucial part of what Abraham terms "Posjudaísmo" (Abraham and

Bleiechmar), somewhat akin to Beasley-Murray's "posthegemony." The use of this prefix is not to suggest that Zionism is a thing of the past, but rather to signal the questioning of beliefs and practices that go along with a self-aware approach to Zionism. In this framework, Zionism presents a paradigmatic opportunity to reflect on what Levinas posits as "vastly differing notions" that nonetheless "share an affinity." Neither Butler nor Abraham rejects self-identification as Jewish; rather they are rejecting Zionism as a default political category with which others presume all Jews are aligned. Both deploy Jewish thought and political figures to contest Zionism. Indeed, Butler proposes thinking through Jewish contestations of Zionism as a possible way out of what she presents as the trap of Zionism's hegemony.

In keeping with the professed pursuits of Latin American filmmakers to challenge assumptions about political beliefs on the basis of Jewish identities, debates on Zionism show that Jewish political subjectivities resist a one-to-one correlation between religion and political identifications. Namely, to be Jewish is not necessarily to be Zionist and to be Zionist does not mean not to question Israeli occupation, particularly in the context of the Zionist left in the heyday of Latin American revolutionary movements. In addition to being often directly at odds with the pro-Palestinian stance of many revolutionary groups, Zionism constitutes a conceptual fault line between the politics and religious identifications of Jews worldwide. Michel Gherman, for example, has stated that in response to the 1967 war: "[The Jewish-Zionist Left and the Brazilian Left] took firm and steadfast positions against Israeli occupation and against the expansionist policies of Israel. Some groups built these relationships on the basis of critical positions against the Israeli occupation. Over the years, the Zionist youth movements began critically to reflect on Israeli policies and the Palestinian occupation" (4). Gherman underscores the point that, among the Brazilian Left in the twenty-first century, Jews are still often conflated with Zionism and Israel. Similarly, in the case of Argentina, Nerina Visacovsky writes, "The intense controversy between progressivism and Zionism was a phenomenon that, although always present, had become solidified during the years of the Cold War" (loc. 262). These phenomena are akin to Schyfter's observation of 1990s Mexico that provided the impetus for her to revisit the 1960s in her film *Novia que te vea*.

The Zionist debate is significant not only as a phenomenon that directly couples Jewish culture with political beliefs, but also because of the particular role that the Israeli-Palestinian conflict played in revolutionary movements in Latin America in the 1960s and 1970s. In 1966 the Solidarity Conference of the Peoples of Africa, Asia, and Latin America, better known as the Tricontinental Conference, issued a proclamation of support for Palestine against Israel. This proclamation became especially important to Latin American revolutionary groups and to the global Jewish community. Over the course of the region's revolutionary movements, Zionism took on a particular valence as it related to national liberation movements. The Argentine philosopher León Rozitchner provocatively asserted in the aftermath of the 1967 war that preoccupation with the State of Israel was but a distraction for the Jewish community from the pressing issues of national politics at home, that is, in Argentina (*Ser judío*). Scholars have also drawn comparisons between the importance of the land in Latin American revolutionary movements and the importance of the kibbutz in Zionist thought, as I discuss further in chapter 1.

The Israeli-Palestinian conflict, mobilized throughout Latin America in the 1960s through Fidel Castro's support of Palestine, came back to the fore in twenty-first century politics, as Pink Tide leaders also avowed their support of Palestine. As part of the Pink Tide's renewed anti-imperialist discourse, allegiance with Palestine and anti-Zionist positions also became more prevalent in the political leadership of this time. Chile's President Michelle Bachelet (2006–2010 and 2014–2018) drew comparisons between her forced exile during Augusto Pinochet's dictatorship (1973–1990) and the situation of Palestinian refugees who were not allowed to re-enter Palestine in the 2010s. For his part, Fidel Castro promised oil to the Palestinians as a way of helping them to maintain strength and visibility as an international power. In addition, Argentine President Cristina Fernández de Kirchner (2007–2015) promised support for Palestine, as did Brazil's President Dilma Rousseff (2011–2016). The Israel-Palestine question continues to have a central role in conversations surrounding the points of contact between Jewishness and political affinities.

Anti-Semitism and Nazism became central factors in the formation of Jewish political identifications. The aftermath of the Holocaust and anti-Semitism in the public sphere in the period immediately following the Second World War created situations in which enmity and ideological affinities became mutually imbued. War, politics, friendship, and religious affiliation are constantly maintained in tension with one another in the films I examine here in detail. In *The Concept of the Political*, first published in German in 1932, the philosopher and jurist Carl Schmitt (1888–1985) argues that enmity and friendship are what determine individuals' political orientations. According to Schmitt, "The specific political distinction to which political actions and motives can be reduced is that between friend and enemy" (26). As Schmitt makes clear here – and as Jacques Derrida later echoes in his *Politics of Friendship* – the possibility of war and the enmity therein allow for friendship and, moreover, without the possibility of war, there may be no friendship. Schmitt elaborates, "A world in which the possibility of war is utterly eliminated, a completely pacified globe, would be a world without the distinction between friend and enemy and hence a world without politics ... there would not be a meaningful antithesis whereby men could be required to sacrifice life, authorized to shed blood, and kill other human beings" (35). Here, the distinction between friend and enemy becomes public, not private. Admittedly, Schmitt's complicity with the Nazi regime makes taking him into account to consider Jewish subjectivities somewhat fraught. On this point, the political theorist and philosopher Tracy B. Strong, in his foreword to the 1995 expanded edition of Schmitt's book, notes "the revival of interest in Schmitt is consequent ... to this increasing distance from the 1930s" (xxvii). The renewed engagement with Schmitt may be understood as a generational phenomenon, which will again be relevant presently to my discussion of the intergenerational transmission of Holocaust memory.[12] In keeping with Schmitt, the Holocaust and lingering anti-Semitism created a matrix in which politics is often negotiated through friendship and enmity.

Schmitt's categories can be somewhat limiting, however, since friendship and politics at times function in an inversely proportional relationship, and there is, of course, a difference between coalition and friendship. The philosopher Gabriella Slomp delineates three types of enmity – and, conversely, friendship – in her reading of *The Concept of the Political*: conventional, real, and absolute. "Absolute enmity," formed out of global revolutionary commitment, leads to what Slomp terms "abstract friendship," and "although the global revolutionary or global terrorist may have physical contacts with some friends, he is equally committed to friends whom he may have never physically met or even seen" (206). The relationship between friendship and politics lends a conceptual category of how personal experience and the political sphere interact with one another. The Second World War and its aftermath, a history that later gave way to Cold War politics and global liberation movements, serve as the backdrop for many of the plots in the films examined here. Fervent political identifications at times impede the realization of friendship and love relationships. Political affinities born out of friendship and religious identification can both facilitate and hinder interpersonal relationships. This phenomenon further underscores the fallacy of extrapolating individuals' political affinities strictly based on their religious identifications for the mechanisms of transfer between the two can function in contradictory ways, particularly when it comes to interpersonal relationships between Jews and non-Jews, Zionists and non-Zionists, or Sephardic and Ashkenazi Jews.

All around the world Jews have encountered political movements that advocate social justice and global liberation. In the 1960s and 1970s the Latin American region as a whole was embroiled in movements calling for revolution – "that great effervescence" to which Schyfter refers. These movements were inspired by the success of the Cuban Revolution in 1959, liberation theology, the Second Vatican Council's call for preferential treatment of the poor, opposition to the Vietnam War, and global decolonization movements. In introducing a 2015 issue of the *Journal of Jewish Identities* dedicated to Jewish youth culture, the editors point out, "Young Jews of the period ... grappled with particularly Jewish issues, such as the repercussions of the Holocaust, the status of Zionism among diasporic Jews, and the effects of the Six-Day War ... they also engaged in the cultural and political rebellions that animated so many others of their age group, joining in struggles against racism, the Vietnam War, sexism and imperialism" (Brodsky et al. 1–2). Participation in both "particularly Jewish issues" and more mainstream, hegemonic cultural/political rebellions characterized the experiences of Jewish youth everywhere in the 1960s. During this period Jewish culture and revolutionary culture converged and increasingly came to inform one another.

Yet, the degree to which Jews participated *as* Jews – that is, without compromising elements of their Jewish identities – remains an open question. For many young people involvement in revolutionary causes was part and parcel of youth culture and often posed an intergenerational tension. For Jews these processes were often more complex: in the first place, it was a matter of fighting for the liberation of a country in which one may or may not have been naturalized as a citizen. At the same time, the Castro regime – the paragon of a communist revolution's success in the Latin American region – prohibited religious practices, although religious principles were often latent in revolutionary culture (as I elaborate in chapter 1). In this context, contradictions arise between supporting revolutionary causes and being Jewish. Rozitchner has sardonically stated, in the context of the 1967 Arab-Israeli War, that one cannot be both Jewish and revolutionary, and he called for Jews to sacrifice "*lo judío*" (that which is Jewish) for the revolution, making direct reference to the Tricontinental Conference. Rozitchner's ironic posturing connotes that he does not, in fact, believe that one must wholly disavow Jewishness in order to be revolutionary; nonetheless, he struggles with how the two may be reconciled.

Filmmakers revisit this moment in history to consider how these tensions continue to inform Jewish political life. Jews have had a crucial role in Latin American cinema, with constant negotiations between specifically Jewish self-representations and representations of hegemonic culture. Filmmakers have vacillated between an apparent will to create stories for their own Jewish communities and, at other times, to depict their Jewish communities with an eye to a broader audience. To this point, in introducing a special issue of *Jewish Film and New Media* dedicated to Latin American Jewish film and media, guest editors Raanan Rein and Tzvi Tal suggest that in these examples of contemporary cultural production, "the representations of Jewish experiences in film and art can also be regarded as test cases for the multiple negotiations of collective identities in Latin America" (6). Jewish filmmaking is, on the one hand, part of a broader constellation of Latin American cultural production and, on the other, specific to Jewish Latin America. In light of this paradigm, I consider how Jewish Latin American cinema cleaves to key precepts of politically committed Latin American cinema more generally.

In twenty-first century Latin American filmmaking, political commitment is often conveyed through themes and forms that carry out memory work. Continuing my focus on Levinas's "sort of affinity" between the religious and non-religious "manifestations of the world," I turn now to the role of memory in bridging religion and politics. The points of contact between the religious and the political spheres can be considered in relation to Marianne Hirsch's theoretical model of postmemory. According to Hirsch, "Postmemorial work ... strives to *reactivate* and *reembody* more distant social/national and archival/cultural memorial structures by reinvesting them with resonant individual and familial forms of mediation and aesthetic expression. Thus less-directly affected participants can become engaged in the generation of postmemory" ("The Generation of Postmemory" 157, original emphasis). The connections that Hirsch articulates between individual and social memory share conceptual affinity with the relationship between the particularity of individual Jewish experience and the collective public political sphere. Individuals come into contact in meaningful ways with the political sphere, a contact often mediated through intergenerational exchange.

My interest in the concept of postmemory is twofold: first, I take into account the intergenerational transmission of Holocaust memory, and second, I am interested in the ways in which postmemory facilitates negotiations of political consciousness between generations. Postmemory functions analogously to Schmitt's categories of friendship and enmity insofar as both posit Holocaust experiences as defining categories for the formation of political affinities for Jews. In Latin American cultural studies, postmemory has gained enormous traction as a theoretical approach – specifically, in the case of the memory of political violence. Yet, to date, existing criticism does not explore the significance of using Hirsch's and other Holocaust models for memory and trauma studies to talk about Jewish experiences in these other contexts, for example, Latin American state violence, that are not confined to Jewish populations. Similarly, despite the preponderance of Walter Benjamin's ideas of rupture and ruins in response to the Holocaust within postdictatorship memory studies, particularly in Chile and Argentina, the implications for Jewish thought and culture have gone largely unexplored.[13] In general, the role of religion in contemporary conversations on memory cultures in Latin America has received relatively little critical attention.[14] In this book, I contextualize religious beliefs and practices within the current "memory boom" of cultural production that takes as its subject matter 1960s and 1970s Latin American revolutionary movements.[15]

Memory has become a twenty-first century corollary to didactic political filmmaking of the 1960s and 1970s. During this time, several prominent filmmakers throughout the region penned manifestos that proposed revolutionary theories as the necessary praxis of filmmaking.[16] The Argentine filmmakers Fernando "Pino" Solanas and Octavio Getino, for example, put forth in their 1969 manifesto *Towards a Third Cinema* that "pamphlet films, didactic films, reports films, essay films, witness-bearing films, any militant form of expression is valid" (qtd. in *Documentary Is Never Neutral*). Solanas and Getino propose these forms of filmmaking to contest hegemonic filmmaking: specifically, they propose "third cinema" as opposed to "first cinema" (Hollywood) and "second cinema" (European auteur film). In the five decades since the release of the Solanas/Getino manifesto, politics and film production continue to inform one another, albeit in different ways. As the film critic Ana Amado puts it, "Since the moment at which film and politics ... unified their criteria, points of view and even action points ... the aesthetic criteria of that relationship have transformed. But the ethical principles remain disseminated in images and narratives still difficult to name: for example, the renovation of forms of film's commitment with social issues [and] the responsibility of memory" (10). In Amado's estimation, politics and cinematic production continue to be co-constitutive, but the ways in which the two interact have changed over time. Namely, according to Amado a preoccupation with memory within film is this century's counterpart of the politically committed forms of revolutionary filmmaking in the 1960s. In this regard the memory of the past that characterizes recent cinematic production, including the films I consider here, becomes vested with particular political significance.

The New Left and 1960s and 1970s revolutionary movements defined a new relationship between politics and cultural production; this interdependence has been part and parcel of revolutionary filmmaking ever since. I use the term "revolutionary filmmaking" to refer to the politically committed filmmaking that flourished at the same time as the revolutionary movements themselves; when referring to films that depict revolutionary movements, I use the term "films about revolution." New Latin American Cinema – manifest in specific national movements such as Nuevo Cine Argentino and Brazil's Cinema Novo – emerged during this time. New Latin American Cinema can be broadly defined as a movement consisting of films that advocated aesthetic forms in line with the ideological principles of revolutionary thinking. In other words, New Latin American Cinema incited audiences to take part in the revolution. The 1960s were the heyday of such militant filmmaking, but film and politics remain intertwined in Latin America. The advent of New Latin American Cinema was both an effect and a cause of the revolutionary fervour throughout the region. As the film critic John King points out, in *Magical Reels*, this moment of filmmaking "contained many utopian elements, fuelled by the maximum utopia of the proximity of social revolution in the sixties" (66). Film both represented and fomented revolution. Production was also directly affected by the demise of these revolutionary movements in the early 1970s. Cynthia Tompkins argues that "as the effervescence of the 1960s was cut short by a series of coups that installed state terrorism ... state censorship ... exile, and self-censorship stymied cinematic production" (17). Critical understandings of revolutionary politics and filmmaking reveal a hugely symbiotic relationship between the two. Tompkins's mention of "effervescence" may be likened to Schyfter's "effervescence" of 1960s political movements that, to her mind, bear indelibly on what it means to be Jewish and Mexican. In other words, a shared, simultaneous "effervescence" links 1960s filmmaking and Jewish experiences with 1960s Latin American politics. Nonetheless, as Rein and Tal note, "The place of Jews in the political cinema that flourished in the sixties and seventies has not been studied" (3).

In light of the continued interdependence between filmmaking and political culture, it comes as little surprise that revolutionary culture should be a recurring theme in Latin American cinema from the late 1990s to the present, particularly given the resurgence of revolutionary culture that undergirded the concurrent Pink Tide.[17] In the past two decades, many of the region's blockbuster films and entries to the Oscars Best Foreign Language Film category have explicitly depicted revolutionary culture and practices. The US-Brazil co-production *O qué é isso, companheiro?* (*Four Days in September*), for example, was released in 1997 and nominated for an Oscar for Best Foreign Film. It recreates the 1969 kidnapping of US Ambassador Charles Burke Elbrick by operatives of Brazil's Marxist-Leninist insurgent group Movimento Revolucionário 8 de Outubro (MR-8). These decades have also seen the production of several films about Che Guevara and his legacy, most notably the Brazilian director Walter Salles's *Motorcycle Diaries* (2004) and Steven Soderbergh's two-part biopic *Che: El argentino* and *Che: Guerrilla* (2008). Benjamín Ávila's award-winning film *Infancia clandestina* (*Clandestine Childhood*, 2012) focuses on the 1979 counteroffensive planned by Montoneros, an Argentine leftist urban guerrilla group, during the country's military dictatorship. As Verónica Garibotto points out, the film's originality lies in the fact that it "openly depicts ... active guerrilla fighters with their guns, their militant rituals, their political affiliations, and their straightforward commitment to the armed struggle" (258). Also from Argentina (and co-produced in Spain), the Oscar-winning 2009 film *El secreto de sus ojos* (*The Secret in Their Eyes*) was set in the turbulent years leading up to the military coup in 1976 and, by many critical accounts, evokes the revolutionary politics that characterized 1970s Argentina (see Hortiguera). Alfonso Cuarón's *Roma*, winner of the 2018 Golden Globe as well as the Oscar for Best Foreign Language Film, is set in Mexico City and features the 1971 Halconazo, a protest in which 120 student demonstrators were murdered by government and paramilitary agents. Renewed interest in revolutionary movements is part and parcel of the return of the left in twenty-first-century Latin American political leadership, which for its part takes conceptual and discursive roots in revolutionary politics. Just as Rein and Tal observe that the place of Jews in 1960s and 1970s political cinema has not yet been a topic of study, neither has the role of Jews within this current panorama of filmmaking that takes up the legacy of revolutionary movements.

Nonetheless, Jews have long been active in the national filmmaking industries of Latin America. In 1897 *La bandera argentina* (*The Flag of Argentina*) was filmed using the first Gaumont camera to arrive in Argentina. Directed by the French-born Eugene Py in collaboration with Jewish Austrian immigrant Max Glucksmann, it has widely been considered to be the first Argentine film ever made. The Argentine filmmaker Raymundo Gleyzer, whose parents founded the Jewish theatre group Idisher Folk Theater, was a member of the armed revolutionary organization Partido Revolucionario de los Trabajadores (PRT). In 1973 he formed the militant filmmaking group Cine de la Base (Cinema of the Base) and is known best for his 1973 film *Los traidores* (*The Traitors*) in which he critiques corrupt Peronist workers' unions.

Gleyzer was disappeared by the military dictatorship in 1976. Within the context of Jewish immigrant groups to Latin America (namely, the Russian Revolution, as I explore in greater detail in chapter 2), Sergei Eisenstein's role in Mexican film production of the 1930s is relevant. Eisenstein was partially of Jewish descent and despite being raised in the Russian Orthodox Church was aware of his Jewish roots and culture, as evidenced specifically in his adept deployment of Yiddish slang and humour (see Bergan).[18] Although he was not Mexican, Eisenstein was a gargantuan figure within the burgeoning film industry in mid-century Mexico, and specifically socialist and political filmmaking. León Hirszman gained notoriety in Brazil as part of the politically committed Cinema Novo movement in the 1960s, although he is better known for his later film *Eles não usam black-tie* (*They Don't Wear Black Tie*, released in 1981). Jews have long had a leading role in Latin American cinema's treatment of national identities and politics.

Films focusing on Jewish characters and their experiences were integral to Latin American cinema in the later part of the twentieth century. In 1975 the Argentine director Juan José Jusid adapted the 1910 novel *Los gauchos judíos* – a chronicle of Jewish settlement of the pampas in Argentina penned by Alberto Gerchunoff, known as the "father of Jewish Latin American literature" (see Hussar 39) – for the screen. This film has long been considered a classic of Argentine cinema and is a touchstone for Jewish culture throughout Latin America. Although it remained a somewhat isolated example of Jewish Latin American filmmaking for quite some time, *Los gauchos judíos* constitutes a cinematic high point for Latin American Jews. In the two decades since the mid-1990s Jewish filmmaking holds a significant place in Latin American film, which has seen a renaissance of innovation and critical recognition and reinvented political filmmaking. A number of directors have attracted considerable critical attention for their films focused on Jewishness in the 1990s and into the twenty-first century, as evidence as well by the attention and acclaim given them in books (see Foster, Cultural Production; Glickman and Huberman) and articles (see Rein and Tal; Rocha; Stein; Goldfine). The majority of these studies focus on issues of identity and belonging. I build on them to argue that filmic self-representations of Jewish political identifications are essential to understanding both Jewish experiences of belonging and how politics and filmmaking are interrelated in present-day Latin America.

My readings of recent cinema chart the persistence of filmmakers in highlighting the importance of political participation as a means of representing their Jewish communities' pasts. Carolina Rocha examines the complexities of cinematic self-representation in her consideration of Jewish Brazilian and Argentine films from 2001 to 2007. She concludes that by choosing to represent Jewish characters, these films "have made visible the diversity of issues facing Jews in Argentina and Brazil, but also ... highlighted a community that has scarcely been represented before in the national cinemas of Argentina and Brazil. In addition, these filmmakers are challenging narrowly defined concepts of what it means to be Argentine, Brazilian and Jewish" (45–6). Through challenging assumptions about Jewish Latin Americans' political affiliations, filmmakers craft cinematic representations of Jewish experiences for broader Latin American and global audiences as a means of rearticulating national and Jewish identities alike.

As I show in my detailed discussions of these films, Jewish and national identities are being negotiated both for Jewish viewers specifically and for broader national or international audiences. Hamid Naficy's concept of "accented filmmaking" examines self-representation and posits that diasporic and exilic filmmakers are saddled with a "burden of representation." Naficy adds that "defensiveness and the desire for counterhegemonic representations often create communal pressure for each film to contain all of the best that the 'original' or the 'authentic' culture is perceived to possess *and* to represent as fully as possible the diaspora community" (65, original emphasis). Natalia Pinázza considers this "burden of representation" in the context of Daniel Burman's *El abrazo partido* (discussed in chapter 4), and Burman himself has bemoaned the "Jewishmeter" used by audiences to determine how Jewish his films are. The "burden of representation" that Naficy identifies recalls Stuart Hall's work on representation. For Hall, with the advent of the "cultural turn" in critical thought and the social constructionist approach, "representation is conceived as entering into the very constitution of things; and thus culture is conceptualized as a primary or 'constitutive' process, as important as the economic or material 'base' in shaping social subjects and historical events – not merely a reflection of the world after the event" (5–6). Representation is not simply a signifier for a fixed referent, then, but rather the constitution of what is itself being represented. In the case of self-representation of identity categories, such as the films I examine here, representation and identities become co-constitutive processes of negotiation. I liken the "constitutive" process of representation to Graff Zivin's notion of Jewishness as a wandering signifier; that is, representation is a site of negotiation for Jewishness as a polyvalent signifier. In thinking of Jewishness rather than Judaism – with the understanding that Jewishness is distinct from the more strictly religious Judaism, although it is intimately related to Judaism – I consider how ethno-religious identifications bear on other aspects of life, namely, political affinities. In the pages that follow, I address how the challenges of self-representation inform Jewish Latin American cinema's engagement with the topic of Jewish political participation as a way of forging identities.

Filmmakers have sought to depict the myriad ways in which throughout the twentieth century Jews encountered the political sphere in various Latin American countries. These directors portray cultural practices specific to Latin America's Jewish communities as a means of both staking a claim in Latin American society as Jews and representing Jewish communities for non-Jewish audiences. Yet, considerable screen time has also been dedicated to projecting the ways in which Latin America's Jews and their communities have striven to become and to be represented as political subjects and citizens of the countries in which they live. This struggle has received less critical attention. Further study of the ways in which cultural productions have represented the involvement of Jews in Latin American politics may lead to fuller, more nuanced understandings of the conceptual links between identity categories and political affinities.

The diversity of experiences and beliefs that characterize filmic portrayals of Jewish life in twentieth-century Latin America is mirrored through a multiplicity of cinematic forms. Levinas's "feeling for oneself a place" finds an analogue in Naficy's reading of "accented cinema.". Both Naficy and Levinas are referring to a sense of engagement with the public sphere as a key phenomenon in diasporic experiences, a feeling that informs how one relates to the political realm.[19] For Naficy, "Multiple sites, cultures, and time zones inform the feeling structures of exile and diaspora, and they pose the representation of simultaneity and multisidedness as challenges for the accented films ... This is achieved by critical juxtapositions of multiple spaces, times, voices, narratives, and foci" (28). Jewish Latin American film grapples with the diasporic condition through a focus on the multiplicity of experiences with political engagement.

Such simultaneity and multisidedness are achieved through a variety of generic and formal approaches to filmic representations of Jewish life. As Cynthia Tompkins submits, "The inscription and subversion of generic conventions provides a useful framework for comparing the range of experimentation of ... films" (45). Not all of the films I discuss blend or subvert generic conventions of film forms. Yet, as I show in this book through close attention to both documentary and fiction films, along with some films that constitute a hybrid between forms, filmmakers have sought to represent Jewish experiences through a variety of conventions. In chapter 2, I consider an array of formal approaches to filmmaking that ranges from conventional documentary forms (Blaustein, Chamecki, and Rodríguez Fábregas) to the most surrealistic, experimental film included in this study (Jodorowsky's *La danza de la realidad*). At the same time that I address generic distinctions within this corpus, I trace how directors working in a variety of forms account for Jewish participation in the political spheres of their various Latin American countries.

In addition to studying discrete cinematic conventions, I am interested in filmmaking that explicitly blends a variety of genres and forms. Burman's *El abrazo partido*, for instance, is a fiction film that incorporates many aspects of documentary film, including voiceover, subtitles to introduce sections, and handheld cameras. Such film forms, as I show, have telling relationships to both the formal and thematic aspects of autobiography and self-representation through cinema. To this point, in his analysis of the relationship between recent Latin American documentary and fiction film forms, the film critic Gonzalo Aguilar asks: "If the inscription of personhood does not principally relate to the difference between documentary and fiction, if personhood is not only a question about inflecting the first person but also appears in 'third-person films' ... if the self is not the origin but a fold and derivative: what is it that brings us the indexical image?" (207–8). Self-representation through fictionalized filmic pursuits has particular implications for the semiotic encoding of audiovisual language.

The blending of documentary and fiction forms in cinema has implications for autobiography and self-expression. Specifically, in my 2016 article "Exposing Mechanisms of Truth and Memory," I focus on Michel Foucault's "regime of truth" within recent Latin American documentary production. According to Foucault, "Each society has its regime of truth, its 'general politics' of truth – that is, the types of discourse it accepts and makes function as true; the mechanisms and instances that enable one to distinguish true and false statements; the means by which each is sanctioned; the techniques and procedures accorded value in the acquisition of truth; the status of those who are charged with saying what counts as true" (131). As I conclude in that piece, hybrid approaches to politically inflected filmmaking question the regime of truth that has conventionally sanctioned what stories individuals may tell about themselves and how those stories are to be told. These films articulate a new model for the relationship between subjectivity and political culture. In the case of Jewish Latin American filmmaking, hybridity of forms constitutes an aesthetic analogue to the thematic hybridity that characterizes the stories and experiences being recounted.[20]

Many of the documentary films examined here evoke the longstanding relationship between political preoccupations and generic conventions established by leftist cinema both in Latin America and around the world. As the film critic David William Foster submits, "The preponderance of documentary filmmaking in Latin America can be identified with specific political movements" (x). As I discussed above in the case of Solanas and Getino, the documentary formats of New Latin American Cinema were directly in line with political objectives. Formal aspects also cleave to aesthetic approaches to documentary filmmaking in line with the global New Left. Specifically, in the documentaries I examine in chapter 2, the directors rely heavily on the interview format. As Thomas Waugh points out, "The seventies revived the interview in the documentary, thanks largely to the feminists [and] the New Left" (70). In keeping with Waugh's assertion, the formal elements of these documentaries – specifically, the use of the interview – are related to a strong preoccupation with political concerns. In particular, Waugh analyses how in documentary film these political concerns are related to personal questions of self-representation. Taking into account the complexities of cinematic self-representation, I demonstrate how recent film has disarticulated monolithic understandings of Jewish political preoccupations. As I argue, these films facilitate a critical reconsideration of, first, how revolutionary groups came to define themselves and allow (or not) for Jewish self-identification and, second, the ways in which Jewishness – alongside other identity categories – comes into contact with the public realm and with specific political movements.

Chapter 1, "Saintly Politics," argues that a preponderance of Catholic beliefs in Latin American revolutionary culture tacitly calls for Jewish filmmakers to consider what space is afforded to Jewishness within filmic representations of the legacy of revolutionary movements. Jews were excluded from full identification with revolutionary movements insofar as these were largely predicated on Christian beliefs. Religion both impeded and facilitated Jewish identification with and participation in revolutionary politics. In addition to the presence of liberation theology and the influence of the Second Vatican Council's ideas of social welfare within revolutionary thought and practices, revolutionary movements were heavily moored in Catholicism. The chapter examines the roles of prophecy, eschatology, and salvation in revolutionary culture (and its legacy in the twenty-first century cultural imaginary) to conceptualize mechanisms of transfer between religious thought and political practices. I conclude with a consideration of the figure of the "New Man," rooted in the New Testament and central to revolutionary thought. The ubiquity of this figure, I argue, implicitly calls for Jews to reckon with their roles in revolutionary politics and in the national projects of their respective countries.

Furthering the focus on the interplays between minority cultures and hegemonic practices, chapter 2, "Here We Are to Build a Nation," examines questions of Jewish assimilation. Here, I shift my attention to filmic depictions of Jewish immigration in 1930s–1940s Latin America. The connections of Jews to socialist and communist movements during these decades laid the groundwork for the tensions in political participation that came up later in revolutionary and guerrilla movements of the 1960s and 1970s, which often called for complex intergenerational negotiations. Postmemory and the transmission of experience across generations are integral to these films. With attention to a variety of film genres, I trace the interwar odysseys of Jews to solidify a place for themselves within the political sphere. Works include Chilean filmmaker Alejandro Jodorowsky's surrealistic autobiographical film *La danza de la realidad*, Argentine documentarian David Blaustein's *Hacer patria*, Uruguayan documentary director Gonzalo Rodríguez Fábregas's *El barrio de los judíos*, and Brazilian documentary filmmaker Cintia Chamecki's *Danken got*. Blaustein's title "Hacer patria" – "to build a homeland" – serves as a guiding concept throughout my consideration of the political participation of recent Jewish immigrants in early twentieth-century Latin America. In these films, Jews are portrayed not only as establishing refuge for themselves, but also as participating actively as political subjects of the respective countries in which they settled. Thus, now in the twenty-first century, cinema serves to inscribe the memory of political activism for broader audiences.

Shifting my focus to how Jews experienced revolutionary political movements in the 1960s and 1970s, chapter 3, "*Poner el cuerpo femenino judío*," argues that Jewish processes of coming to feel a sense of belonging in revolutionary movements were often incomplete. Jeanine Meerapfel's *El amigo alemán* and Guita Schyfter's *Novia que te vea* are examined in detail here. I introduce the term "poner el cuerpo judío femenino," a modification of "poner el cuerpo," an expression commonly used among 1960s and 1970s revolutionaries. "Poner el cuerpo" means "to place the body" in reference to putting one's body in the streets, in battle, or on the line for the cause. For Jewish women in these films, belonging in their respective countries necessarily takes into account negotiations with revolutionary politics. In this chapter, my interest is in how these films depict gendered Jewish embodiment against the backdrop of the characters' embroilment in Latin American revolutionary struggles. The protagonists in these films navigate spaces in which femininity and Jewishness are often taken for granted. My attention is on how the characters are presented in coming to understand themselves as Jewish women and as citizens of Mexico and Argentina. The patently gendered elements of Judaism and Jewishness force them to grapple with how to occupy the category of femaleness "correctly."

To consider the present-day intergenerational legacy of Jewish involvement in these 1960s and 1970s political causes, chapter 4, "Lost

Embraces," examines films about Jewish children whose parents left them to fight for their political beliefs. Hamburger's 2006 *O ano em que meus pais saíram de férias* is set against the backdrop of Brazil's insurgent movement, and in Burman's 2004 *El abrazo partido* the 1973 Arab-Israeli War has a central role. My interpretation of *El abrazo partido* hinges on protagonist Ariel's fraught relationship with his father who left Argentina to fight in that war, in Ariel's words, "to save all the world's Jews except for one." The film thus posits conflicting points of contact between family commitment and Jewish-Argentine identities. Similarly, Mauro, the protagonist in *O ano em que meus pais saíram de férias*, is left behind in his father's childhood Jewish neighbourhood while his parents go underground as part of the insurgent movement in 1970. In both films, historically Jewish neighbourhoods – Bom Retiro in São Paolo and Once in Buenos Aires – serve as loci of identity and community formation that are presented to the spectator as insular microcosms. The chapter argues for the continued importance of the defence of Israel and the anti-dictatorial insurgence for twenty-first century considerations of what it means to be Jewish in both the Argentine and Brazilian contexts. This younger generation of Jewish filmmakers are positioning themselves as heirs to a legacy of filmmaking, national identity, and Jewishness with which they have a vexed relationship. For them, filmmaking is a process of coming to terms with familial, religious, and national identities and of projecting this process for a broader audience.

To conclude, I return to Levinas's "sort of affinity" to propose that there are "affinities of all sorts" between the religious and political "manifestations of the world." At the same time, one cannot fully understand either Jewish life or the legacy of 1960s and 1970s revolutionary politics in the Latin American region without taking them into critical account *together*.

Jewish identification with revolutionary struggles continues to be a complicated negotiation and constitutes a critical lacuna within cultural studies. As I underscore in the epilogue, Jewish experiences with progressive politics must be examined if we are to have a full understanding of both Jewish life and political culture in Latin America as well as in other regions of the world. I conclude this book with a brief look at recent innovations in Jewish film and media as well as salient moments in recent political movements that distil the central questions of how Jews are or are not able to identify wholly with progressive politics.

Chapter One

Saintly Politics: Christianity, Revolution, and Jews

In an interview I conducted in 2015, former Montonero and Buenos Aires Senator Gabriel Fuks stated that, for Jews such as himself, participating in Montoneros meant assimilating into lay culture. Fuks's use of the word "lay" (*laico* in Spanish) seemed to mean not "secular" per se but, more precisely, "non-Jewish." As Fuks went on to underscore in our conversation – decades after forming part of Montoneros and working now as a self-identifying progressive Jewish politician in Argentina – the revolutionary group that he had been affiliated with was heavily steeped in Catholic beliefs and culture. Yet, from his perspective as a Jew, Montoneros was laico. His assertion shows that, in joining revolutionary groups of the 1970s, some Jews went through a process of assimilation into a culture that they termed "lay" but that at the same time was saturated with elements of Catholicism.

If revolutionary culture had been wholly secular, religious difference would presumably have had little effect on Jews' experiences with it. Revolutionary practices were, in fact, laden with manifestations of religious beliefs and thought. Because of the ubiquity of Christianity within Latin American revolutionary politics, revolutionary filmmaking from the 1960s and 1970s and twenty-first-century films depicting revolutionary politics are both marked by Christian tropes. Film's focus on Catholicism in revolutionary culture tacitly marginalizes – or even excludes – Jews from the legacy of revolutionary politics. The role of religion within political conversations and cultural productions dealing with the politics of memory has received surprisingly scant critical attention. Nevertheless, Christianity heavily undergirds conversation surrounding the legacies of revolutionary culture.

The Christian underpinnings in Latin American revolutionary culture meant that Jews were perhaps less familiar with some elements of revolutionary life and that revolutionary commitment was, therefore, less accessible to them.[1] Meanwhile, the pervasiveness of Christian thought within revolutionary culture created pathways through which religious identification could inform political action, fostering affinities with revolutionary politics on the basis of religious beliefs. Christian thought and culture in revolutionary movements created a space in which religion could enter into politics. Many of the Christian tropes present in cultural understandings of revolution are also integral components of Jewish culture, recalling the ways in which the two are enmeshed. Thus, the conceptual slippage that comes up between secular, Christian, Jewish, and Judeo-Christian beliefs can be critically productive.[2] As I show in this chapter, religion both impeded and facilitated Jewish identification with Latin American revolutionary politics.

Revolutionary practices in this region explicitly evoke religious paradigms. As the Mexican historian Enrique Krauze writes in *Redeemers: Ideas and Power in Latin America,* "In Latin America, the religious background that stems from an overwhelmingly Catholic culture has always suffused its political reality with moral categories and paradigms" (loc. 78). Krauze's model is akin to Levinas's "sort of affinity" between the religious and non-religious "manifestations of the world," for which the "suffusing" of the political realm with Catholic culture constitutes a conceptual analogue. For Krauze religion is brought to bear on politics by lending it moral categories and paradigms. Elements of religious culture entered the political sphere in such a way that political action was made more intelligible and compelling through familiarity with these religious elements. Insofar as these were predicated on Christian beliefs, Jews were excluded from full identification with revolutionary movements. As cultural depictions of these movements continue to remind us, Jews were situated ambiguously vis-à-vis revolutionary practices in Latin America.

In my examination of these ambiguous positions, I first take a look at the roles of prophecy, eschatology, and salvation in Latin American revolutionary culture so as to conceptualize mechanisms of transfer between religious thought and political practices. From there I consider the importance of the Second Vatican Council, liberation theology, and the preferential option for the poor in 1960s and 1970s Latin America. These schools of thought were integral to revolutionary practices and continue to inform the cultural imaginary surrounding revolution. Next I present an overview of present-day debates on the legacy of armed revolutionary movements that explicitly include religious paradigms. After considering briefly how religion informed and continues to inform these movements, I turn my focus to 1960s and 1970s revolutionary filmmaking and its use of overtly religious images and tropes as a means of inciting solidarity. Finally, I discuss some examples from twenty-first-century Latin American cinema that revisit the role of religion in the region's revolutionary politics. My argument is that Judeo-Christian religious paradigms are worked into filmic representations of revolution in a way that does not wholly exclude Jews but does privilege Christian thought and Catholic culture. To conclude, the chapter considers the "New Man" – ubiquitous to documentary and fictional depictions of revolution – and what that figure has meant for Jews, given the obvious New Testament origins of the term. In light of the ambiguities of this figure and the role of religion more generally in these events, iconic 1960s and 1970s revolutionary cinema as well as recent film productions that revisit this moment in history have implicitly created a call for Jews to create cinematic representations of their own roles vis-à-vis revolutionary politics in Latin America.

Revolutionary Prophecy, Eschatology, and Salvation

Cultural understandings of revolution take into consideration prophecy, eschatology, and salvation. At different points each of these may assume different valences as they relate to Jewish, Christian, and secular cultures. For purposes of my analysis I understand a prophet to be someone connected to a divine source, able to shape history through exegesis, and vested with an intercessory role in the courts of terrestrial rulers. Of particular importance is the self-positioning of prophets as mediators of political authority. In broad terms, these paradigms are lent to revolutionary culture in the 1960s and 1970s in the Latin American region through the presentation of prophet-martyrs for the cause of liberation. The most iconic of these prophet-martyrs is Che Guevara. Guevara and other "saviours" are presented as prophets who were able to see the promise of a better, more just world and who were murdered for defending their cause. Within the broader history of religious and cultural thought, this model is unusual insofar as it conflates the figure of the prophet and the martyr into one person, whereas the Church generally has regarded Christ as strictly a martyr.[3] This conflation suggests a conceptual hybridity between the Old Testament (Jewish) figure of the prophet and the New Testament (Christian) martyr. Elsewhere, real-life and fictional figures associated with revolutionary movements have been vested with the prophetic role of having foreseen the cataclysmic events of dictatorship and repression that put an end to Latin America's revolutionary movements. As I will show, this narrative is presented with varying degrees of religious tenor, ranging from overtly religious to apparently secular. The distinctions between Jewish, Christian, Judeo-Christian, and secular beliefs become blurred in this model, for prophecy and eschatology may be understood as part of both Jewish and Christian beliefs, whereas salvation is more exclusively Christian. In Latin America, prophecy had the paradoxical role of both facilitating and impeding Jewish identification with revolutionary movements.

In Latin America and around the world, scholars have tried to account for the prevalence of eschatological thinking in twentieth-century revolutionary movements, or to use religious historian Norman Cohn's term, "revolutionary millenarianism" (286). The doctrine of the end of things, eschatology is concerned with the final events of history, with humanity's ultimate destiny. The "end of the world" or "end times" are common terms for the realm of eschatology. The idea that the current world would end and give way to another was integral to revolutionary culture and facilitated intellectual affinity between eschatological thinking and revolution. In *Sobre la violencia revolucionaria: Memorias y olvidos* (*On revolutionary violence: Memories and forgetting*), his 2009 analysis of revolutionary practices in his home country of Argentina, the historian Hugo Vezzetti argues: "In coexistence there are limited struggles for specific objectives and a combat of another nature, sacred and essential, limitless in its aspirations, headed towards a prophecy of a cataclysm from which a new man and a new world would emerge. That sense of the imminence of an event, [one] that would reveal itself in different signs, edifies a true *revolutionary eschatology*" (166, original emphasis). As Vezzetti's retrospective reflection points out, however specific they may have been in their avowed objectives, revolutionary movements were often conceived of and discussed in prophetic terms that transcended any particular goals.[4] Prophecy provided a conceptual framework through which to articulate the goals of specific political projects.

Vezzetti uses the term "revolutionary eschatology" to situate the revolution's coupling of religious tropes and political culture within a long history of political action predicated on eschatological thinking. Vezzetti has borrowed from Cohn who uses that term in his seminal work *The Pursuit of the Millennium: Revolutionary Millenarians and Mystical Anarchists of the Middle Ages* (1970). Cohn lays out five criteria for a millenarian sect's end times thinking:

> (a) collective, in the sense that it is to be enjoyed by the faithful as a collectivity;
> (b) terrestrial, in the sense that it is to be realized on this earth and not in some other-worldly heaven;
> (c) imminent, in the sense that it is to come both soon and suddenly;

(d) total, in the sense that it is utterly to transform life on earth, so that the new dispensation will be no mere improvement on the present but perfection itself;
(e) miraculous, in the sense that it is to be accomplished by, or with the help of, supernatural agencies. (15)

To a great extent, these categories are applicable to revolutionary practices in Latin America in the 1960s and 1970s. Figures such as Che Guevara are thought of as individuals vested with a unique vision into the promise of an imminent, miraculous transformation that is to come about as a result of revolution.

These paradigms play out in filmic portrayals of prophetic characters associated with revolution. Krauze views Latin American politics through prophecy, dedicating the first section of *Redeemers* to historical figures he terms "prophets" that, in his estimation, "configure the revolutionary vocation of the continent with an apostolic zeal and a spirit of sacrifice" (loc. 78). The Cuban poet José Martí (1853–1895) is one of the "prophets" Krauze analyses. Martí takes on a prophetic role within revolutionary cinema insofar as his writings lent titles to the films of the iconic directors Santiago Álvarez (1919–1998) and Fernando "Pino" Solanas (b. 1936) and Octavio Getino (1935–2012), whose work is discussed at greater length later in this chapter. The verses that Álvarez and Solanas and Getino borrow for their film titles not only are overtly revolutionary in their tenor, but they also have strong prophetic – and, in the case of *La hora de los hornos* (*The Hour of the Furnaces*), directly biblical – overtones. Martí's role as a prophetic voice cannot be understated because he was, in many ways, a pioneer in Latin America's cultural and intellectual spheres as a turn-of-the-century voice against the informal empire of the United States and its economic imperialism that 1960s and 1970s revolutionary movements in the Latin American region would later contest.

The eschatological thinking in revolutionary politics, I submit, is evidence of the secularization of religious paradigms. To this point, Cohn concludes his analysis by drawing parallels between the millenarian thinking that fuelled the Crusades and revolutionary thinking in the 1960s and 1970s (when he was writing his book): "The old religious idiom has been replaced by a secular one, and this tends to obscure what otherwise would be obvious. For it is the simple truth that, stripped of their original supernatural sanction, revolutionary millenarianism and mystical anarchism are with us still" (286). Revolutionary thinking in the 1960s, for Cohn, was a paradigm born out of the secularization of an "old religious idiom." I liken Cohn's model of the secularization of religious idioms to Krauze's position that Catholic culture suffuses politics with religious and moral paradigms, as well as to Levinas's "sort of affinity." Such "religious idioms" are mobilized within secular politics both implicitly and explicitly. Some revolutionary movements and their participants are avowedly atheist, while at the same time they, in fact, rely on figures and tropes of Christianity as organizing principles; in other instances, Christianity is referenced explicitly. This connection between secular and religious practices is manifest in the pervasive role that prophecy had in Latin American revolutionary practices and that it continues to have in cultural representations that revisit this moment in history.

The role of prophecy helps foreground religious thought within heated contemporary conversations about the memory of revolutionary politics. Moreover, prophecy conjures one of the biggest tensions that remains unresolved within existing understandings of Latin America's revolutionary culture, namely, the division between elite intellectuals or politicians, on the one hand, and the working class they purport to champion, on the other. As Vezzetti elaborates in his reading of Cohn's revolutionary eschatology, the politician is supplanted by the prophet, whose authority rests largely on his intimate knowledge of ideas and images of a different order than the status quo. Intellectuals and professionals in Latin America who fulfilled the role of prophet in this schema of revolutionary eschatology often became the leaders of revolutionary groups. This division between the working class and intellectuals was a point of contention within revolutionary movements throughout the region as well as in the student and worker protests in Paris in 1968.[5] In critical studies that revisit the importance of 1968 and radical politics worldwide, this division continues to be a conceptual thorn in the side for leftist politics. Thus, the role of prophecy, for the "prophets" were almost always intellectuals, is intimately linked to central debates on the legacy of 1960s revolutionary politics, highlighting the need to parse out the role that religious thinking played in them.

To be sure, prophecy and eschatology are more closely linked to Judaism than is salvation. As Cohn points out, prophecy and eschatology were readily embraced by new Christians and almost seamlessly came to constitute key parts of Christian beliefs and culture. Yet, these concepts had earlier been and have remained elements of Jewish beliefs as well, stemming from the books of Daniel, Ezekiel, and others in the Hebrew Bible (whereas Christian apocalyptic thinking stems from the New Testament Gospels, Pauline epistles, and the Book of Revelation). The distinction that Cohn draws underscores that prophecy and apocalyptic thinking are not necessarily Christian to the exclusion of Jewish beliefs and culture. Many examples of eschatology and prophecy within the cultural imaginary of revolution do, however, try to work out the idea of salvation and rely on the visual trope of a Christlike martyr figure as the key to salvation. Neither the term "Jewish" nor "Christian" nor "Judeo-Christian" should be taken for granted as monolithic or as wholly exclusive of one another. Rather, the points of contact between Jewish, Christian, and the secular are constantly in flux and come to bear on political practices in different ways.[6] What, then, do these shifting points of contact between religious beliefs and the political sphere mean for Jews as they grapple with self-identification and revolutionary politics in Latin American film?

The Preferential Option for the Poor and Liberation Theology

Revolutionary eschatology, in both religious and secular discourse, resided within and sometimes interacted with the revolutionary thought espoused by the clergy and the Church, particularly in the context of John XXIII's papacy and the Second Ecumenical Council of the Vatican, or Vatican II (1962–1965). Indeed, Vatican II was held with the express purpose of addressing the relationship between the Church and the modern world, a Catholic counterpart for Levinas's "sort of affinity" between the religious and non-religious "manifestations of the world." As a way of treating this relationship, the Catholic Church and Catholics themselves became increasingly concerned with the rights and well-being of impoverished people. In many countries, the resolutions propounded by the Church galvanized young Catholics in a way that inspired solidarity with revolutionary groups that sought a more equal distribution of resources and wealth.

Argentina's Guardia de Hierro (Iron Guard) was a grassroots organization that emerged in the 1960s. It self-identified first and foremost as a Catholic group that "essentially conceived of Justicialism [Peronism] as the political expression of faith" (Peiro). Although Guardia de Hierro does not receive much scholarly attention in comparison with other leftist groups, it was crucial for revolutionary culture in both Argentina and the Latin American region more generally. Eventually it came to form the basis of the Peronist Left, with many of its members ultimately joining the more radical Montoneros once Guardia de Hierro itself disbanded in 1970. Much of their Catholic discourse would change once its members joined with Montoneros. All the same, a sizeable contingent of Montoneros came from Guardia de Hierro that, by Juan Perón's own estimation, constituted the ideological backbone of the Peronist Left and that saw its militancy as the political expression of faith.[7] In this regard Montoneros, which was one of Latin America's most influential revolutionary groups, drew heavily from a fundamentally Catholic base. Jews in Montoneros were placed in a process of reckoning, as Senator Gabriel Fuks underscored in his interview with me.[8]

In keeping with the idea of a "political expression of faith," the most obvious manifestation of the connections between religion and revolutionary politics in Latin America is liberation theology: the importance of liberation theology cannot be overstated, although most revolutionary groups did not align themselves with it, strictly speaking. Across Latin America, there were variations on liberation theology, such as "teología del pueblo (theology of the people)" in Argentina, that were largely in line with liberation theology yet did not avow a Marxist tendency, in part so as to avoid alienating potential supporters who were more conservative leaning. Furthermore, as the Brazilian sociologist Michael Löwy states, liberation theology "is only one aspect (though an important one) of this broad socioreligious reality" that he terms "Christianity of Liberation" (351). Importantly, Löwy argues that liberation theology is better understood as an effect of the widespread influence of the Church on the secular world in Latin America than as the singular phenomenon that it is often thought to be, that is, as a single movement limited to the 1960s and 1970s. Put another way, liberatory politics and Christian beliefs mutually inform one another in more ways than people might generally think.

Liberation theology encapsulates a paradigm in which politics and Christianity converge, and it continues to inform how revolutionary movements are conceptualized in the cultural imaginary. One of the most renowned liberation theologians, the Colombian priest Camilo Torres, who was assassinated by Colombia's military forces in 1966, stated that in order to "love thy neighbour," as the Bible commands, a true Christian must also be a revolutionary. Father Torres is credited with coining the slogan, "Si Cristo viviera sería guerrillero (If Christ were living, he would be a guerilla)." He formed part of the Ejército de Liberación Nacional (National Liberation Army), a Marxist-Leninist guerrilla group in solidarity with the Cuban Revolution. After his death, all over Latin America Camilo Torres was almost immediately taken up as a martyr for revolutionary causes. The magazine *Cristianismo y Revolución* appeared for the first time in 1966 and included messages from Torres before his death and extolled his model of sacrifice for the revolution. Today, the memory of Father Torres continues to have an enormous presence in Colombia and great significance for present-day politics; in 2016, President Juan Manuel Santos agreed to exhume his remains as a key initiative in moving towards peace talks within the country.

In Argentina in 1974 Padre Carlos Mugica was assassinated by the paramilitary Alianza Anticomunista Argentina (Argentine Anticommunist

Alliance). Padre Mugica was part of Movimiento de Sacerdotes para el Tercer Mundo (Movement of Priests for the Third World). He spearheaded a contingent of *curas villeros*, priests who dedicated themselves to working with impoverished and uneducated inhabitants of *villas* – shantytowns – in Buenos Aires. Although unlike Torres, Mugica did not subscribe to liberation theology nor identify with guerrilla groups, he is commonly associated with "teología del pueblo." As I show in my later analysis of *Elefante blanco*, Padre Mugica continues to be a crucial figure for memory and politics in Argentina. In 2014 Mugica became the second person, after only Eva Perón, to have a sculpture by artist Alejandro Marmo erected in his likeness along Buenos Aires's central artery, Avenida 9 de Julio. For Hugo Vezzetti, Mugica represents not only the paradigm of the cura villero, but also the Peronist Left's militant struggle more broadly ("Archivo y memorias del presente" 180). In these cases, an interdependence remains between spiritual – religious – leadership and revolutionary culture.

"Thou Shalt Not Kill"

If Church doctrine and biblical teachings undergirded revolutionary beliefs during the heyday of revolutionary movements in the Latin American region in the 1960s and 1970s, religious thought continues to have a pervasive role within contemporary historical revisions of the history of these revolutionary movements. Oscar del Barco (b. 1928) was once part of the Ejército Guerrillero del Pueblo (People's Guerilla Army), an armed revolutionary group in Argentina in 1963–1964. In 2004 he sparked a heated debate on the ethics of armed violence with the publication of an open letter titled "No Matarás ("Thou Shalt Not Kill," published in English translation in the *Journal of Latin American Cultural Studies* in 2007). In this letter, del Barco abjures his fellow militants' taking of lives after reading statements of armed revolutionary violence that prompted him to consider that those killed could have been his own loved ones. Based on the biblical commandment, the letter also includes several implicit biblical references and brings to mind Emmanuel Levinas. Del Barco states: "Evil, as Levinas says, consists of exempting oneself from the consequences of one's reasoning, saying one thing and doing another, supporting the killing of other people's children and invoking the commandment when it comes to the killing of our own" (115). The letter does not, however, cite Levinas directly nor ever gesture towards Levinas's Jewishness.

Although the commandment "thou shalt not kill" derives from Exodus 20:13, del Barco's references throughout his letter are largely secular. He does not invoke the Bible or God other than to reference that "thou shalt not kill" is a commandment and to assert: "But beyond everything and everybody, including whatever God there might be, there is the *Thou shalt not kill*. Faced with a society that kills millions of human beings in wars, genocides, famines, illness and every kind of torture, at the base of each of us can be heard weakly or imperiously *Thou shalt not kill*" (115, original emphases). The immanence of the "thou shalt not kill" that del Barco posits here as being "beyond ... whatever God there might be" reads first as an appeal to his readers' familiarity with the Ten Commandments.[9] Alternatively, most critics have read it as an affirmation of the ethical implications of "thou shalt not kill." If one accepts the former, the biblical basis for considerations of the legacy of revolutionary armed struggle becomes clear. The latter, for its part, speaks to the secularization of biblical thought as a matrix for critical understandings of revolutionary culture. In either case, the underpinning is the Bible. Clearly, "thou shalt not kill" derives from the Bible, and it therefore merits analysis within that context – a critical response that so far has not yet been offered. The lack of discussion of the overtly religious implications of del Barco's letter speaks to the ways in which religious thought has seamlessly been incorporated into Latin American revolutionary culture in such a way that, as I soon show, situates Jews precariously.

In his response to del Barco's letter, published first in 2006 in *El Ojo Mocho*, León Rozitchner specifically addresses the intersection of Jewish and Christian thought. He claims that del Barco's use of "thou shalt not kill" (although it is the fifth of the Ten Commandments and to be found in the Old Testament) is both inherently Christian and paternal.[10] Rozitchner then moves towards a model that he proposes as maternal and Jewish predicated on "thou shalt live," which he asserts supersedes both "thou shalt kill" and "thou shalt not kill." He argues that, although the Bible commands "thou shalt not kill," God also enjoins, "thou shalt live," which, Rozitchner argues, supersedes the maxim not to kill. The Argentine philosopher asserts that the Christian interpretation of "thou shalt not kill" on which del Barco bases his letter is rooted in a Christian understanding of the Old Testament Jewish god, which Rozitchner couches as paternal in contrast to the maternal maxim of "thou shalt live." Rozitchner concludes his reply to del Barco's letter with: "Prior to the maternal and the paternal the *no matar* was the murmur of life that cries out for the absolute respect of Life as absolute. I believe that the call or beseeching of *no matar* is life itself and the possibility of life presenting itself and persevering as life" ("Intercambio Rozitchner–Del Barco"). Del Barco does not respond here directly to the genealogy that Rozitchner posits of "thou shalt live," "thou shalt kill," and "thou shalt not kill." Nor does he engage with the dichotomy that Rozitchner articulates as between the Christian, paternal "thou shalt not kill," on the one hand, and the Jewish, maternal "thou shalt live," on the other.

Del Barco does, however, directly discuss God's call of "thou shalt kill" to Abraham in the Bible in his reply to Jorge Jinkis's, Juan Ritvo's, and Eduardo Grüner's responses to "No Matarás."[11] His comments on these three authors' responses to his letter were published in English alongside Jinkis's, Ritvo's, and Grüner's letters in a special 2007 issue of *Journal of Latin American Cultural Studies*. Del Barco writes, "I think that God, on staying Abraham's hand through the intermediary of his angel, might have said: How dare you disobey my commandment? Not even in obedience to my order should you have tried to violate it! To which Abraham could have replied: I never thought to kill Isaac, even though I was going to do it, because You have ordered that we should not kill" (161). Del Barco returns to the Bible to relativize the injunction "thou shalt kill" that Rozitchner submits God also commands. He thus further entrenches within biblical thought his abjuration of the taking of human lives by revolutionary movements.

Del Barco's original letter ends in such a way that both secularizes Christian beliefs as a framework for conceptualizing revolutionary culture and directly interpellates Jews within the Christian matrix of salvation in keeping with Paul's epistles.[12] He ascribes to his friend and fellow militant, the Argentine Jewish poet Juan Gelman (1930–2014), the idea that the only path to salvation is through accepting one's culpability – specifically, the culpability of having been complicit in armed violence. Del Barco ends his letter with: "This is the basis of salvation, says Gelman. I think so too" (117). The "this" to which del Barco refers here is the acceptance of responsibility in having taken lives. That del Barco should end his letter speaking of salvation, along with the move towards secularization that he shows, is more in key with personal redemption – that is, assuaging his own guilt – than with salvation in a religious sense. Yet, he appeals to his Jewish friend to speak of salvation, calling his Jewish peer into his own Christian belief system as he enjoins him to reflect on his militancy. This aspect of the letter speaks to the ways in which Jews involved in Latin American revolutionary politics were interpellated into the Christian habitus within these movements as well as within recent conversations that have revisited these movements. Del Barco's invocation of Gelman mobilizes New Testament thinking to talk about truth, memory, and justice. The conversation on the memory of revolutionary politics thus draws strength from Christian beliefs and tropes in such a way that it echoes the secularization of Christian paradigms within Latin American revolutionary politics during their heyday. Doing so subtly changes memory by using religiosity to revisit the role of militancy within present-day political culture. The terms in which del Barco couches his reference to salvation have more to do with secular notions of justice than with salvation in a religious sense. In this way, del Barco's letter engages implicitly with the ubiquitous conversations on truth, memory, and justice that pervade postdictatorship societies in Latin America.[13]

Elsewhere in his letter, del Barco ascribes to himself a prophetic clarity of vision that is common among militants who joined armed struggles in good faith in the belief that doing so would lead to a better society. They did not know and could not have known that the violence would escalate so much or that dictators would take over their countries. Yet some, like del Barco, in their revisionist views of their militant involvement, claim in an implicitly prophetic tenor that they all *should* have known what was going to happen next. In his response to del Barco's letter, Jorge Jinkis seizes on this prophetic role that del Barco has vested himself with, finding in his letter "the anguish of the soul of a penitent, one who, enlightened by conversion, adopts a biblical tone for the language of his missionary voice" (120). Jinkis's reading of del Barco also suggests a correspondence between religion and revolutionary action, in this case moving from revolutionary commitment to religious faith.[14] Similarly, Chilean Hernán Vidal (1937–2014) – a literary critic and pioneer of academic theorizations of the testimonial genre – revisited the role of violence in Latin America's revolutionary left in such a way that he, too, implicitly vests his own voice with a prophetic role of having been able to foresee the brutality and cruelty that were to come in the form of Pinochet's dictatorship (Vidal).[15]

In his response to del Barco, Jinkis also posits a dichotomy between apocalypse and defeat. He enjoins del Barco: "Let us be less apocalyptic and say that it goes by the name of Defeat" (120). Here, Jinkis is indicting del Barco's self-fashioning as a prophetic voice after first stating that del Barco has taken his open letter as an opportunity for confession in front of a public audience. Like del Barco, Jinkis is deploying religious terms to talk about personal redemption. But Jinkis strips the "apocalyptic" tenor with which del Barco writes of its redemptive value. The circumstantial defeat of the left at the outset of dictatorship has been central to political and cultural understandings of the left in Latin America. In keeping with the conceptual slippage between secular and religious tropes, the (circumstantial) defeat of the left in the 1970s is often presented in apocalyptic terms. Jinkis's move from "apocalypse" to "defeat" speaks to the eschatology contained within the left's culture of defeat. In his 1999 study of postdictatorship, *The Untimely Present* (the Spanish title, it is worth noting, is *Alegorías de la derrota*, "Allegories of defeat"), Idelber Avelar offers a "genealogy of defeat." His analysis of defeat is presented using prophetic language. In Avelar's estimation, by the mid-1960s "several of the period's most lucid minds had already seen the dead-end street [of revolutionary politics] and warned against it" (39). Here Avelar is speaking specifically of Brazil, but he notes that both the success of the Cuban Revolution and the traction that the Peronist Left was gaining in Argentina at the time were influencing factors in the armed left's decision not to retreat.[16] The rhetoric of defeat that the left adopted is bound up in ideas akin to Cohn's "revolutionary eschatology." Here again, latent Catholic thought underpins leftist politics in such a way that necessitates a process of reckoning among Jews as they grapple with their identification with these movements.

Within this diachronic framework in which religious thought informs both the revolutionary heyday of the 1960s and 1970s in the Latin American region and conversations on the memory of these political movements, I turn my focus to the ways in which Christianity is presented both implicitly and explicitly in filmic representations of revolution. I thus consider the role that religion continues to play in filmic depictions of revolution in such a way that has, in turn, called for Jews to come to terms with their places within these movements and, finally, to invite Jewish filmmakers to revisit this moment in history and their place therein through their own filmmaking.

La hora de los hornos and the Christification of Che

If Latin American revolutionary movements had a singular icon, it was and remains Che Guevara, the Argentine-born leader of the Cuban Revolution who was killed in Bolivia in 1967 by the US Central Intelligence Agency. Che is often presented in messianic terms. As Krauze points out, "The history of Latin America foreshadowed – almost in the religious sense of the term – a figure like Che Guevara. And he duly arrived, at the right time and place" (loc. 5172). The messianic quality that Che's figure has taken on in the years since his death shows the degree to which Latin American revolutionary culture was imbued with Catholic tropes. In the prologue to his 2008 *For They Know Not What They Do: Enjoyment as a Political Factor*, Slavoj Žižek issues a warning regarding what he calls the "Christification of Che": "Although we should be aware of the dangers of the 'Christification of Che,' turning him into an icon of radical-chic consumer culture, a martyr ready to die out of his love for humanity, one should perhaps take the risk of accepting this move, radicalizing it into a 'Cheification' of Christ himself" (xlvi). Žižek draws comparisons between Che's assertion that the true revolutionary is guided by love, on the one hand, and the radical potential of Christ that derived from Luke 14:26 in which Christ states that anyone who does not hate their own family "and even their own life" cannot be his disciple, on the other. Žižek signals a biblical origin for the "Cheification of Christ," that is, the use of Christ to justify radical politics.

Indeed, the phenomenon that Žižek terms the "Christification of Che" underwrote much of revolutionary culture. Fernando "Pino" Solanas and Octavio Getino's iconic 1968 film *La hora de los hornos* is a treatise in three segments addressing neocolonialism, violence, and liberation, respectively.[17] The film's title is taken from a line from José Martí, as mentioned, one of the "prophets" Krauze analyses: "It is the hour of the furnaces and all that is to be seen is light." The title thus strongly suggests a prophetic vision, in keeping with Martí's poem, of freedom and equality; it also recalls the fiery furnace episode in the Book of Daniel.[18] The first part of *La hora de los hornos* ends with a ten-minute shot of Che Guevara's corpse, taken from below. Angled up towards Che's face, these final minutes of the first segment conjure up images of Christ on the cross.[19] One half of the frame is a still shot, and the other side is a time-lapsed image of Che's decaying face. This composite image of Che – simultaneously decaying and living on – is coupled with the aural component of a drumbeat increasing in intensity in both volume and frequency. Simultaneously with the crescendo of the beating drum and the split image of Che's corpse, Solanas's voiceover instructs viewers that he who chooses to sacrifice his life for the cause, as Che Guevara did, will not die in vain but will have chosen his own death that will generate his life anew.

The final segment of *La hora de los hornos* is footage of Indigenous populations coupled with a narration recapitulating the film's eighty-minute description of the genocide caused by poverty and colonialism. The narrator then asks us: "What is the only option left to the Latin American?" And he answers: "To choose, through his rebellion, his own life, his own death. When one joins the fight for liberation death is no longer the final instance. It becomes an act of liberation. He who chooses his death is also choosing a life." Thus, Solanas and Getino represent Che as a martyr whose example is to be followed if the decimation caused by the genocide of poor and Indigenous populations in Latin America is to be stopped. Here, Che has become both prophet and martyr. These two aspects of his image – as I show later in this chapter in my discussion of *San Ernesto nace en La Higuera* (*Saint Ernesto Was Born in La Higuera*) – will often become conflated into a more simplistic image. *La hora de los hornos* deploys Che as an exemplary model for others to follow.[20]

In addition to film, such models of Che permeated revolutionary culture through *nueva canción* ("new song"), the folk music movement that gained immense popularity throughout Spain and Latin America in the 1960s transmitting strong political messages. Argentine singer-songwriter Atahualpa Yupanqui (1908–1992) offered an elegy to Che Guevara in his song "Nada más (Nothing more)." The short song includes the verse:

> Some people die
> To be born again
> And he who doubts that
> Should ask Che.

As in *La hora de los hornos*, "Nada más" posits Che's death as leading to a rebirth. Víctor Jara (1932–1973) – the subject of Santiago Álvarez's 1973 documentary *El tigre saltó y mató pero morirá, morirá* (*The Tiger Pounced and Killed but It Will Die, It Will Die*), which I discuss presently – also elegizes Che in his 1969 song "Zamba del Che" in which he dubs him "San Ernesto de La Higuera." The epithet is in reference to Che Guevara's death (and beatification) in La Higuera, Bolivia, from which the title *San Ernesto nace en La Higuera*, explored later in this chapter, also stems.

Religion in Cinema Novo and ICAIC Films

Elsewhere, revolutionary cinema explicitly rejects false prophets. Fernando "Pino" Solanas and Octavio Getino's famous 1969 essay *Hacia un tercer cine* (*Towards a Third Cinema*) became a touchstone text for Latin American revolutionary film more broadly, together with the 1965 document by Glauber Rocha (1939–1981) entitled *Estética da Fome* (*Aesthetics of Hunger*), long considered a manifesto of Brazil's Cinema Novo movement. The relationship between manifesto and film for such committed directors as Rocha, Solanas and Getino, and also Cuban director Julio García Espinosa (in his essay "Por un cine imperfecto") became essential to the imbrication between politics and filmmaking throughout 1960s Latin America. Rocha's main thrust in *Aesthetics of Hunger* is to establish hunger as the basis for and rationalization of violent political action. As he expounds here and puts into practice in his filmmaking, violence is the only recourse for those who are starving – a direct result of the economic and political imperialism visited upon Latin America. Rocha's 1964 film *Deus e o diabo na terra da sol/Black God, White Devil* treats religion explicitly in its exploration of false prophets, hunger, and violence. This film has been glossed as a "fable" (Xavier 35). In *Black God, White Devil*, Rocha questions religion as his protagonists, Manuel and Rosa, struggle to make sense of and to find guidance in an unjust world. Manuel first follows a false prophet, Sebastião (the "god" to whom the film's title ironically refers), to whom he turns after being wrongly accused by his boss. He later finds a bandit, Corisco (the "devil"), who tells him "man on this earth is only worthy when he takes up arms to change his destiny; not the rosary ... but the rifle, the dagger." Corisco forwards an interchangeability between religion and armed struggle. Although from the protagonists' perspectives Corisco's voice is not entirely to be trusted, this assertion is in keeping with Rocha's aesthetics of hunger.

Religious themes are present not only through the spoken language of Rocha's film, but also in the religious undertones of his aesthetic approach to filmmaking. As Ivana Bentes submits, "[Rocha] moves away from critical realism and classical narrative, creating a kind of aesthetic apocalypse" (123). Indeed, the chaotic and disorienting approach that characterizes Rocha's aesthetics of hunger – and to which he would return even more forcefully in his later film, *Terra em transe* (*Land in Anguish*, 1967) – serves to create a sense of urgency in viewers through largely apocalyptic overtones. For Bentes, this "aesthetic apocalypse" is transmitted through "images of unbearable power." Aesthetic forms are thus a way of transmitting apocalyptic visions of the decimation caused by global forces of imperialistic power.

Akin to Argentina's Third Cinema and Brazil's Cinema Novo, revolutionary cinema in Cuba also reckoned explicitly with religious tropes and themes. For Castro and his supporters, film was a vital medium for inculcating both revolutionary beliefs and national pride in the Cuban people. Within the first months of his rule, Castro established the Instituto Cubano del Arte y de la Industria Cinematográficos (Cuban Institute of Cinematic Art and Industry, ICAIC). Although religion had a complicated role in Castro's Cuba, Christianity and revolutionary politics are often presented as interchangeable in ICAIC filmmaking.[21] Tomás Gutiérrez Alea (1928–1996), a founding member of this institute, asserted: "The idea of communism had seemed pretty similar to me to that of paradise ... It was no longer ... a matter of preaching the virtues of Christ so as to improve man and suppress social injustices, but of admitting that man is moved by his interests and that the economic factor is determining *in the final instance*" (qtd. in Bosteels loc. 2129, original emphasis). Continuing his conflation of paradise and communism, Gutiérrez Alea's works present communism and the revolution as interchangeable with religion through both explicit thematic elements and aesthetic forms.[22]

Religion has a role in the state-supported work of Santiago Álvarez, another ICAIC founding member. Like *La hora de los hornos*, Alvarez's 1973 film *El tigre saltó y mató pero morirá, morirá* takes its title from one of José Martí's writings. The tiger here – as was common in Martí's writings, most notably his essay "Our America" (1891) – represents neocolonialism, specifically on behalf of the United States. This fifteen-minute film was supported by the ICAIC and released shortly after the Chilean coup that took place on 11 September 1973. This moment in history was crucial not only for Chile, but also for leftist-leaning and revolutionary movements across Latin America and indeed the world. The brutal end to Salvador Allende's government came to signal, for many, a definitive defeat of the left in Latin America. *El tigre* (as I will refer to this film from here on) transmits a strong sense of urgency. Similar to the ending sequence of the first segment of *La hora de los hornos*, this film ends in a crescendo that seeks to incite revolutionary action through themes of sacrifice and salvation in what has been dubbed a "nervous montage" (Hess qtd. in Mahler, "The Global South in the Belly of the Beast" 99). Much of the film's urgency is couched in overtly religious codes.

Described from its outset as "an homage in four songs," *El tigre* begins with the Violeta Parra song, "¿Qué dirá el santo Padre? (What will the Holy Father say?)." Parra wrote this song as a tribute to Julián Grimau, a Spanish socialist executed by Franco's regime in 1965. By this time, Pope John XXIII had largely alienated Franco because of his regime's brutal totalitarianism. Parra's appeal to the Pope, therefore, makes sense literally. The song derives its lyrical force from its use of antitheses to highlight the hypocrisy of a government that positions itself as a bastion of Catholic morality yet acts counter to Christian principles. Parra's song begins: "Look at how they talk to us about freedom / When they deprive us of it in reality." In Álvarez's film the song is relevant to the brutality of the Pinochet regime in Parra's home country. *El tigre* juxtaposes this song with images of military violence against Chilean citizens. Álvarez's use of Parra's invocation of the Pope recalls his use of Lena Horne's song "Now" in his 1966 documentary film *Now!* to invoke the founding fathers of the United States in signalling the hypocrisy of that country's actions.[23] Anne Garland Mahler, in her reading of *Now!* argues that Álvarez uses Horne's lyrics not because he believes that the United States of America's founding fathers would disapprove of violence against African Americans in the 1960s, but rather to suggest that the oppression of racial minorities has always been part of US history ("The Global South" 103). Similarly, using Parra's invocation of the Pope reminds audiences that, at this point, the Church had taken no direct action against the Pinochet government. The lyrics thus take on both an ironic and a damning meaning. I would further the comparison between *El tigre* and *Now!* insofar as both films position resistance against (military) police brutality in a particular place (Cuba in *Now!* and Chile in *El tigre*) in line with broader liberation and anti-colonial resistance on a global scale, including in Vietnam. The pairing of the song with images of the military government's brutality furthers the antitheses that Parra suggests through her lyrics.[24] Thus, unlike Parra's appeal to the Pope, who had disavowed Franco, Álvarez's use of Parra's song takes on a more ironic, antithetical meaning in the first minutes of *El tigre*.

The film then transforms into an elegiac homage to Víctor Jara presented in a framework of prophetic eschatology. After opening with Parra's song, the rest of the film's soundtrack consists exclusively of Víctor Jara's music. Jara was kidnapped and killed by Chile's military dictatorship almost immediately after the coup. In one of the dictatorship's most infamous acts of brutality, Jara's torturers broke his fingers and forced him to play the guitar before killing him. Already an iconic voice for the revolution, Jara's death rendered him a martyr for the cause, particularly once he was taken up in this way in cultural productions such as Álvarez's *El tigre*. The ways in which Álvarez uses Jara's own music create a sense of the singer-songwriter as a prophetic voice. The last song in the film is Jara's "Plegaria a un labrador (Prayer to a worker)." The lines of the song evoke the Lord's Prayer: "May your will be done on earth / Give us your strength and your courage to fight." Elsewhere in this song's lyrics revolutionary prophecy is present through, "today is the moment that could be tomorrow." The imminence of a coming future through the invocation of a worker explicitly brings together prophecy and workers' struggles. Jara's words – and Álvarez's use of them in film – invoke the divine and eschatological thinking so as to incite solidarity. Revolutionary eschatology allows Álvarez to mobilize this moment of crisis to posit the idea of a future event.

Álvarez incorporates imagery of devastation to buttress his depiction of Víctor Jara so as to create a sense of urgency that will, in turn, incite solidarity. Akin to the drum crescendo with which Solanas and Getino end the first part of *La hora de los hornos*, the last verses of Jara's song increase in intensity at the same time that Álvarez's images transition from footage of Jara peacefully singing to images of destruction and violence in the world's colonized lands in an apocalyptic audiovisual composition. This juxtaposition of sound and image – the aforementioned "nervous montage" that characterizes Álvarez's works – draws its strength from the coupling of the prophetic prayer to a labourer with visual images of brutality. The montage serves to radicalize the film's audience into action through the strong sense of urgency that stems from the prophecy of Jara's lyrics at the same time that it consecrates Jara as a martyr and the workers to whom he sings for liberation as saviours for the cause. Thus, like Che Guevara, within revolutionary cinema Víctor Jara is represented as both a martyr and a prophet. The juxtaposition of this image with apocalyptic brutality and destruction makes Álvarez's *El tigre* immediately intelligible through overtly Christian concepts.

Che's Afterlife: *San Ernesto nace en La Higuera*

Filmmakers immediately took up the deaths of Che Guevara and Víctor Jara to radicalize audiences in 1960s and 1970s revolutionary film. To this day, Che's image as a martyr for the cause remains a central icon in cinema. Over the past two decades, this image has been revitalized in film production, most notably through Walter Salles's *Motorcycle Diaries* (2004) and Steven Soderbergh's two-part biopic *Che: El argentino* and *Che: Guerrilla* (2008). Che's figure has been revived through a litany of documentaries that focus on various moments and aspects of his life and the mythic personality that his life and death generated.

Much critical attention has been paid to the "afterlife" of the iconic image Che Guevara. Such studies include Michael J. Casey's 2009 book *Che's Afterlife: The Legacy of an Image* and Héctor Cruz Sandoval's 2008 documentary film *Kordavision*. Both of these focus on Alberto Korda's photograph of Che Guevara and how the image has been used in the decades since Che's death. Here, I consider a filmic representation of the model of Che Guevara's afterlife that perpetuates the Christlike figure posited in *La hora de los hornos*. Nearly forty years later, Isabel Santos and Rafael Solís's 2007 documentary *San Ernesto nace en La Higuera* takes up Che's legacy in La Higuera, Santa Cruz, Bolivia, the town where he was killed by CIA operatives in 1967. This film was co-produced in Cuba and Bolivia. The collaboration between the two countries during the early days of Evo Morales's presidency underscores the importance of the Castro regime for Morales, who held the presidency from 2006 to 2019, and for the Pink Tide more broadly, as Keith Richards notes in his study of Bolivian film in the twenty-first century (152). At the same time, the co-production speaks to the ways in which Che's image was revitalized for the Pink Tide. The film consists mainly of interviews. The model that the townspeople create of Che centres not only on the parallels between his death and the death of Christ, but also on the Christian principles with which locals explicitly equate Che's life and actions. The film's sustained emphasis on the religious implications of Che's legacy in La Higuera and across all of

Latin America suggests that the strong Christian overtones of his life and legacy are also central to cultural understandings of revolution within the Pink Tide.

The interviews focus expressly on how and why Che's image has been compared to Christ. The film begins with shots of the little town juxtaposed to an elegiac song composed and performed by one of its native sons, Policarpio Cortez. The song begins: "Ernesto Guevàra was a courageous man / But many people have betrayed him / So his life ended right here." The film thus introduces Che in this place through his death in this place. Then it moves to a shot of an enormous bust of Che Guevara atop an altar at the end of the "ruta del Che," a veritable pilgrimage that visitors can make to the spot where the revolutionary leader and icon was assassinated. This giant bust is shrouded by an even larger cross, and the retaining wall beneath it bears the following words: "Your example lights up a new dawn."

Given the iconic significance of the presentation of the corpse of Che Guevara as a strategy to mobilize revolutionary action in the 1960s and 1970s, it comes as little surprise that a great deal of the film focuses on this very image. Similar to my reading of the final scene of the first segment of *La hora de los hornos* in which Che is compared to Christ, many of the interviewees in *San Ernesto nace en La Higuera* discuss the image of Che's corpse and draw comparisons to Christ on the cross. One townsperson tells viewers that it is important to remember that Christ's eyes, unlike those of Che Guevara, are not open but rather closed and covered with coins before he is entombed. He goes on to say that they should have closed Che's eyes after they killed him since the comparisons to Christ – both physical and in his life – were so many. Yet, other interviewees' accounts focus on how alive the corpse seemed days after Guevara's execution precisely because his eyes remained open. As one of the women comments, "When a person dies, they usually lose their colour, change, but not him, he was alive." As in Solanas and Getino's juxtaposition of the decaying half of Che's face and the preserved half, in *San Ernesto nace en La Higuera* the antitheses between life and death in which Che's image is couched underscore the belief that Che would live on through the revolutionary principles that his life and death instilled and propagated throughout Latin America. Here again, Che Guevara is conflated as a prophet-martyr, a continuation of the image put forth earlier in Solanas and Getino's *La hora de los hornos*.

The interviews included in *San Ernesto nace en La Higuera* turn from the physical comparisons between Che Guevara and Christ to a focus on the principles he espoused, which became a revolutionary gospel for many of Che's followers. One of the men interviewed points out that it would be easy for any bearded man to be compared to the image of Christ in a country such as Bolivia – in which few men have beards – but that in the case of Che Guevara, the comparison was more to be based on Che's principles. He asserts that Che was like Christ because of his generosity, his sacrifice of his life, and his passion for ideals. Another interviewee is quick to point out that Guevara, in fact, took issue with a great deal of what the Church was doing at that time in Latin America and other parts of the world. Yet, this same man goes on to suggest that Che probably learned the term "New Man" not from reading Marx but in his readings of scripture and that, as Saint Paul does in Ephesians, Che used the term to refer to a person who was "generous and altruistic, unfettered by the circumstances that surrounded him." These points create an almost tautological model in which Che Guevara was like Christ and therefore died like Christ, and vice versa.

This possible tautology is important not because it is a logical fallacy. Indeed, I submit that it is not a logical fallacy, but rather a strong example of how Christian paradigms made Che Guevara's life and death intelligible and meaningful in a predominantly Catholic culture, specifically through the Catholic emphasis on the exemplary lives of the saints. People in La Higuera read Che Guevara typologically in line with Christ; that is, they saw his beard, witnessed his death, and drew comparisons. These similarities also led some townspeople to speak of Che as a Christian. One interviewee explains, "He's a Christian and a human just like us." Through this utterance, Che Guevara enters a narrative of belonging on the basis of shared Christianity. Such depictions of Che implicitly exclude Jews from full identification with Latin American revolutionary culture. In particular, as I discuss further in this chapter's conclusions, Che Guevara is taken up as a paragon of the New Man in a way that is explicitly couched in biblical terms. Adrián Krupnik constructs an analogy between Che's "New Man" and the austere life of the kibbutz in his essay "Cuando camino al Kibutz vieron pasar al Che," translated as "When on their way to the kibbutz they saw Che walk by" (311). For Krupnik's model, Che was, on the one hand, in keeping with Jewish culture because of the importance of the kibbutz and working the land and, on the other, a distraction from Jewish youths' obligation to work on the kibbutz. The cultural model of Che as the New Man meant that Jews were tacitly "Othered" vis-à-vis one of the most iconic figures associated with Latin American revolutionary culture.

Twenty-First-Century Filmic Depictions of Priests in Revolutionary Politics

The strong religious valence of revolutionary culture continues to appear in fictional films from Latin America that revisit revolutionary culture of the 1960s and 1970s. The 2004 film *Machuca* garnered considerable critical acclaim. It centres on two youngsters, Gonzalo Infante and Pedro Machuca, who become unlikely friends at St. Patrick's School for Boys in Santiago, Chile, in the days leading up to the 1973 coup. Pedro and Gonzalo live in different worlds, and only come to meet each other as part of a socialist dream come true (then turned nightmare) of the school's rector Father McEnroe to bring students from a *población* (shantytown) in the outskirts of Santiago into the wealthy school. Based primarily on the childhood memories of the director and co-author Andrés Wood when he himself was a young boy at a parochial school in Santiago, the setting evokes the sympathies of priests committed to socioeconomic equality during this period, in line with the liberation theologians and *curas villeros* (a term for priests who work in slums) discussed earlier. Most analyses of *Machuca* focus on the importance of class conflict (see Martín-Cabrera and Voionmaa; Rocha, "Children's View"), memory (Yim), and trauma (Traverso). As Antonio Traverso notes, the film "seems driven by a desire to 'remember' fixed memories that 'act out' the traumas of the military coup" (1). In contrast, little attention has been paid to the film's overt and salient religious themes (other than in a footnote in Martín-Cabrera and Voionmaa's article noting the importance of the Second Vatican Council), although these elements are certainly implicit in the film's critical focus on class struggle. The film conflates Catholicism and class equality in the context of the socialist, pro-Allende movement.

Indeed, the religious elements of *Machuca* show that the socialist dream was inexorable from Catholic teachings at this time. As the film begins, Father McEnroe is entering the classroom with the young boys from the shantytown, and he enjoins the other students to treat them as they do one another and to love their neighbour. At this time Father McEnroe is hopelessly struggling to keep a self-sustaining garden in the school's courtyard, but the pigs that he has brought in to do so are dying. The pigs never stood a chance at surviving in this school and the rector's dream was doomed to failure, just as his attempts to integrate the boys from the shantytown into the school were never to succeed. This element of the film is a quite literal illustration of the common Chilean expression "chancho en misa (pig in Mass)," meaning something that is completely out of place. As with the efforts of many progressive priests in the Latin American region at the time, Father McEnroe's endeavour to foster social justice and equality through the project with the pigs fails.

Machuca explicitly couples faith in Christianity with faith in Allende's political project. In one of its most poignant moments, soldiers have taken over the school following Pinochet's coup and ousted socialist sympathizers, wresting Father McEnroe's authority. In reaction Father McEnroe consumes all of the available communion hosts. After doing so he proclaims to one of the soldiers, "This is no longer a sacred place. The Lord is no longer here." The clergyman is thus protesting the presence of the soldiers by consuming the body of Christ so that others who are not worthy cannot have the consecrated host. His proclamation that the chapel is no longer a sacred place now that the military has taken over the country posits that Catholic faith and military rule are incompatible, evoking the complicated role of the Church in Pinochet's Chile.[25] Father McEnroe resists the takeover of the school and its chapel by denying the sacrament of communion to the military men and to others whom he deems unworthy of the Eucharist now that the school – like the entire country – is no longer a sacred place.[26]

Rather than an apocalypse, the narrative force of the ending of the film *Machuca* lies in the impossibility of salvation. Released some thirty years after Álvarez's documentary, Wood's *Machuca* includes images of the military regime's brutality but does not include the apocalyptic images of the destruction that *El tigre* uses to depict the military coup. Rather, the visual representation of Pinochet's takeover is relegated to images of annihilation (as Martín-Cabrera and Voionmaa adroitly discuss). The audience sees this annihilation through the eyes of Gonzalo after the shantytown where Machuca and his family live is razed and they have disappeared. At the end of the film, the co-author of the screenplay, the Jewish Chilean writer Roberto Brodsky, speaks directly to this disillusionment. Interestingly, he does so in Christian terms of salvation, stating that Gonzalo's escape from repression at the film's end is ironic insofar as there is no actual salvation at this point. He adds, "What is interesting is that there is no salvation ... we had reached a point in which our old mythologies seemed bankrupt ... What remained? What shred of truth might remain in that great accumulation of events, which seemed to bespeak the apocalyptic *Aguirre, Wrath of God*, coming to tell us that this is the dream?" (qtd. in DiGiovanni and García-Caro, "The Uncertain Territory of Memory"). Carolina Rocha also takes up Gonzalo's role as witness to conclude her reading of *Machuca* stating that "the wound produced by his witnessing of the repression is still an unresolved consequence of political violence" ("Children's View of

State-Sponsored Violence in Latin America" 90). In *Machuca*'s ending, prophecy and salvation are supplanted by witnessing, as Brodsky submits, through Gonzalo's role as protagonist and Wood's reimagining of his country decades later.

Brodsky's discussion of the impossibility of salvation recalls the secularized terms in which Oscar del Barco speaks of salvation in reference to his Jewish peer, Juan Gelman. Like del Barco, Brodsky and Wood evoke salvation as a way of considering justice in the context of the memory of revolutionary politics. In his novel *Bosque quemado*, published in 2007, three years after release of the film *Machuca*, Brodsky directly treats his family's Jewish identity within a story of childhood during the days leading up to the coup and, later, their exile in the United States. Yet, these aspects are missing from *Machuca* and Brodsky's discussion of the film, both of which are couched in more overtly Christian terms. In his role as co-author of Wood's largely autobiographical story set in a parochial school, Brodsky assimilates some of Wood's religious beliefs. For Brodsky and Wood, a retrospective consideration of Chile's socialist revolutionary moment necessarily takes into account the role of religion, specifically the Church's preferential option for the poor.

Unlike *Machuca*'s setting in the early 1970s, Pablo Trapero's *Elefante blanco* is set entirely in the present but draws explicit parallels with 1970s progressive politics in Latin America. Released in 2012, *Elefante blanco* is dedicated to the memory of Carlos Mugica, Padre Mugica. The film takes place in present-day Buenos Aires in a *villa* (shantytown) and centres on two priests. The older one, Julián, is portrayed by iconic Argentine actor Ricardo Darín. The younger, Belgian priest, Nicolás, is disillusioned after having worked in the Amazon only to be run out of the small village to which he was ministering by men with rifles. The title, *Elefante blanco* (*White Elephant*) refers literally to the eyesore that looms over the villa in many of the film's shots: a partially built hospital whose construction was halted. In addition to being a monstrosity, the structure recalls broken dreams of social equality and well-being. Class difference is brought into sharper relief when the film shows Julián in a modern, efficient doctor's office as he is being diagnosed with a terminal illness. He has access to quality health care in this space that towers above the villa putting the other, unfinished hospital in its shadow. This contrast reminds viewers that Julián, like Padre Mugica, comes from a privileged background yet spends his life in the villa among people of far humbler means. Once he knows that he is going to die, Julián becomes more devoted to his parishioners and to training Padre Nicolás so that he may leave them all for the better. Padre Julián thus serves as a model of martyrdom for social justice and the well-being of the poor.

In addition to being dedicated to Padre Mugica, the film itself draws clear parallels between Julián and Padre Mugica. Julián dies tragically from being shot by a police officer as he is attempting to help one of the *villeros* (shantytown dwellers) who has been involved in drug trafficking and the murder of a police officer to surrender. His death recalls that of Mugica, also at the hands of government forces. The film equates the injustices of poverty in today's society with the social ills that Mugica sought to correct in his time. In a sense, *Elefante blanco* evokes not only Mugica but also the well-known present-day shantytown priest José María di Paola, commonly referred to as "Padre Pepe," renowned for his work with drug addiction and decriminalization. As with the figure of Che Guevara in *San Ernesto nace en La Higuera,* cultural understandings of Padre Mugica create a cultural model of the relationship between Christian principles, the revolutionary left, and twenty-first century leftist leadership in which a personage associated with Christianity serves to link past and present political movements. The Kirchnerist politician and documentary filmmaker Gabriel Mariotto asserted in a 2014 homage to Padre Mugica that the spirit of the deceased priest now lives in the Casa Rosada, the government house which at the time was occupied by Cristina Fernández de Kirchner, president of Argentina (Vezzetti, "Archivo y memorias del presente"). As Vezzetti points out, Mariotto's position is not critically significant, and it is propagandistic (ibid.). Yet, for some, like Mariotto, the use of Padre Mugica links together the 1970s revolutionary left, the preferential option for the poor, and the Pink Tide leadership. Like in del Barco's and Brodsky's writings of salvation, twenty-first century Latin American memory politics are bound up in the legacies of revolutionary movements through both implicit and express invocations of Catholic beliefs and practices.

Conclusions

These depictions of revolution predicated largely on Catholicism situate Jews uncertainly vis-à-vis revolutionary culture. Specifically, I consider what the place of the New Man means for Jews. Within Latin American revolutionary cinema, the model of the New Man is also integral to Tomás Gutiérrez Alea's films *Fresa y chocolate* (*Strawberry and Chocolate,* 1994), an adaptation of the Senel Paz novella *El lobo, el bosque y el hombre nuevo* (*The Wolf, the Forest, and the New Man,* 1990), and *Memorias del subdesarrollo* (*Memories of Underdevelopment,* 1968), both of which explore the idea of the New Man who emerges in the context of the Castroist government. Returning to the interviewee in *San Ernesto nace en La Higuera* who commented that Che learned the term "New Man" not from Marx but from the Bible, one can see how New Testament thought works its way, if subtly, into conversations about revolutionary politics. In the specific case of the use of New Man in its biblical roots, New Testament thinking situated Jews ambiguously within (or outside of) Latin American revolutionary culture. Paul's New Man in Ephesians puts forth a model Christian who is opposed to the "old man," the Jew, lending itself to a model of biblical interpretation in which the Old Testament prefigures the New Testament.[27] The New Man is often presented in secularized terms through retrospective analyses of the life of Che Guevara such as in the interviews in the film *San Ernesto nace en La Higuera*. Yet, the figure of the New Man lends itself to cultural models of revolutionary thought in which Christians find affinity with one another and take anyone who touts himself or herself as the New Man to be "a Christian and one of us."

For Marxism, the New Man has a particular meaning considering that Marx famously proposes the extirpation of religious beliefs as a necessary component for the revolution and, by extension, for self-identification with the revolution. Yet, Marx also explains in his responses to Bruno Bauer's "Jewish Question" that this process is wholly different for Jews from what it is for Christians.[28] Within this context, Marx's use of the New Man is another indicator of the multilayered and contradictory implications of the use of religious terminology within revolutionary politics. Just as Marx notes that disavowal of religious beliefs is a different experience for Jews than for non-Jews, the New Man means something different for Jews than for Christians.

Similarly, Bruno Bosteels has asked: "Whether the creation of 'new man' necessarily obliterates the 'old man' as Jewish ... or ... to what extent is the construction of a new militant subjectivity ... a process that would be constitutively Christian, if not also anti-Semitic?" (loc. 2101). Whether or not the model of the New Man is patently anti-Semitic, Christianity most definitely enjoys a strong hegemonic status that creates exclusionary categories when it comes to considering the place of religious minorities within revolutionary politics in the Latin American region. Through these cultural depictions of revolution, Jews are positioned tenuously in the face of these movements that many of them perceived as "laicos" (to use Senator Gabriel Fuks's characterization), that is, lay or more precisely, non-Jewish, despite the presence of Old Testament beliefs, references, and tropes. In effect, the visual and semiotic logics by which Christianity comes to be taken as secular within revolutionary politics and their filmic representations eschew any religious difference. At the same time, they foreground signifiers heavily laden with New Testament thought, such as the Christlike image of Che Guevara and the term "New Man."

Throughout these depictions of revolutionary beliefs – whether from the time of revolutionary action in Latin American in the 1960s and 1970s or through more recent works that have revisited the place of these moments within the cultural imaginary – slippages occur between Jewish, Christian, "Judeo-Christian," and secular cultures. Religion informs politics in differential and contradictory ways that are inexorably inseparable from broader questions of ideology and hegemony. As a result of these vexed matrices, as I show in the following chapters, Jews have assuredly been compelled to grapple with their place in these movements and in the cultural imaginary representing their legacy.

Chapter Two

Here We Are to Build a Nation: Jewish Immigrants to Early Twentieth-Century Latin America

Recent filmic representations of Jewish immigration emphasize the significance of identifications with global and national political issues as integral to Jewish life in Latin America. In the early decades of the twentieth century, Brazil and the Southern Cone region (Chile, Argentina, and Uruguay) saw a sizeable influx of Ashkenazi Jews, most of them fleeing pogroms and persecution in Russia and elsewhere in Eastern Europe. Not long after these Jews arrived in their new countries, many formed businesses and began to participate in the local political sphere. They not only found refuge, but they also became active in the mainstream communities in which they were establishing themselves. The surrealist fiction film *La danza de la realidad* (dir. Alejandro Jodorowsky, Chile, 2013) and the following documentaries represent Jewish families who immigrated to Latin America: *Hacer patria* (dir. David Blaustein, Argentina, 2007), *El barrio de los judíos* (dir. Gonzalo Rodríguez Fábregas, Uruguay, 2011), and *Danken got/ Estamos aqui estamos/Here We Are* (dir. Cintia Chamecki, Brazil/USA, 2013). Particular attention is devoted to Jewish businesses and political organizations. These films share a common focus on the national, regional, and international issues that influenced Jewish identities and beliefs in Latin America in the period leading up the Second World War, its horrors, and its aftermath. They show how political orientations strongly inflect patterns of assimilation. Encounters with local, national, and global political movements were a key component of Jewish integration into local life in various Latin American countries. These experiences oriented Jewish political beliefs and, later in the century, created possibilities for identifications with revolutionary culture. This chapter looks exclusively at Ashkenazi communities that immigrated to Latin America from Eastern Europe; I address filmic representations of Sephardic communities, specifically tensions and misunderstandings between Ashkenazi and Sephardic characters, at length in the following chapter.

Jewish life as seen in these films is characterized by such issues as Zionism, assimilation into non-Jewish culture, exile, and embodied difference. Emmanuel Levinas's "feeling a place for oneself in the economy of being" – understood here as gaining a sense of belonging in the public spheres of the countries in which Jewish families gain refuge – becomes manifest through Jewish participation in political groups as well as through their newly formed businesses. These films portray how Zionist, anarchist, and socialist political groups informed Jewish identities in these new communities. Early twentieth-century experiences in Latin America set up paradigms of political participation that lent themselves to the Jewish affinity with revolutionary politics that would arise later in the century. Yet, at the same time, these paradigms of political identifications also meant that Jewish involvement in the more extreme aspects of revolutionary politics presented a disruption to Jewish life, as did the Catholic elements of revolutionary culture discussed in the previous chapter. These films depict some of the ways in which Jews came to understand themselves as citizens of their Latin American homelands with regard to hegemonic racial and ethnic categories and Otherness. Depictions of anti-Semitism and the persecution of Jews centre Jewish experiences within the national identities of their respective countries.

As a way of engaging with the points of contact between family and politics, the films discussed in this chapter dedicate significant attention to exploring the transmission of memory from older generations of family and community members to younger ones. Many aspects of these films evoke Marianne Hirsch's understandings of postmemory, loosely defined as the memory held by subsequent generations who did not live through an event but grew up with their parents' and ancestors' memories about an event or events as told to them. Postmemory bridges the conceptual divides between familial and "more distant" constructions of social memory. Although the term has received some criticism, postmemory has been widely discussed within contemporary cultural studies as a theoretical model for conceptualizing the relationship of present-day culture to Latin America's recent past. Beatriz Sarlo expresses her objection: "There is not then, a 'postmemory,' but rather forms of memory that can be attributed directly to a simple division between those who lived the experiences directly and the children of those who lived them" (*Tiempo pasado* 157). Hirsch's emphasis on the importance of intergenerational transmission of memory is relevant here, because these films show that memories passed down through generations are integral to the self-understandings and self-representations of the Jewish communities they portray. Families' transmission of memories, experiences, and histories regarding anti-Semitism and Nazism are central in all of these films and depicted as an important process through which Jewish individuals and communities came to understand their place in relation to the national project of their new country and to global politics.

The political implications of a variety of cinematic genres are analysed here as I discuss the ideological multiplicities these films represent in various Latin American Jewish communities. Inexorably linked to the political sphere since the heyday of 1960s revolutionary filmmaking praxis (e.g., Solanas and Getino, Rocha, and Álvarez, all discussed in the previous chapter), the documentary form has been and continues to be of great significance. Writing in 1990, Julianne Burton asserts that 1960s cinema "accorded to documentary a privileged status," adding that "today's Latin American artists and activists continue to embrace documentary as an instrument of cultural exploration, national definition, epistemological inquiry, and social and political transformation" (6). The documentaries examined in this chapter explore these issues from a distinctly Jewish position. The documentary form uses Jewishness as a lens through which to view various expressions of national culture and identity; moreover, Jewish filmmakers use it to inscribe themselves into the national histories and political spheres of their respective countries. Although his focus is on the North American documentary and not on Latin America, Michael Renov argues, "Current documentary self-inscription enacts identities – fluid, multiple, even contradictory – while remaining fully embroiled within public discourses" (178).

In addition to the long history of the documentary's overt thematic engagement with politics, formal aspects of the documentary carry their own political valence. As Vinicius Navarro and Juan Carlos Rodríguez, in introducing their 2014 publication *New Documentaries in Latin America*, assert, "If filmmakers in the 1960s and 1970s used the camera as a weapon, as a political weapon, today veteran filmmakers ... push the boundaries of the documentary tradition as they tackle the sociopolitical complexities of the present" (4). These innovations, as Navarro and Rodríguez point out, correspond to the emergence of a new generation of filmmakers – to which the documentary makers I discuss here belong. Importantly, they submit that "the convergence of politics and aesthetic experimentation is perhaps most obvious in works that connect personal and historical realities, while foregrounding the role of the filmmaker as discursive agent" (8). The Jewish Latin American documentaries examined below offer multifaceted representations of individual identities in relation to broader sociopolitical concerns and challenge hegemonic understandings of identities and of national histories. Jewish documentary filmmakers engage with ideological multiplicities in line with Hamid Naficy's model of exilic and diasporic filmmaking, explored in this book's introduction.

In documentary and fiction cinema alike, experimentation with genres and aesthetic forms allows filmmakers to grapple with the national projects of the countries their ancestors arrived in as immigrants and, ultimately, to represent their Jewish communities as integral participants in these national projects. If, as Renov posits, documentary enacts multiple identities while remaining committed to social issues, Jodorowsky draws from his long entrenchment in surrealist filmmaking to fulfil a similar objective in narrating the story of his own life with an eye towards the political and historical contexts in which he grew up. Jodorowsky uses quintessentially surrealistic precepts of cinema to explore Jewish embodiment and Chilean national identity in his semi-autobiographical *La danza de la realidad*, a departure from his previous films where no mention whatsoever is made of his home country. Jodorowsky maintains his patently cosmopolitan aesthetics as a way of dealing with national politics, and his formal approaches to filmmaking are related to both his (trans)national and his Jewish identity. Despite the significant formal differences between documentary and surrealist cinema, these films all share in an endeavour to leverage generic qualities to explore the points of contact between Jewishness and participation in the respective national projects, whether of Chile, Brazil, Uruguay, or Argentina.

Hacer patria

David Blaustein's *Hacer patria* (*To Build a Homeland*, Argentina, 2007) opens with his visit to the national museum of immigration in Buenos Aires. This opening, which embeds his personal family history within a space of institutionalized national history, sets the tone for the rest of the film's focus on the points of contact between the history of Blaustein's Jewish family and the history of Argentina. Comprised primarily of interviews with family members who emigrated from Poland to Argentina in the 1920s, the emphasis in Blaustein's film is on citizenship and participation in the political sphere as significant elements of his family's identity. As the director's brother points out, at the time their ancestors immigrated, Argentina "was a very seductive country. It was a country still being constructed." Through sustained attention to the ways his family encountered life and political developments in Argentina over the course of the twentieth century, Blaustein provides a document showing a country that "seduced" new immigrants who then helped to construct the nation through their active participation in the political sphere. Blaustein makes it clear that many of the Jewish immigrants completely assimilated and forgot not only that they were Russian or Polish, but also that they were Jewish. Coupling Jewishness and nationality, Blaustein prompts viewers to reflect on the ways in which religious identification and citizenship come to bear on one another. The dangers of forgetting, against which Blaustein implicitly warns, is the impetus for the film. Blaustein reminds viewers, whether they are Jewish Argentines or not, of his community's origins and history. *Hacer patria* retrieves Argentina's Jewish communities from the margins and centres them within the country's national history and politics.

David Blaustein is a prominent political filmmaker in Argentina. He is well known as the award-winning director of political documentaries, including *Cazadores de utopias* (*Hunters of Utopias*, 1996), about Montoneros and the revolutionary culture of the 1970s, and *Botín de guerra: La historia de una búsqueda infatigable* (*Spoils of War: The Story of an Indefatigable Search*, 2006), a film about the children of Argentina's *desaparecidos*, "the disappeared." Desaparecidos were the victims of state terror during Argentina's last military dictatorship. Jorge Rafael Videla was the military junta leader who deposed Isabel Perón and became Argentina's president from 1976 to 1981. When at one point he was asked about political prisoners, Videla infamously claimed that they were neither dead nor living but rather "disappeared," thus coining the term. *Cazadores de utopías* and *Botín de guerra* are crucial for the periodization of memory politics in the 1990s and into this century. Blaustein's 2012 short film *Las Abuelas de la Plaza de Mayo* (*Grandmothers of Plaza de Mayo*) is about the grandmothers who fought to identify the children of desaparecidos. The release of *Cazadores de utopías* coincided with a moment at which the political presence of activists for memory and justice, including the human rights orgnizations Abuelas de la Plaza de Mayo, set up in 1977, and Hijos por la Justicia y contra el Olvido y el Silencio (Children for Justice and Against Forgetting and Silence), established in 1995, was growing exponentially. In a 2008 essay "La mirada del cine," Blaustein writes of the importance of memory for filmmaking, calling for more fiction films to engage memory politics in postdictatorship Argentina. Since that time, by all counts, Argentine cinematic production has largely filled this lack, as evidenced by the commercial and critical success of films such as *Infancia clandestina* (2012) and *El secreto de sus ojos* (2009), each named Argentina's official entry for the Oscar for Best Foreign Language Film (a prize the latter did win). Jeanine

Meerapfel's 2012 film *El amigo alemán* and Daniel Burman's 2004 film *El abrazo partido*, discussed in detail in the next chapters, are examples of fiction films focused on Argenitne postdictatorship memory politics from a patently Jewish perspective. In his consideration of the importance of memory in film, Blaustein does not, however, mention his own *Hacer patria* or a need to foster Jewish memory in particular.

In the late 1990s and early 2000s, Blaustein emerged as a seminal voice inaugurating a new generation of political cinema. *Hacer patria* furthers his earlier endeavours to document Argentina's history and politics but here incorporates a more intimate focus – on his own family members – at the same time that he recounts the history of Argentina's Jewish communities more broadly. Moving beyond the clichéd "the personal is political," *Hacer patria* shows how the Blaustein family's involvement in the political sphere in twentieth-century Argentina becomes a form of nation building and foregrounds Jews as integral citizens of the nation.

Hacer patria sets out to instil historical consciousness in its viewers. On the cover of the film's DVD and on the disc's title screen is the following caption: "Dare to learn about your past." This tagline suggests that the film will reveal not only the Blaustein family's history, but also the history of Jewish Argentina and, perhaps, that of non-Jewish Argentina as well. Tzvi Tal is emphatic in stating that "the cinematic history of the Jewish family is also the history of the Argentine people ... Despite the xenophobic anti-Semitic attitudes of a residual minority, most of the Argentine population recognizes itself in these cinema images of the people once known as '*rusos*' and can identify with the small successes and misfortunes of the Jews in the film" ("The Other Becomes Mainstream" 387). A review in *La Nación* adapts the axiom "Paint a picture of your village and you'll paint the picture of the world" and turns it into "Paint a picture of your immigrant family and you'll paint the picture of the evolution of Argentina during a good portion of the twentieth century" (Battle).[1] In keeping with Blaustein's political concerns in his earlier filmmaking, *Hacer patria* offers a model of Argentine history and citizenship through focusing on his family's political affinities and activism, which began in Poland and Russia a good century ago and continue to this day.

What immediately differentiates *Hacer patria* from Blaustein's other films is the low-tech, homemade quality of much of the footage, shot by Blaustein himself, giving the documentary a more intimate aesthetic. As do his other documentaries, *Hacer patria* incorporates a lot of historical footage, which is of varying quality; however, the technical aspects of the scenes in which Blaustein interviews people or goes to archives and museums have a far less sophisticated feel to them than the interviews in his other documentaries. The lighting and angles used in the interviews with Blaustein's family members give a less formal feel than in *Cazadores de utopías,* further emphasizing the film's personal and intimate aspects. The footage begins with Blaustein himself entering Buenos Aires's Museo de la Inmigración, a museum on the former site of the port of entry into Argentina. He is looking up information about his family members. In these opening scenes, Blaustein juxtaposes images of his visits to the *conventillos* (tenements) where his family lived and images of the same sites in the more distant past. Elsewhere, we see him walking down the street as he interviews his family members telling their stories, visually inscribing his family within the urban spaces of Buenos Aires, and through these visual inscriptions Blaustein is building a *patria,* a homeland.

Blaustein draws attention to Jewish negotiations with global and national politics using these family interviews. His mother, aunt, and cousins expressly underscore the importance of their family's political principles and participation. Members of the older generations talk to him about the influence of the Russian Revolution in fostering the political views of Jews worldwide. But, as the contradictions revealed by their accounts show, members of Blaustein's family did not all have the same take on the Russian Revolution. One interviewee asserts that the Russian Revolution awoke the political spirit in Jews. Blaustein's maternal grandparents were actively involved in political groups in Poland, yet his paternal cousin Bubi tells how his Russian grandfather on his father's side was displeased when his children became active in socialist organizations in Argentina. Another cousin describes his parents' political thinking as "a formation that wasn't exactly socialist but something like it." He explains that his mother was one of the first members in Hashomer Hatzair (Young Guard), the foundational Jewish Zionist socialist group previously introduced. Hashomer Hatzair also comes up in Gonzálo Rodríguez Fábregas's *El barrio de los judíos,* as I explore later in this chapter, and is integral to the plot of *Novia que te vea,* discussed in detail in chapter 3. Attention to the Blaustein family's beliefs and responses to various political movements over time shows Jewishness informing political affinities in contradictory ways: for some family members, experiences with politics before emigrating meant that they were already actively embroiled in politics, while others felt a need to maintain a low profile when it came to political activity because they were immigrants and feared persecution.

Hacer patria especially underscores the vexed relationship between Jewishness and political identifications that characterized Jewish experiences with Peronism. References to Juan Domingo Perón abound in the film. One of Blaustein's cousins laments the family's presence, including the director's father and the father's four siblings, in the Plaza de Mayo in 1955 celebrating the so-called *revolución libertadora* that ousted Perón. This cousin points to the family's hypocrisy in claiming solidarity with the Peronists when, in fact, on that occasion they stood alongside the oligarchy celebrating Perón's defeat. The family story is thus rife with the political struggles and controversies that characterize twentieth-century Argentina as a whole. The Blausteins' complicated relationship with Peronism was the experience of many Jewish Argentine families, as Perón was sometimes an ally of Argentina's Jewish communities, helping in the establishment of Jewish organizations and labour initiatives, while he also allowed Nazis to enter the country.[2] As an additional complicating factor, explored in the previous chapter, the Peronist leftist guerrilla group Montoneros was strongly undergirded by Catholic beliefs and culture.

The discussion of Peronism in *Hacer patria* is important for understanding revolutionary culture. Peronist working-class hegemony in the 1940s and 1950s gave way to a proliferation of fervent liberation movements, and Jewish relationships to Peronism would only become more complicated as the Peronist Left became increasingly militant through the 1960s and 1970s. Assimilation into the Argentine national project in this particular moment had salient implications for political participation. On this issue, and drawing on the Argentine political theorist and philosopher Ernesto Laclau (1935–2014), Jon Beasley-Murray submits, "The working class becomes hegemonic by also being populist ... A 'socialist populism' is not the most backward form of working-class ideology but the most advanced – the moment when the working class has succeeded in condensing the ensemble of democratic ideology in a determinate social formation within its own ideology" (*Posthegemony* 51). Although Peronism is perhaps the most hyperbolic example of how hegemony-cum-populism cedes to later revolutionary politics (i.e., the Peronist bases of 1960s and 1970s revolutionary movements), this paradigm of assimilation into working-class populism is significant beyond Argentina's borders. The assimilation of Jewish immigrants into their countries' national projects was a crucial step in a broader process of political participation, as Jews came to be involved in these countries' local politics.

Not only does *Hacer patria* document the immigration and assimilation of Jewish Argentines as part of their role in the national project, but Blaustein also reminds viewers that cinema itself is a way of articulating national identity. In concluding her analysis of *Hacer patria*, Daniela Goldfine writes, "Blaustein allows himself and us to question our role as citizens and protagonists of our stories and of History. The space that the director offers should be taken up as a point of departure for this exploration and not only as a static document. Ultimately, a meaningful way to build a nation is by telling the stories that formed it" ("*Hacer patria* de David Blaustein"). As Goldfine suggests through her characterization of the film as a "point of departure," *Hacer patria* invites Jewish viewers to reflect on how their own families' histories helped shape their country's history in contributing to the national patrimony. By focusing on Jews and Argentine politics in the twentieth century, demonstrating how Jewish experiences with the political sphere shaped the history of his family and his country, Blaustein makes *Hacer patria* relevant to a wide variety of audiences.

Conversations in the film show memory being transmitted across generations, and several moments in *Hacer patria* comprise a veritable mise-en-scène of Hirsch's model of postmemory. This is accomplished through shots of the director sitting with members of a younger generation of his family as they listen to his mother's accounts of her life as a Polish woman living in Argentina. One of the children asks Blaustein's mother, presumably the child's grandmother, about the difficulty of having two children who were exiled during Argentina's dictatorship, a point to which I return presently. In another scene, one of Blaustein's cousins recounts his own mother's journey to Argentina and in doing so he points out, "I am repeating my mother's version of the story. I wasn't present." *Hacer patria* emphatically conveys the importance of oral histories and the transmission of memory within this family and for Jewish communities more broadly, and indeed, for other families and other communities, for that matter. Many of these stories of family history are bound up in difficult moments of national history, such as the family's experiences during the dictatorship. Blaustein's own presence as a listener to his mother's stories alongside members of younger generations signifies his charge as a filmmaker to facilitate and participate in these conversations. I direct my attention to exile as it relates to Jewish experiences in my readings of *El abrazo partido* and *O ano em que meus pais saíram de férias*, in chapter 4.

In *Hacer patria*, David Blaustein draws attention to postmemory through explicit consideration of the capacity his filmmaking has to foster collective and intergenerational conversations on memory. One scene shows him with Ariel, his brother. Ariel informs David that after seeing the 1996 film *Cazadores de utopías*, his teenaged son became irate with him in talking about the documentary. The son asked Ariel whether Argentina was under a military government or a dictatorship in the years that film discusses (1976–1983). When Ariel responded, saying the government had indeed been a dictatorship, his son stood up from the table and ran to his bedroom upset. Ariel had briefly been detained during the dictatorship and subsequently gone into exile. As he now tells his brother, his son was upset not only because he had just learned about the dictatorship, but also because his father had remained silent about it. The son admonished his father, "If you don't explain it to me, I can't understand!" This comment by the son highlights the problematic silences surrounding the dictatorship that characterized much of the 1990s political climate under the presidency of Carlos Menem (1989–1999), during which time *Cazadores de utopías* was realized. Within this culture of silence, it was even more incumbent upon parents to discuss the country's dictatorial past lest their children never learn. This anecdote about Ariel and his son underscores the capacity of documentary film to arouse historical consciousness among Argentine citizens and, perhaps especially within families, a main purpose of *Hacer patria*. In this scene with his brother who is discussing his nephew, Blaustein engages the complicated subject of the particular experiences of Jews during Argentina's military dictatorship.[3]

This scene with Ariel also evokes Hirsch's notions of postmemory with regard to Blaustein's self-referential consideration of the conversations that his own filmmaking prompts. Hirsch posits that postmemory is "a very particular form of memory precisely because its connection to its object or source is mediated not through recollection but through an imaginative investment and creation" (*Generation of Postmemory* 22). Such imaginative investment and creation are seen through Blaustein's reflections on the intergenerational conversations within his family prompted by his own films.[4] Postmemory has become a common way to interpret how writers and filmmakers approach Argentina's dictatorship (see Blejmar; Maguire; Nouzeilles). *Hacer patria* differs from other discussions of postmemory in that Blaustein uses the aesthetics of postmemory in the specific case of a Jewish family, a point I develop further in my discussions of *Danken got* and *El barrio de los judíos*.

The documentary brings politics to the fore of conversations about Jewish life in Argentina and situates Jews at the centre of discussions of national politics. Additionally, *Hacer patria* uses postmemory to explore the family's relationship to national history within the context of a film that is considering ethno-religious identities. For Blaustein's family, to build a nation means to populate the land with immigrants whose children and grandchildren will not only actively participate in the political sphere of that nation, but also understand their identities as being inexorably linked to national belonging. For Blaustein to build a nation means to document in cinema these processes of negotiation of identity and make them accessible to a wide audience.

Danken got/Estamos aqui

Like *Hacer patria*, the Brazilian director Cintia Chamecki's *Danken got/ Estamos aqui* focuses on the roles of Jewish immigrants in national and local politics, specifically in Chamecki's hometown of Curitiba, the largest urban centre in the southern Brazilian state of Paraná and its capital. Chamecki's exploration of Curitiba facilitates a unique consideration of Jewish political life, given the Jewish community's particular history there. In the 1950s the city saw the founding of the Jewish political organization Sociedad Cultural Israelita Brasileira, and in 1971 it elected a Jewish mayor, Jaime Lerner, who was later to become the governor of Paraná. The film follows Chamecki, who currently lives in New York City, back in Curitiba to interview her family and community members as the city works on a Holocaust Museum, the inauguration of which provides the film's ending sequence. *Danken got* represents the history of Jewish immigration and everyday life in Curitiba.

Danken got offers a quintessentially cosmopolitan impression of Curitiba. Shown in film festivals worldwide and now available online through the Vimeo platform, the bilingual title *Danken got/Estamos aqui* immediately garners attention. The use of both Yiddish and Portuguese underscores the hybridity of Latin American Jewish existence – the first line of the film's description refers to Chamecki as "searching for her own identity as a cosmopolitan (Jew)." The gloss of "cosmopolitan (Jew)" evokes notions of Jewish exile and wandering. Rather than translate the Yiddish expression "Danken got!" ("Thank God!"), the film's Portuguese title is *Estamos aqui* and its English title is *Here We Are!* Through these changes in the title's translations from Yiddish into Portuguese and English, the film's subject matter is suggested to be less religious. At the same time, the Portuguese and English versions of the title nevertheless bring to mind the Hebrew "Heneni (Here I am)" that in Genesis Abraham utters to God to indicate that he is ready to be called upon to be God's servant, thus coupling being present in a place to a divine, religious meaning.[5]

In addition to the title's religious implications, the literal meaning of *Here We Are!* denotes a filmic endeavour to write Jewish immigrants into the national histories of their countries of refuge. In this way, the title dovetails with Renov's emphasis on the capacity of the documentary for self-inscription that allows its subjects to enact their identities while remaining embroiled in social discourse. Chamecki's film certainly proclaims that her Jewish community is here in Curitiba and involved in local happenings. The English title *Here We Are!* draws attention to the status of the subjects as immigrants who, partially as a way of defining who they are, proclaim *where* they are. The film opens with a black screen on which the definition of the verb "to immigrate" appears: "To establish oneself in a foreign country." The act of establishing oneself is key to the stories included in *Danken got/Estamos aqui*. Jewish immigrants and their descendants interviewed in Curitiba emphasize the roots they planted almost immediately upon their arrival in that city, particularly through their political participation. The historian Jeffrey Lesser has stated that "Brazil's Jewish Question was really a struggle by Brazil's leaders to fit the bigoted images of Jews that filtered in from Europe with the reality that the overwhelming majority of Jewish immigrants ... were rarely active politically, and rapidly acculturated" (*Welcoming the Undesirables* 3). *Danken got* does depict a Brazilian Jewish community that, in keeping with Lesser's model, is neither rich nor poor and acculturated quickly into Brazilian society, but contrary to Lesser, this is a community that was, in fact, quite politically active. The film thus nuances understandings of Jews in twentieth-century Brazil.

Danken got/Estamos aqui brings to the fore the importance of Jewish businesses in Curitiba. As was common throughout Latin America in the early twentieth century, many Jewish immigrants who are mentioned in this film worked first as peddlers when they arrived. Over the next decades, they established brick-and-mortar storefronts where they sold textiles and furniture. Chamecki interviews former Governor Jaime Lerner, as they walk past buildings that used to house Jewish enterprises. Lerner waxes nostalgic over his childhood as the two stand next to one that used to be a furniture store owned by a local Jewish family. Lerner nods towards another one nearby and informs viewers that it was in front of that buiding that he was sworn in as mayor of Curitiba. *Danken got* thus visually demonstrates the convergence of community, economic activity, and political leadership that characterizes Jewish life in Curitiba.

In addition to the significance of the brick-and-mortar storefronts, *Danken got/Estamos aqui* follows the inscription of Jewish life in Curitiba's urban space through focus on the new Holocaust Museum there. In a sense, memory of the Holocaust is the culmination of the documentary's narrative, insofar as the film ends with the inauguration of the museum. Unlike in *Hacer patria*, the interviewees in *Danken got* do not mention political affinities in Poland or Russia (such as supporting or not supporting the Russian Revolution) before their immigration to Brazil. Instead, discussions of Poland and Russia focus on the difficulty of life there in

Figure 2.1. Cintia Chamecki speaking with Jaime Lerner in the streets of Curitiba in *Danken got*.

contrast with life in Brazil, described by one interviewee as "um paraiso (a paradise)." In comparison with the other documentaries discussed here, *Danken got* devotes substantial time and attention to the response of Curitiba's Jewish community to the mounting Fascism in Europe in the 1930s and the impending Holocaust. The film also focuses on Jewish encounters with local Curitiba politics and with Brazilian national politics. Interviewees speak of their experiences with the Integralist movement, a fascist nationalist movement that began in 1932 in Brazil. One of the interviewees, when asked about the Jewish community's reaction to Integralist street demonstrations, affirms that there was no community reaction, for the Jews were too scared to react publicly. This fear of reacting publicly may be attributable to a need to continue to appear apolitical. The writer and journalist Bernardo Schulman (1902–1990), however, is mentioned in *Danken got* for his condemnation of Brazil's anti-Semitism as well as Brazil's neutrality during much of the Second World War (although Brazil eventually did declare its opposition to the Axis, in 1942). Schulman had published a book in the 1930s – *Em legítima defeza: A voz de um judeu brasileiro* (In legitimate defense: The voice of a Brazilian Jew). Today, the Instituto Cultural Judaico Brasileiro Bernardo Schulman in Curitiba is named for him. The testimonies in *Danken got* first focus on how overjoyed the Jewish citizens of Curitiba were when the war was finally over, but then Chamecki transitions to a litany of accounts of the heartbreaking news that they later received informing them of loved ones who had perished in the Holocaust.

Another salient difference between this documentary and the others discussed in this chapter is the exotic tone with which *Danken got/ Estamos aqui* introduces Brazil and Curitiba to viewers. The other documentaries also include footage of early twentieth-century life in the countries depicted, but *Danken got* begins with exotic, tropical images of palm trees, people on the beach and surfing juxtaposed with the sound of interviewees' stories of the unbearable heat they encountered on arriving in Brazil. Chamecki also includes a comical anecdote about a misunderstanding between her grandparents: Her grandfather, who had left for Brazil first, wrote to her grandmother back in Europe saying that he loved bananas. But her grandmother, as the woman states, at the same time that the soundtrack plays tropical music from the 1940s, took this to mean that her husband had fallen in love with someone named "Banana." These superimpositions of sound and image create an exoticized picture of the country that suggests an exogenous viewpoint, not unlike the film's use of subtitles in English for a non-Brazilian audience.

As part of this exoticized depiction of Brazil, *Danken got/Estamos aqui* also explicitly addresses Jewish encounters with racial alterity and embodied difference. These include provocative suggestions of encounters that the European Jews had with Brazil and with issues of race. One interviewee tells how when she was a child, upon seeing an Afro-Brazilian person for the first time, she exclaimed, "He's black! He's dirty!" to which her father responded by taking her hand and the Afro-Brazilian man's hand and touching them to one another, telling his daughter, "See? He is not dirty. He is clean. He is just like you and me." Thus begins the film's chronicle of Jewish life in Brazil through incorporating Otherness and exoticism. These depictions of race and difference set up a consideration of Brazil as a melting pot that is largely in keeping with the fraught notion of *democracia racial*, as I discuss in chapter 4 as it relates to *O ano em que meus pais saíram de férias*. Questions of race, if not explicitly political, nonetheless figure into notions of citizenship and political participation as Jews came into contact with other categories of racial alterity.

Far more overtly political is Chamecki's attention to the establishment of the Sociedade Cultural Israelita Brasileira. In one interviewee's estimation, the SOCIB encapsulates a phenomenon that was affecting every Jewish exile worldwide at the time: the tension in the 1940s and 1950s between communism and Zionism. When the film turns its focus to the SOCIB, Chamecki introduces onscreen the word "*roite*," and its definition: the Jewish reds. At this point in the film, Chamecki explores the Jewish community's encounters with communism and Zionism in Brazil after the Second World War. The communities embodied a tension between what one interviewee describes as the Zionist, anti-Soviet position, and a more pro-Soviet position affirmed by another interviewee's declaration that she believed that Russia was going to save them all. Within the SOCIB there were a number of conflicting stances regarding solidarity with Soviet Russia. As one interviewee asserts, "Any time there were ten Jews in a room, there were ten different stances."

In comparison with Blaustein's *Hacer patria*, Chamecki devotes little attention to the experiences of Jews with Brazil's most recent dictatorship (1964–1985). *Danken got/Estamos aqui* does, however, address the repression of Jewish dissidence through the testimonies of those who opposed the Integralist movement and were arrested during the era of Getúlio Dornelles Vargas (1930–1945). In addition to the film's sustained focus on Holocaust memory as well as postmemory of the Holocaust, *Danken got* works to sustain the collective memory of Jewish experiences with repression in a situation that was not the Holocaust,

The film's narrative culminates in the inauguration of the Holocaust Museum in Curitiba. Like *Hacer patria, Danken got* depicts Holocaust memory as central to filmic endeavours to depict Jewish life in Latin America. Both directors couple the institutionalization of the intergenerational transmission of memory – whether through the conversation about filmmaking in *Hacer patria* or through creating a museum in *Danken got* – with national history and politics in Argentina and Brazil, respectively. Chamecki's focus on this museum's inauguration reveals another mode through which memory work is carried out: museumification. Although not as self-referential as Blaustein's use of postmemory in his film, the use of documentary film to depict another medium's institutionalization of Jewish life and history in Curitiba evokes postmemory. This phenomenon raises a woefully underexamined question within Latin American Jewish studies, namely, the role of the critical concept of postmemory – ubiquitous in conversations about Latin American postdictatorship – in the specific case of Jewish individuals. That notions of Holocaust postmemory have become integral to critical conversations on memory in post-conflict Latin American societies demonstrates a powerful way in which Jewishness has come to be foregrounded in Latin American political life. I return to the role of postmemory in my discussion of *El barrio de los judíos*.

In *Danken got/Estamos aqui*, the Holocaust Museum space becomes a site of national politics when we are shown President Dilma Rousseff at that the museum's inauguration. The film was released before the political upheaval of 2016, in which Rousseff was ousted in what some call an impeachment and some call a coup. The images of Rousseff in attendance at the museum's inauguration are a visual reminder of the Pink Tide that characterized Latin America at the time. As I outlined in the introduction and in the previous chapter, the Pink Tide brought an enormous amount of popular and critical attention to issues of memory. Moreover, memory became patently politicized within this recent movement. Through the inclusion of Rousseff's presence at the events inaugurating the Holocaust Museum in Curitiba, Chamecki visually blends national politics with the institutionalization of Holocaust memory, calling into question the extent to which the Holocaust can be considered a specifically Jewish issue. The ending of *Danken got/Estamos aqui* with the inauguration of this museum visually inscribes Curitiba's Jewish community into national history.

But perhaps the concluding argument of the film comes in the statement made by one of its interviewees who, in response to being called a Jew, says, "No, I am a Brazilian of Jewish faith." This self-identification speaks to a more widespread phenomenon in Brazil in which ethnicity and nationality are conflated, and often mistaken. As Lesser has shown, "normative 'Brazil' cannot include ethnicity that differs from nationality," and he adds, "Public definitions of group identity and otherness – what may be called a negotiation between in-group and popular discourses – allow members of both minority and majority groups to create identity by holding deep stereotypes even as tolerance is asserted" ("How the Jews Became Japanese" 10). The connection between Jewishness and nationality that often comes up is attributable to broader questions of belonging and acceptance, akin to Blaustein's statement that many people arrived in Argentina and eventually forgot not only that they were Russian or Polish, but also that they were Jewish. As *Danken got/Estamos aqui* emphatically makes clear, Curitiba's Jewish community is comprised of Brazilians who, as one interviewee asserts, love Brazil, and whose roots and beliefs as Jews inform their self-understanding as Brazilians and as political subjects. As Jewish Brazilians, they have striven for inclusion and have also participated actively in the political life of the country in which they have established communities.

El barrio de los judíos

Like the other two documentaries, *El barrio de los judíos* (*The Jewish Neighbourhood*), directed by Gonzalo Rodríguez Fábregas, relies heavily on interviewees' childhood memories and people's recountings of their parents' memories as immigrants to the neighbourhood. These memories are transmitted predominantly through conventional interviews in which immigrants and their children offer their testimonial accounts of their families' histories. Unlike the other documentaries, *El barrio de los judíos* focuses on just one neighbourhood in a city – specifically, Montevideo's Jewish neighbourhood of Barrio Reus, established in the late nineteenth century and named after Emilio Reus, a Spanish banker who immigrated to Montevideo in the 1880s. One interviewee describes the neighbourhood as "a sort of Jerusalem." *El barrio de los judíos* emphasizes the importance of the transmission of memory across generations though its interviews with the children of immigrants. Another interviewee repeatedly refers to his parents who "vinieron como vinieron (came as they came)" as a way of defining his parents as immigrants to the Reus neighbourhood and to Uruguay. Almost a century later, most Ashkenazi Jews have now moved out of this neighbourhood, many of them to the Pocitos neighbourhood on the beach in Montevideo. The dark comedy *Mr. Kaplan* (2013), directed by Álvaro Brechner, centres on a Jewish family in Montevideo and was filmed in the Pocitos neighbourhood. The Sephardic community, for its part, largely confined itself to the historic city centre. The history of Barrio Reus, central to both the urban history of Montevideo and to the history of Uruguay's Jewish populations, runs the risk of being relegated to oblivion, giving this documentary a sense of urgency in transmitting the neighbourhood's history, akin to Blaustein's pointing out in his film that with time some of his family members forgot that they were Jewish.

Like Blaustein, throughout his career Gonzalo Rodríguez Fábregas has directed documentaries focused on revolutionary culture. In 2009 he made *Cuando Liberarce se escribe con C*, a biographical documentary about Líber Arce, a student activist executed in 1968 by Uruguay's military forces and widely considered a martyr for anti-dictatorial causes. Released in 2011, *El barrio de los judíos* is, in a sense, an expansion of the 1969 short film *Líber Arce, Liberarse* by Mario Jacob and Mario Handler, a seminal work for revolutionary Uruguayan filmmaking. Rodríguez Fábregas has an established relationship to political filmmaking in his country and to the experiences that he brought to bear in his approach to telling the history of Barrio Reus. Unlike Blaustein and Chamecki, Rodríguez Fábregas does not himself identify as Jewish; rather, he married a Jewish Uruguayan woman and found himself increasingly interested in recurring stories about the "Jewish neighbourhood" that he often heard from his father-in-law, the son of Lithuanian Jewish immigrants who grew up in Barrio Reus. Like Blaustein and Chamecki, however, Rodríguez Fábregas uses his family's story as a point of departure to explore the broader history of his country's Jewish communities.

El barrio de los judíos alternates between historical documents, including photographs, maps, and historical footage, filmed interviews with inhabitants of the neighbourhood, and footage of present-day events in Jewish life, such as bar mitzvahs, weddings, and Shabbat dinners. The film opens with shots of an old man walking through Barrio Reus juxtaposed with an audio recording of him stating that his parents left Poland because Poland was a very Catholic country in which the Church held enormous power, meaning that Jews were not wanted there. *El barrio de los judíos* thus introduces a theme that the other two documentaries do not address, namely, the role of Christianity in Jewish experiences of belonging in predominantly Catholic countries. The man's testimony suggests that the Catholic Church was less forceful in Uruguay. Minutes later, a voiceover giving the historical overview of Barrio Reus informs viewers that many Jews found refuge in Uruguay after escaping religious persecution in Eastern Europe.

El barrio de los judíos focus is family and community in the history of Jews in Barrio Reus. Akin to Blaustein's focus on his own family and Chamecki's emphasis on the tight-knit community of Jews in Curitiba, the interviewees in *El barrio de los judíos* repeatedly mention the family-like bonds that during their childhood characterized the entire Reus neighbourhood. They speak of the smell of typical Jewish foods everywhere and playing together in the streets. One interviewee recalls, "My mother always said, 'blessed country!' For my mother it was always, 'blessed country!'" This woman's repetition of "blessed country" is similar to the description in Chamecki's film of Brazil as "a paradise." Rodríguez Fábregas depicts Uruguay and the Barrio Reus in particular as a sanctuary for the Jews who arrived there.

El barrio de los judíos, like the other films I have been discussing here, highlights the importance during the Second World War of relationships to family members still living in Europe as well as how local politics affected the Jewish community. One of the film's few voiceovers reminds viewers that Uruguay, like Brazil, maintained a neutral position almost until the end of the war. President Alfredo Baldomir broke ties with Germany in 1942 and only in 1945 did Uruguay join the Allied Forces to declare war on Germany and Japan. Like *Danken got*, *El barrio de los judíos* makes clear how little communication and information there was at the time from relatives still in Europe.

Rodríguez Fábregras's attention is on the political activity of the Jewish community. *El barrio de los judíos* begins with an overview of the arrival in Montevideo of Jews from Eastern Europe. The narrator informs viewers that three opposing currents of thought divided this Jewish community from the outset: religious orthodoxy, Zionism, and communism. For Rodríguez Fábregas, the history of Montevideo's Jewish community is marked by active political affiliations and by significant divisions among a multiplicity of ideological affinities. One interviewee says that the founders of Israel were not right-wing political leaders but leftists and that the Jews who left Russia for Uruguay were all "socialists, communists, or anarchists." These categorizations, however, are contradicted by other interviewees' claims that, when it came to ideological affinities, there was plenty of variety among members of the community.

El barrio de los judíos devotes even more attention to the neighbourhood's responses to the creation of the State of Israel than the other two documentaries do. Before the creation of Israel, one man recalls, "We weren't Jews; we were *rusos*." But with the establishment of Israel, he states, "*Then* we became Jews." This man describes the creation of Israel almost as a psychological change within the Jewish community, and he declares that with the establishment of Israel people in the community began to take pride in being Jewish and in defining themselves as such. Similar to the assertion in Chamecki's film that wherever there were ten Jews there were also ten stances, a woman in *El barrio de los judíos* affirms, "Some were Zionist, some weren't, but we were all Jews," thus highlighting that there were different positions regarding Zionism within the same Jewish community. This assertion also evokes the Blaustein family's divergent views on their children's political activism. Another interviewee remembers his opposition to Luis Alberto de Herrera (1873–1959), a nationalist who over the years made several bids for the presidency, reminding viewers again of the importance of local and national politics within Jewish communities. *El barrio de los judíos* represents a high volume of political participation among Jews in the 1940s and 1950s but does not posit a homogeneous or monolithic understanding of Jewish political affinities.

Akin to *Hacer patria*'s and *Danken got*'s images of the director with her children and her parents, *El barrio de los judíos* includes moments of intergenerational transmission of history, with shots of grandchildren seated with grandparents. Rodríguez Fábregas includes footage of adolescents taking a field trip to the Barrio Reus in which the group leader informs them that they are going to learn about the neighbourhood in which their grandparents and ancestors lived. In contrast to the sunny shots of older adults standing on the sidewalk recalling their childhoods, the students' visit shows grey, rain-soaked streets with closed storefronts. Barrio Reus in the present is portrayed as a vestige of an erstwhile

Figure 2.2. Bus driver looking in rearview mirror in *El barrio de los judíos*.

thriving Jewish neighbourhood. The mise-en-scène of the younger generation's visit to Barrio Reus thus constitutes a visual metaphor to remind audiences of the urgency of remembering and of representing the history of Montevideo's Jewish communities. Abel Bronstein, the director of the Kehilá Synagogue, informs the children that they are going to learn about their grandparents' roots in Montevideo, which are fundamental to their own identities as Jews. The adolescents seem largely uninterested in Bronstein's spiel – looking out the window or drinking mate – while Rodríguez Fábregas also shows the bus driver's silent facial responses to what Bronstein is saying. The driver serves as a witness to Bronstein's endeavour to foster intergenerational memory of Montevideo's Jewish history, just as the film's viewers are witnesses to Rodríguez Fábregas's pursuits to do the same.

The visual inclusion of the bus driver's outsider gaze, I argue, corresponds to Rodríguez Fábregas's avowed endeavour to promote awareness of Uruguay's Jewish history for non-Jewish audiences. In an interview, Rodríguez Fábregas explained, "I'd like for this documentary to have more resonance in the non-Jewish community, because it talks about human rights, humanity, a ton of values that are really meaningful and important to understand" (Jerozolimski). This sequence in the film evokes Hirsch's postmemory in its subtle gesture towards self-awareness through the gaze of the bus driver as he witnesses a conversation about the need to promote intergenerational memory. Through both the content of what Bronstein is saying and the scene's visual composition, Rodríguez Fábregas is pointing to the significance of the transmission of memory across generations and across insider/outsider groups. Hirsch notes in her article "The Generation of Postmemory" that conversations about memory between Jews and non-Jews become a salient element of postmemory.[6]

Although the film incorporates these aspects of postmemory, *El barrio de los judíos* focuses much less on the Holocaust than is the case for *Danken got* or *Hacer patria*. Similarly, the film does not make reference to Uruguay's own dictatorship. Comparing the relative lack of attention that Rodríguez Fábregas devotes to the Holocaust and to Uruguay's dictatorship, the focus on both of these phenomena in *Danken got* and *Hacer patria* becomes suggestively linked in the shared element of persecution against Jews. That is, within this corpus of documentary filmmaking on Jews in Latin America, there is a correlation between discussing the Holocaust and discussing local authoritarianism. In this way, the question that I posited above about dictatorship and Holocaust memory becomes more pressing. As Hirsch submitted in 2008, "'Memory studies'... have, in large part, been fueled by the limit case of the Holocaust and by the work of (and about) what has come to be known as 'the second generation' or 'the generation after'" ("Generation of Postmemory" 105). Hirsch's idea that the Holocaust is a "limit case" reveals the paradigmatic role that the Holocaust has for memory studies. Yet, in her 2012 book, Hirsch amends her 2008 position to state, "At the beginning of the second decade of the twenty-first century – after the brutal dictatorships in Latin America, after Bosnia, Rwanda, and Darfur; during the aftermath, globally, of the events of September 11, 2001; and in the midst of the Israel/Palestinian conflict *the Holocaust can no longer serve as a conceptual limit case* in the discussion of historical trauma, memory, and forgetting" (18, my emphasis). The extent to which the Holocaust may or may not be considered a "limit case" is called into question by the issues of trauma and memory that Latin American dictatorships have created. The role of Holocaust memory as a "limit case" raises the question of what it means to use Holocaust theory in entirely distinct cases – as Brazilian, Argentine, and Uruguayan dictatorships might appear to be – as opposed to cases in which there are clear carryovers from the Holocaust, such as the targeting of Jews within these same instances of state repression. Blaustein and Chamecki directly grapple with the intergenerational transmission of Holocaust memory, whereas Rodríguez Fábregas treats the issue more obliquely through focusing on Uruguay's neutral position during the Second World War. The treatment of Holocaust memory in these films is focused on intergenerational conversations within families at the same time that it serves a broader purpose of positioning Jewish experiences within national conversations. In this sense, Holocaust memory serves to orient Jews within the public spheres of the countries to which they immigrated, a topic I explore further in later chapters.

El barrio de los judíos ends with present-day images of the neighbourhood's vibrant street life during the day, consisting mostly of commercial activity among people who are not interviewed and whom the former inhabitants who are interviewed in the film describe as non-Jews. As one of the older interviewees who spent much of her life in the neighbourhood points out, unlike when she was a child and there was always vivacity in Barrio Reus, nowadays activity disappears from the streets at night and on weekends. Rodríguez Fábregas thus explicitly underscores the shifts in urban spaces that have characterized many formerly predominantly Jewish neighbourhoods in cities throughout the Americas, a theme I will explore in further depth in chapter 4's discussion of São Paolo's Bom Retiro neighbourhood in *O ano em que meus pais saíram de férias*. As Rodríguez Fábregas reminds viewers, however, not all Jews enjoyed economic success or the upward social mobility that allowed them to move to more affluent neighbourhoods. Yet, as the documentary's ending highlights, Barrio Reus is no longer *the* Jewish neighbourhood of Montevideo. In this context, *El barrio de los judíos* is offering a diachronic consideration of the neighbourhood as the erstwhile Jewish neighbourhood of the city, bringing memory into the living present and blending Jewish and non-Jewish portions of the neighbourhood's past and present.

La danza de la realidad

Through a vastly different aesthetic approach, the Chilean-born director Alejandro Jodorowsky's 2013 film *La danza de la realidad* (*The Dance of Reality*) focuses on the points of contact between immigrant families' Jewish identities and their political affinities in 1930s Latin America. It is the first instalment in a planned series of autobiographical films portraying the director's own childhood (the second film of this series, *Poesía sin fin/Endless Poetry*, was released in 2016). In addition to being his first autobiographical film, *La danza de la realidad* is the first of Jodorowsky's cinematic works to be set in Chile in his decades-spanning corpus of film production. In returning to the scene of his own childhood, Jodorowsky grapples with national identity: the figure of the child, here the writer-director's alter ego, becomes vested with a particular valence of nationhood. The film explores the trappings of the father's allegiances to Stalin at the same time as he rises up against, and eventually attempts to assassinate authoritarian leader General Carlos Ibáñez del Campo, president of Chile from 1927 to 1931 (and again in 1952–1958). From the child's perspective, these three mustachioed men – Stalin, Ibáñez, and Jodorowsky's father – are visually equated as they are all depicted as authoritarian figures with whose influence the child must reckon. Similarly, Jodorowsky's perspective of Psychomagic, his own school of shamanic psychotherapy, complicates the film's treatment of Judaism and specifically of Jewish mysticism. *La danza de la realidad* chronicles the director's coming of age as well as a significant portion of the history of politics in 1930s Chile. Through an original filmic and narrative style, Jodorowsky shows that an active role in the political sphere was inextricable from growing up as a Jewish boy in Chile.

Jodorowsky has a complicated relationship with his Chilean nationality. Having long formed part of a distinctly cosmopolitan contingent of filmmakers, like fellow Chilean filmmaker Raúl Ruiz, Jodorowsky immigrated to Paris in the 1950s (by his own account, in search of André Breton), where he was imbued with surrealist filmmaking. He went on to make a remarkable career for himself producing surrealist films in Mexico that generated a cultlike following around the world. His novels and films are often catalogued as Mexican or French, seldom as Chilean. His categorization as a Chilean filmmaker is vexed. *La danza de la realidad* creates a narrative of national history and identity that reaches back to the years shortly after this director's parents, along with many other Jews, immigrated to Chile.

Jodorowsky's identification as Jewish is also fraught. Ariana Huberman notes in her analysis of Jodorowsky's autobiographical *Donde mejor canta el pájaro* that Jodorowsky "has never really been part of a Jewish community. His family's connection to Judaism is also filled with conflict. His father and several of his grandparents tried to distance themselves from a Judaism that they associated with the Russian pogroms" (loc. 692–6). In light of his troubled relationship to Judaism, it comes as little surprise that earlier instalments in Jodorowsky's oeuvre have not dealt explicitly with Judaism. However, it is possible – and, I maintain, critically productive – to revisit Jodorowsky's earlier works to foreground Jewish aspects of his corpus; indeed, some critics have shown that Jodorowsky's earlier works are suffused with aspects of his Jewish upbringing. Naomi Lindstrom has argued that the director's documented interest in and depiction of apocalyptic narratives (most prevalently in the cult classic *El Topo*) must be taken into account within the framework of the apocalyptic genre's origins in Jewish, and not Christian, apocalypse – akin to the previous chapter's discussion of the blending of Old and New Testament thinking. Lindstrom points out that "a strain of Jewish thought is present even in Christian apocalypses" (127). In his earlier work, Jodorowsky mixes Jewish visionary and mystical themes. Similarly, Huberman submits, "Some of Jodorowsky's main sources of inspiration are Jewish mysticism, Kabbalah, and Jewish popular beliefs" (loc. 692). Aside from Lindstrom and Huberman, however, Jewish aspects of Jodorowsky's earlier works have received little critical attention. *La danza de la realidad* treats Judaism and Jewishness in ways that make these cultural practices explicit. Specifically, Jodorowsky engages with Jewishness through uncanny representations of its embodiment.

La danza de la realidad is the first of Jodorowsky's films to deal explicitly with Jewish identity. The director did take up the topic in his earlier written works, namely, the autobiographical novel *Donde mejor canta el pájaro* and his later biography *La danza de la realidad*, from which he adapted his film. As Huberman suggests, because of Jodorowsky's distance from his own Jewish roots and his fascination with Christian and Eastern spiritual paradigms, Jodorowsky's corpus runs the risk of exoticizing Jewish thought. Yet, Huberman concludes her reading of *Donde mejor canta el pájaro* refuting an interpretation that Jodorowsky exoticizes the Other insofar as "he does not depict the Other in opposition to the norm. When he merges the strange and the familiar he instills strangeness in what is familiar. He achieves this by portraying the supernatural within the familiar context of a wake, or a potential marriage" (loc. 838). Although Huberman does not explicitly make the connection between what she suggests here and the uncanny, the idea of the uncanny is certainly implicit in her explanation of Jodorowsky's integration of strangeness into the familiar. My reading of the film adaptation of *La danza de la realidad* argues that Jodorowsky's depiction of the place of Jews within Chilean society is intimately linked to his exploration of the uncanny, understood, in Freud's terms, as "on the one hand ... what is familiar and agreeable, and on the other, what is concealed and kept out of sight" (223). A preoccupation with the uncanny and the dreamlike is to be expected in light of Jodorowsky's established tradition of surrealist filmmaking. In the case of this film, as in Huberman's reading of *Donde mejor canta el pájaro*, not only is he continuing in a surrealist tradition of filmmaking, but also he incorporates uncanny elements into his film in a way that explicitly couples Jewish identity with the uncanny. In *La danza de la realidad*, uncanny signifiers are related to the political identifications that provide a point of tension between the child Alejandrito and his father Jaime. Jodorowsky puts to use surrealist film aesthetics in a way that implicitly joins Jewishness with political beliefs.

La danza de la realidad highlights Alejandrito's difference from other young boys on the basis of his circumcision. During a scene at the beach, other young boys tell Alejandrito, "Pinocchio, come over here" (they call him Pinocchio because of his nose), and then they tell him, "We are going to jerk off," to which Alejandrito responds with confusion and asks what that means. While the other children vigorously rub bananas, Alejandrito is shown with a mushroom between his legs. The boys notice his difference and ridicule him. Jodorowsky thus evokes tropes of Jewish difference in the circumcised versus uncircumcised penis through giving Alejandrito the mushroom-shaped phallus while the other boys' bananas more closely resemble uncircumcised penises. The film's use of various produce and the shaming of Alejandrito on the basis of genital difference evoke common tropes of circumcision as a marker of Jewish difference. At the same time, the visual language of this scene is quintessentially surrealist. Elsewhere in the film, Alejandrito's mother, Sara, urges him to be more inconspicuous, going so far as to shake him and proclaim, "Out Jew, Out Pinocchio!"

This visual composition in *La danza de la realidad* of the masturbation scene on the beach is also significant for its racial markers of difference, related to broader questions of belonging. Alejandrito is notably lighter-skinned than the other boys. In the scene immediately prior, the film shows boys around Alejandrito's age of different shapes and sizes (all dressed alike in shorts, whereas Alejandrito is wearing long pants). Yet, in stark contrast, the group of boys who goes over to the cove to masturbate are all the same size and have the same haircut and are virtually identical. This scene thus visually couples the Jew's appearance of whiteness with the difference connoted by his circumcision, which forms the basis of social ostracizing. That is, the same shot that depicts the embodied difference of circumcision also strongly contrasts Alejandrito's phenotypic ethnic composition with that of the other boys in the scene. The visual composition of this scene suggests that Alejandrito does not fit in because he is circumcised and the other boys are uncircumcised and darker-skinned; specifically, the others are more phenotypically Indigenous. In this regard, the film evokes questions of how *mestizaje*, being of mixed race, informs Jewish feelings of belonging in Latin America, a topic I explore further in the next chapter.

The circumcised penis is also presented in *La danza de la realidad* as part of Alejandrito's coming of age as it relates to his strained relationship with Jaime, his father. Identification and competition between son and father on the basis of their penises are related to the film's exploration of the father's political pursuits. Regarding circumcision, Melvin Konner posits, "All Jewish circumcision since Abraham's symbolize the continuity of the male line ... the symbolic wound of circumcision will confirm the lineage of all Jews back to Abraham" (33). Circumcision serves as a bodily signifier of male Jewish lineage that links fathers and sons. Yet, the circumcised phallus can also conjure intergenerational tensions, a recurrent issue in recent Jewish Latin American cinema, as I show in chapter 4. Within the context of the film's sustained emphasis on Alejandrito's vexed relationship to his father, this marker of difference is integral to his psychological journey to overcome his father. Indeed, in his homonymous autobiography upon which *La danza de la realidad* is based, Jodorowsky recounts spying his father's penis while he lay sleeping: "His circumcised member was in the shape of a mushroom, but, incredible! It was much smaller than mine. More than a phallus it looked like a pinky finger. Suddenly I understood the reason for Jaime's aggression ... he made fun of my long nose because he knew that between his legs he was short" (57–8). The shared mushroom comparison unites Jodorowsky and his father, while the realization that his father has been compensating for his small penis size serves as a point of disidentification and intergenerational competition. Both the beach scene – through the juxtaposition of "Pinocchio" in reference to Alejandrito's nose and the mushroom phallus – and the narrator's description of his father's taunting him because of his long nose couple the nose and the penis as bodily markers of Jewish masculinity.

Although I do not focus as deeply on gendered embodiment in this chapter as I do in the next two, Jewish embodiment is innately linked to questions of gender. Jodorowsky's exploration of childhood subjectivities and the Jewish body in *La danza de la realidad* evokes Kathryn Bond Stockton's notion that childhood is an inherently queer experience, as she argues in her book *The Queer Child,* an idea that I explore further in relation to Jewish embodiment in chapter 4. Alejandrito's process of coming to understand his own body in relation to others is marked by the patently gendered difference that is directly related to his Jewish body, particularly as his parents emasculate him – his mother by coddling him and his father by challenging him. These markers of embodiment serve as points of both identification and disidentification with his father within the broader matrix of the film's exploration of Chilean citizenship and processes of identifying with national and global politics.

In the film *La danza de la realidad,* unlike in Jodorowsky's written autobiography, Alejandrito never spies on his father's penis. Yet, Jodorowsky does equip Jaime's character with a small gun in an all-too-Freudian sequence. Once Jaime has resolved to attempt to assassinate Ibáñez, the director himself appears in the frame and hands Jaime a comically small pistol. That Jodorowsky – who appears in other scenes to embrace and console the young Alejandrito as he grapples with feelings of hurt and loneliness – should himself enter the frame to hand the character depicting his father such a small weapon visually recreates the moment of catching a glimpse of his father's small penis in *Donde mejor canta el pájaro*. These jabs at his father's penis size serve as moments in which Jodorowsky is able to overcome the abuse and repression that characterized his relationship with his father. Such gestures are typical of Jodorowsky's Psychomagic through which he seeks to heal the pain instilled in individuals over the course of their lives, and particularly during childhood.

Intergenerational tensions surrounding Jewishness and masculinity are also manifest through Jaime's political affinities. Despite the tensions between father and son and in contrast to many coming-of-age stories, *La danza de la realidad* depicts the protagonist's father as a character who also grows and changes over time. At the film's beginning, Jodorowsky presents Jaime as a strongman who abuses and challenges his young son. Although his efforts to make a man out of Alejandrito do toughen the young boy, Jaime becomes less of a strongman over the course of the film. His character changes coincide with his process of overcoming staunch party affiliations.

Jaime's fervent political opinions define him. Viewers first learn of his opinions as he urinates on a radio that he has thrown into the toilet of the family home. General Ibáñez's voice is speaking as Jaime's urine breaks the radio so that the transmission stops; Jaime exclaims "Lying milico!" (*Milico* is a pejorative term for a soldier or someone in the army.) Through this sequence, Jodorowsky underscores both Jaime's opposition to Ibáñez and his strongman persona that frightens the young Alejandrito and the audience alike. Notably, in this scene Jaime exposes his phallus to assert his political beliefs. Once Jaime decides that he must assassinate Ibáñez, the film depicts Jaime's journey on the ship from Tocopilla to Valparaíso en route to Santiago. There, he encounters another radical who is irate with him because, in his estimation, Jaime is not fit to assassinate Ibáñez because he is Jewish. The man exclaims to him, "You are Jewish. A Chilean must kill him. He who kills him is going to go down in history. I must go down in history." The juxtaposition of the sentences "You are Jewish" followed immediately by "a Chilean" connotes that, from this man's perspective, Jewish and Chilean are mutually exclusive. In this regard, the film resonates with Lesser's observation in "How the Jews Became Japanese" that, in Brazil, ethnicity is often impossible to disentangle from nationality. In *La danza de la realidad*, this character's anti-Semitism would suggest that the same was true for some Chileans. Within the context of this anti-Semitic belief, the necessity for film to revisit Jews' sense of national identity becomes more apparent.

Through Jaime's exchange with this man on the ship, Jodorowsky's film takes on the urgent purpose of debunking stereotypes about Jews and their place in the national project. The man's assertion that a non-Jewish Chilean must kill Ibáñez recalls widespread anti-Semitic ideas that Jews are not citizens of the countries to which they immigrate. His additional "He who kills him is going to go down in history," furthers this anti-Semitic stance. The character asserts that Jews cannot form an integral part of national history. Through this scene, Jodorowsky brings to light the pervasiveness of this anti-Semitic belief and counters this stereotype through his depiction of a Jewish immigrant character's fervent political commitments. Such instances remind viewers of the need for filmmakers to address the anti-Semitic attitudes that have long existed in their countries and the need to demystify these anti-Semitic beliefs by representing Jews at the fore of national history and identity. The idea of "going down in history" may be likened to filmmakers' endeavours to inscribe themselves within the national projects of their countries through cinematic depictions of Jewish involvement in politics.

Yet, for Jaime, it is necessary to move past his staunch political identifications. He does not assassinate Ibáñez; rather, he attempts to sabotage Ibáñez's life by killing his beloved horse but finds that he cannot bring himself to do so and eventually begins to admire Ibáñez. Later, he returns to Tocopilla after a byzantine journey home – including a brief capture by Nazis – has left him changed and his fingers immobile. Sara reveals to him three portraits: one of Stalin, one of Ibáñez, and one of himself. Upon unveiling these photographs, she explains to him that he has found in Ibáñez all that he admired in Stalin, adding that he is the same as both of them. She then sings to him, "return to yourself" and hands him a pistol (markedly larger than the small one he wielded earlier) as she belts out "Jaime." He grips the gun and is once again able to move his fingers as he pulls the trigger and shoots the portrait of himself square between the eyes, at which point all three portraits go up in flames. Here, Jaime's masculinity is restored through both Sara's support and his letting go of his staunch allegiance to tyrannical figures, including himself. Alejandrito's coming of age hinges on his father's moving past his fascination with these strongman-type political leaders, including the then-figurehead of the Russian Revolution. Stalin's photo bursting into flames is a strong visual rejection of the conflation between Jewish and Bolshevik in Chile that Moisés Senderey documented and that I discussed in the first pages of the introduction.

Figure 2.3. Portraits of Stalin, Jaime, and Ibáñez in *La danza de la realidad.*

Through Jaime's character arc, Jodorowsky portrays a political subjectivity that engages with and demystifies stereotypes of Jewish political identifications. The film ends with the family's leaving Tocopilla for Santiago, marking the end of a chapter in Alejandrito's childhood. Alejandrito's coming of age is defined by his father's fraught and unsuccessful attempts both to emulate and to assassinate tyrants. At the end of the film, Alejandrito's father is finally at peace, having left behind his allegiance to Stalin and his hatred (and later admiration) for Ibáñez. Jaime's adoration of Stalin recalls Senderey's consideration of the term "rusos" that connotes both Jewish ethnicity, albeit imprecisely, and solidarity with the Russian Revolution. Ibáñez, for his part, is a typical caudillo (leader). Jodorowsky nonetheless recounts a tale in which political affinity and enmity are integral parts of Jewish experience as immigrants and as Chilean citizens. Yet, in the beginning of the film's sequel, *Poesía sin fin / Endless Poetry,* Jaime's tyrannical tendencies resurface shortly after the family's move to Santiago. Whereas the political climate of 1930s Chile is the focus of *La danza de la realidad, Poesía sin fin* chronicles Alejandrito's journey to become a poet. In the chapter of Alejandrito's childhood recounted in *La danza de la realidad,* Jodorowsky shows paradigms of identification with national and global political leaders among families of Jewish immigrants. Moreover, the film emphasizes the effects of these political affinities on processes of identity formation for young Jews through a sustained focus on the embodiment of Jewishness. This topic will come to the fore in my next chapter's exploration of gender and embodiment in Jewish women's solidarity with revolutionary politics.

Conclusions

The works of the filmmakers discussed in this chapter show an impulse to articulate and maintain Jewish and national identities through intergenerational negotiations. These memories are by no means limited to religious identity, but include the polyvalent and sometimes contradictory stances that members of the Jewish community took regarding national and global political issues. The respective films' attention to Ibáñez (Chile), Vargas (Brazil), Perón (Argentina), and Herrera (Uruguay) highlight the importance and pervasiveness of national politics in the South American countries to which Jews immigrated. In my discussion of these films, I have traced the complexities of processes of assimilation into hegemony and the national projects of these respective countries. Meanwhile, discussions of reactions in Jewish communities to Nazism and the creation of the State of Israel emphasize the transnational aspects of Jewish identities and political affinities. As I explored in my discussion of Carl Schmitt in the introductory chapter and as I elaborate in the next chapter, encounters with the Holocaust and Nazism created categories of friendship and enmity that served as orienting paradigms for the individual and collective formation of political affinities. At the same time, the diversity of stances espoused by members within a single Jewish community – or even within a single family, as in Blaustein's case – shows that there are many ways Jews can be political. Cinematic emphasis on the actions of Jews within the political spheres of the countries to which they immigrated move beyond narratives of belonging to represent Latin America's Jews as full-fledged citizens who do not live on the margins of society, but rather form part of the backbone of their nations.

I have not discussed postmemory in Jodorowsky's film as I have for the documentaries; neverthelss, intergenerational negotiations between parents and children regarding political affinities are importantly related to the notion of postmemory, a theme I explore further in chapter 4. As with my consideration in the previous chapter of the implicit role of Christian thought in memorial or remembrance culture, the pervasiveness of postmemory in conversations on postdictatorship denotes a way in which Jewish experiences have come to inform cultural understandings of national politics. The use of Holocaust postmemory in talking about Jewish experiences with state repression serves an analogously tautological function to the use of the Pauline "New Man" that underwrites the memory of revolutionary culture and the memory of Che Guevara. Yet, unlike the role of the New Man in revolutionary culture, Holocaust experiences relate more strictly to Jewishness than to Judaism, such that it is already a somewhat secularized notion. There is also the crucial difference between Christian habitus in predominantly Catholic countries versus the role of critical concepts related to an ethnic group that forms a small minority, such as Jews in Latin America.

I offer the analogy here because, as I underscored in the previous chapter, much work remains to be done on thinking through the patent roles that religion plays within the ubiquitous present-day conversations on memory politics in Latin America. In relation to Jewish culture and the transmission of memory, one may think of *l'dor v'dor* (literally, "from generation to generation") a concept Daniela Goldfine develops in her discussion of memory in recent Jewish Argentine fiction, where she writes, "The force of imagination and narrative within Jewish Argentine literature at the turn of the century beholds the possibility of finding an authoritative voice that (re)shapes the imaginary of this community within the nation" ("L'dor V'dor" 1). I expand on Goldfine's discussion of l'dor v'dor with a specific focus on Jewish political participation. The transmission of memory refigures the place of Jewish communities within the national imaginary at the same time that Jewish understandings of memory refigure national identity.

The filmmakers discussed here engage with tropes and traditions integral to cultural understandings of Jewish political identifications throughout Latin America in the twentieth century. Experiences of immigration, assimilation, and anti-Semitism abound in these stories alongside negotiations of solidarity with the Russian Revolution, anarchist affinities, socialist movements, and the State of Israel within various Latin American countries. These political experiences bridge particularly Jewish experiences and issues with the broader public sphere as a way in which families of Jewish immigrants, in keeping with Levinas's assertion, begin to feel a place for themselves in the economy of being. For its part, film offers a space for self-representation in which these directors inscribe Jewish identities within the histories and political matrices of their countries. Both documentary filmmaking and surrealist fictional cinema bridge personal and political experiences in the Jewish diaspora. These films' retrospective depictions of the early twentieth century chart patterns of political participation that continue to inform identity and belonging in Latin America and that, as I show in the following chapters, guided paradigms of political identifications in the decades characterized by revolutionary politic

Chapter Three

Poner el cuerpo femenino judío: Jewish Women's Bodies and Revolutionary Movements

Guita Schyfter's *Novia que te vea* (1993) and Jeanine Meerapfel's *El amigo alemán* (2012) portray how politics came to bear on the lives of Latin American Jewish women in the 1960s and 1970s. Produced nearly two decades apart, these two films are largely autobiographical depictions of the intersection of Jewish women's friendships and encounters with leftist politics. The friendships are between individuals from distinct categories: Schyfter centres on inter-Jewish groups in her story of two young women in 1960s Mexico, one Sephardic and the other Ashkenazi, whereas Meerapfel explores the more polarized relationship between the daughter of a Jewish German immigrant family and the son of a Nazi immigrant in Argentina. The main focus of both films is interpersonal relationships, while issues to do with political identifications and gender repeatedly surface to problematize them. The directors share a dtermined effort to convey their own histories with revolutionary and leftist causes. As both films demonstrate, the simultaneous and often conflicting categories of Jewishness, femininity, and revolutionary politics converge in creating matrices of identities too vexed for their protagonists to participate in revolutionary struggles actively as non-Jewish men might. Yet, they show solidarity with revolutionary causes. For these Jewish women belonging in their respective nations of necessity entails negotiations with leftist politics. For them Levinas's "feeling a place for themselves" in national identity means grappling with whether and how to put their very bodies on the line for political causes.

Gendered Jewish embodiment is depicted in *Novia que te vea* and *El amigo alemán* against a backdrop of the protagonists' embroilment in Latin American revolutionary struggles. The characters are navigating spaces in which femininity and Jewishness are largely taken for granted. Throughout this book, I try to explore the construction of Jewishness in a way that makes no assumptions about it. My attention in this chapter is on how some of the characters in *Novia que te vea* and *El amigo alemán* come to understand themselves as Jewish women. Patently gendered elements of Judaism and Jewishness force them to struggle with how to occupy the category of femaleness "correctly."

Female embodiment has come to bear on representations of revolutionary practices in part because the body has been widely understood as integral to leftist social movements and communist revolutions in Latin America. These practices may be traced back to Che Guevara, whose autobiographical writings often mention his struggle to transform himself from a scrawny, asthmatic adolescent into a strong and virile warrior. In addition to his ideological principles, Guevara came to be widely respected and admired for the physicality of his leadership. Valeria Manzano, a historian of revolutionary youth culture, discusses Che Guevara's dedication to transforming his body. She notes that, for some revolutionaries, "Guevara was a hero because he had left 'intellectualism' aside and showed that Latin America was 'ripe for what counts: action'" (212). The body is positioned at the fore of the revolutionary struggle in the training manual of Argentina's Montoneros, a group heavily influenced by Guevara. Published in fragments between 1975 and 1976, the manual allocated one daily time slot to physical exercise and another to hygiene. It emphasizes that the physical exercises are to be taken seriously since they are "military aspects" of the training. Put another way, in revolutionary practice the body achieved precedence over ideas. The emphasis that revolutionaries placed on one's body as the centre of action spawned the widely used term "*poner el cuerpo*" (literally, "putting one's body," or committing one's body to the cause). The sociologist Barbara Sutton studies the use of this term with regard to women activists in Argentina, and she writes, "With respect to political agency, *poner el cuerpo* means not just to talk, think, or desire, but to be really present and involved; to put the whole (embodied) being into action, to be committed to a social cause, and to assume the bodily risks, work, and demands of such a commitment" (161–2). Sutton explains that, for women, poner el cuerpo at times constitutes a "forced sacrifice," while at other times it is empowering. In *Novia que te vea* and *El amigo alemán* the act of putting one's body on the line takes on ambiguous meanings because of the complex ways in which Jewish women's bodies are socially coded.

Putting one's body on the line in the struggle for a political objective constitutes both a physical and a literal manifestation of citizenship. The Chilean author and critic Diamela Eltit analyses gendered embodiment among members of Chile's Movimiento de Izquierda Revolucionara, a far-left guerrilla organization established in 1965. She asserts that women were obligated to "place their biological bodies in the cultural codes of masculine bodies and [...] to participate epically in history from the place of dominant power to which they hope to grow gradually closer in order to achieve a possible identity" (66). As Eltit shows, placing one's body on the line became a way to insert oneself into history, a phenomenon I liken to "feeling a place for oneself in the economy of being" (Levinas). To put one's body into the act of resistance was a manifestation of the values and practices of the militant woman's commitment to the revolutionary struggle. The act of inserting one's body into the struggle most definitely takes on a gendered valence. In *Novia que te vea* and *El amigo alemán* placing one's body on the line comes more easily to non-Jewish men than it does to Jewish women, despite the latter's solidarity with revolutionary politics.

For two reasons the idea of poner el cuerpo is significant for Latin American Jewish women as they came to reckon with revolutionary movements. First, the practice of putting one's body on the line can be thought of as another instance of the secularization of Christian practices, namely, asceticism for the higher purpose of spiritual purity or the physicality of Christ's crucifixion in which his body is sacrificed for the salvation of Man. Second, female embodiment and Jewishness conjure vexed ethno-religious stereotypes. Sutton points out that the sacrificial element of poner el cuerpo "resonates with prevailing gender expectations" (180). In traditional – to be sure, stereotypical – understandings of the female Jewish body, as Riv-Ellen Prell has shown, "whether the Jewish woman is portrayed as sweating in sports, or not sweating at all, playing sports, or refusing to move, desire for her and her desire are always frustrated by the lack of the active body or physical productivity" (354).[1] *Novia que te vea* and *El amigo alemán* partially debunk the stereotypical image prevailing since the Second World War that Prell posits of the "Jewish princess that doesn't sweat" by depicting Jewish women's erotic desire and desirability. Yet, both of these films run the risk of perpetuating this image of the passive Jewish woman insofar as the female characters portrayed do not place their bodies on the line for the causes with which they sympathize to the same degree that their non-Jewish male partners do. The process of grappling with the decision of whether to "poner el cuerpo judío femenino" is fraught by both religious and gender differences. In *Novia que te vea* and *El amigo alemán* Jewish women sympathize with revolutionary politics, but unlike the gentile male love interests, they do not fully put their bodies on the line for the causes in which they believe. Yet, these women do navigate the codes of their embodied identities in establishing their place both in the national project and in revolutionary politics.

Novia que te vea

Novia que te vea (*Like a Bride*) tells a coming-of-age story of two young Jewish women in 1960s Mexico: Oshi, who is Sephardic, and Rifke, who is Ashkenazi. Rifke meets Saavedra, a young, non-Jewish revolutionary, a man who will become a love interest for her. When Saavedra has difficulty pronouncing "ídish," she ridicules him and says that most people mispronounce her language. She tells him that it is supposed to be pronounced "sh, not ch-" to which the young man comically responds "ch-, like 'Che' Guevara." The two discuss the similarities between working on a kibbutz in Israel and militating for a revolution at home in Mexico. Rifke again teases Saavedra (whom she will later marry) when he states, "Oh, yeah, Jewish socialism, kibbutzim, and things like that" by sarcastically repeating, "Yeah, Jewish socialism, kibbutzim, and things like that." The film provocatively couples revolutionary commitment with non-Jews' lack of understanding of the Yiddish language and, by extension, Ashkenazi life. *Novia que te vea* articulates a cultural model of Jewish Mexicanness predicated on active political participation. Oshi's and Rifke's activism is presented in tension with their families' respective expectations of them as young Jewish women, especially in the case of Oshi's traditional family, which throughout her childhood tells her that they cannot wait to see her "like a bride" (hence the film's title).

Novia que te vea depicts political participation as a way of reconciling multifaceted Jewish identities with national belonging. Many analyses, for example, those by Teresa Alfaro-Velcamp, Elissa Rashkin, and Coonrod Martínez note in *Novia que te vea* the importance of Mexican national identity with respect to the protagonists' processes of creating a sense of belonging. What these interpretations overlook, however, is the importance of active political participation for these characters' understandings of themselves as Mexican citizens while they do mention their involvement in socialist and Zionist groups. Let me point out here that it is precisely through their embroilment in negotiations with their Zionist and communist peers that the characters in this film are able to see themselves as part of the broader national project. *Novia que te vea* makes it clear that all areas of Jewish life in Mexico – intergenerational conflicts, citizenship and belonging, differences between Ashkenazi and Sephardic cultures, gender, and stances on Zionism – are pervaded by issues of active political participation both within Mexico and in a pan–Latin American context.

My reading of *Novia que te vea* situates the film in relation to the novel from which it was adapted and to other 1990s Mexican cinema within the context of the shifting landscape of cultural production and politics at this point in Mexico's history. From there I consider Mexico's climate towards Jewish refugees in the 1920s, when the film's storyline begins, and relationships between Sephardic and Ashkenazi Jews. I then turn my attention to the film's treatment of Mexican ethnic identity and the place of Jews therein to argue that ethnic and ideological aspects of Jewish women's identities create a model of citizenship that in one's youth necessarily takes into account involvement with radical politics.

Guita Schyfter vested her film with overtly political themes by making significant changes to the novel from which she adapted it. Yet, the film retains the explicitly gendered title *Novia que te vea*. As I addressed in this book's opening lines, the film exists *because* the director wanted to highlight the importance of 1960s political movements for her Jewish community. To write a film script as a loose adaptation, Schyfter worked with Rosa Nissán (b. 1939), who had recently penned the novel of the same title under the tutelage of renowned Mexican author Elena Poniatowska (b. 1932). The major change that Schyfter made in her film was to move the time setting from the 1950s to the early 1960s in order to place the main characters' encounters with socialist movements inspired by the Cuban Revolution. Moreover, the film grapples directly with anti-US imperialist sentiments through its depiction of President John F. Kennedy's visit to Mexico City in late June 1962. Schyfter has stated that her motivation to make a film set in the 1960s stemmed from a desire to change common perspectives of Jews as being conservative and Zionist. She explained to the film critic Ilana Luna, "All the friends I had who were more or less leftist, criticized Israel a lot ... well, until then, but let's say that then things got ugly and people always associated Jews with more conservative positions. Then I said, 'Oh, I'm going to talk about the sixties' so as to show, you know, the leftist part and how that also influenced the Jewish community. So I set the film in the sixties" (295). In other words, *Novia que te vea* exists because Schyfter wanted to reclaim a chapter in Mexican Jewish history that had been lost, namely, Jewish involvement in leftist revolutionary movements of the 1960s. The process of adaptation between Nissán's novel and Schyfter's film has been studied at length in Ilana Luna's book, *Adapting Gender: Mexican Feminisms from Literature to Film* (2017), and by Ilene S. Goldman in her chapter entitled "Mexican Women, Jewish Women: *Novia que te vea* from Book to Screen and Back Again." As a Jewish woman filmmaker, Schyfter identified with Nissán's novel and made changes to emphasize how the leftist movements of the 1960s affected Jews.

Produced earlier than the other films discussed in this monograph, the timing of the release of *Novia que te vea* is relevant to its consideration of socialist and nationalist movements. The film premiered as the

North American Free Trade Agreement was being negotiated, a policy that directly affected cultural productions, including film. Schyfter's focus on the legacy of left-leaning politics for present-day Mexican identities may be likened to Gabriel Retes's *El bulto* (1992), or Juan Carlos de Llaca's *En el aire*, released two years after Schyfter's film, insofar as both of them chronicle erstwhile leftist politics in Mexico. *Novia que te vea* is less cynical, however, in that it does not overtly posit a loss of or disillusionment with left-leaning ideals over the years. *Novia que te vea* forms part of a broader panorama of 1990s Mexican (and Latin American) cinema that engages with the neoliberal present through a consideration of the importance of leftist and revolutionary movements throughout the country's history.

By centring Jewish experiences, Schyfter's film revises twentieth-century national history through cinema. In this capacity, *Novia que te vea* contributes to Mexican national cinema, a current of filmmaking that was experiencing particular challenges at the time. As Ignacio Sánchez Prado argues, by 1994, "The cultural economy of so-called national cinema had faded away. I understand 'national cinema' as a cultural genre that acts around the idea of 'national culture,' as a repository of those signs that define the polity, and as a site of contestation for definitions of national sensibilities" (*Screening Neoliberalism* loc. 116–22). Sánchez Prado attributes this "fading away" to the fact that "the ideologies of the Mexican self – or *Mexicanidad* – that were instrumental in the emergence of national cinema and the national culture of the 1930s and 1940s no longer carried the same social significance, particularly with middle-class audiences" (127). In this sense, *Novia que te vea* is a crucial intervention not only for filmic representations of Jewish Mexican identities or those of Mexican identities writ large, but also for the capacity of cinema as a medium to engage with the Mexican condition, particularly at this watershed moment for Mexico's film market.

Sephardic Jews, Ashkenazi Jews, and Non-Jews in Mexico

Novia que te vea articulates a model of Mexican citizenship from a distinctly Jewish position that places attention on Sephardic and Ashkenazi experiences. As the film shows, in the early twentieth century new waves of Ashkenazi Jews from Eastern Europe and Sephardic Jews (from Turkey, in this film) arrived and added to the Mexican Jewish population, which traced its ancestral origin to the Jews accompanying the conquest of Mexico. Their arrival helped not only to sustain a critical mass of Jews in the country, but also to foster Jewish memory in Mexico.

The film identifies both the challenges and the opportunities presented to Jews who immigrated to Mexico. In the opening sequence of the film, Oshi's parents and their siblings arrive at a train station in Mexico City. In this very space, they immediately find a community that welcomes them when other Ladino (Judeo-Spanish, spoken by some Sephardic Jews from the Mediterranean area and based on medieval Spanish) speakers overhear them and offer them a place to stay. Yet, at the same time, the train station is flanked with posters celebrating the transatlantic flight of known anti-Semite Charles Lindbergh and praising him as a hero. These posters both situate the film's temporal setting and evoke the anti-Semitism that was rampant worldwide at the time. *Novia que te vea* thus visually reminds viewers of the conflicting messages that simultaneously welcomed and excluded Jews. Such conflicting messages were commonplace during the presidency of Plutarco Calles (1924–1928), according to the historian Jacob Levitz, who asserts that anti-Semitism abounded in Mexico City during the 1920s. Yet, Levitz quotes Calles as stating, "The Government of Mexico is prepared to welcome most warmly the immigration of Jews from Eastern Europe to engage there both in agricultural as well as industrial pursuits ... I am very warmly interested in the situation of the thousands of Jewish immigrants stranded in Europe" (10). In keeping with this paradigm, the visual composition of the opening scene in *Novia que te vea* sets a bittersweet tone in which both opportunity and hardship are constantly present for these Jewish residents of Mexico City.

Rifke and Oshi find solace in one another and in their political activism as they both struggle with their encounters with anti-Semism. Rifke is shown as a child in a park as other children are yelling at her, "Jews who killed Christ!" In a voiceover conversation, as adults, Rifke and Oshi remark to each other that it is incredible they had never met in that same park in La Lagunilla many years ago, since they both had been there often as children. Had the two been friends in their childhood years, their friendship may have helped mitigate the anti-Semitism that they both had experienced, as well as their feelings as outsiders. The anti-Semitic trope of "Jews who killed Christ" will continue to come up throughout their lives. In their college years, Oshi and Rifke witness a religious procession that depicts Jews as killers of Christ. Rifke is upset by this, yet unlike when they were children, the two girlfriends can now relate to each other regarding their experiences with anti-Semitism. Post-Holocaust experiences and anti-Semitism, together with the categories of friendship and enmity that Carl Schmitt postulated in 1932, are relevant here. The solidarity and refuge that Oshi and Rifke find in each other is made possible by their meeting one another through

Hashomer Hatzair. This socialist Zionist youth group had chapters throughout Latin America and was a key agent in familiarizing Jewish youth in the region with sociopolitical issues – and thus also with each other. In *Novia que te vea* affiliation with the group not only facilitates the protagonists' friendship, but also allows them to acknowledge and express their shared condemnation of overt acts of anti-Semitism.

One of the film's greatest and unique contributions to cinematic representations of Jews in Latin America lies in its sensitive treatment of the differences between Sephardic and Ashkenazi communities in Mexico. Indeed, *Novia que te vea* is the first film from the region to focus on a friendship between Ashkenazi and Sephardic individuals. Although both women's families are shown to be rather conservative in comparison with the young protagonists themselves, Oshi's Sephardic family is more focused on tradition and heritage than is Rifke's Ashkenazi family. In scenes of Oshi's childhood, the older women in her family are often seen embroidering her trousseau. In contrast, Oshi herself is typically seen drawing. Oshi's entire life, from the perspective of her older female relatives, has always been tied up with her eventually becoming a bride and marrying – again, as in the title *Novia que te vea* (*Like a Bride*) – despite her interests in art and self-fulfilment. Schyfter remains faithful to Nissán's novel in her rendering of the Sephardic family's traditionalism, yet she moves beyond stereotypes of Sephardic communities. Similarly, Rifke's family is also portrayed as bound to tradition; in their case there is less of a sense of isolation between the family and the rest of the neighbourhood, particularly with regard to non-Jews.

In an effort to debunk monolithic understandings about Mexico's Jewish communities *Novia que te vea* directly addresses stereotypes of Sephardic Jews that are held by other Jews. Before Oshi comes to Rifke's home for the first time, Rifke's mother tells her that Sephardics are "behind the times" and "ignorant." At this point, Rifke's father enters the room to quip ironically that Sephardics are indeed ignorant, such as Maimonides and Spinoza – who, of course, are anything but ignorant. In some moments, the film works to undo negative stereotypes of Sephardic Jews. Yet, Schyfter's portrayal of Oshi's Sephardic suitor León as being overly traditional and chauvinistic despite being educated as a physician does run the risk of reifying such negative stereotypes, and here, tensions also arise between ethnicity and gender. *Novia que te vea* shows viewers some of the perhaps smaller differences between Ashkenazi Jews and Sephardic Jews. During their dinner, Rifke's mother points out typical Ashkenazi cuisine, and Oshi delights in trying these new dishes, such as gefilte fish. As I address later in my discussion of Zionist affinities, *Novia que te vea* also draws parallels between acceptance among differing groups of Jews and broader themes of welcoming towards immigrants and refugees.

"La gran familia Mexicana": Jews and (the Cosmic) Race

Schyfter's film reckons with the notion of the "gran familia mexicana," or the great Mexican family, and the place of Jews in it. The term "la gran familia mexicana" is coined in the film by Rifke's boyfriend Saavedra, as he uses it ironically to counter an anti-Semitic elder when Rifke is invited to dine at his family's home. In that same scene, Saavedra's father assures Rifke that she is welcome in their home because, in his words, "Some of my best friends are Jewish." Rifke asserts that "la gran familia mexicana" is inclusive of cultural minorities, as she enumerates "the otomís, the coras, the Tarahumaras, the huicholes, the náhautls, the Jews." Rifke includes herself among the ethnic groups that are broadly understood to form part of Mexico's national identity. The older man scoffs and says that Jews are not the same as Indigenous groups and leaves the room; Saavedra's parents escort him out.

Elsewhere, Rifke commiserates with fellow Hashomer members over others' assumptions that they are not Mexican because they are Jewish, which she counters with her interest in Indigenous cultures. She proclaims that she is so Mexican that she is learning Nahuatl, the Indigenous language of most Aztecs, currently spoken by an estimated 1.5 million people in Mexico. Rifke's insistence on learning Nahuatl shows that knowledge of both national history and Indigenous populations is essential to her self-identification as Mexican. Earlier in *Novia que te vea* Rifke listens attentively as her archaeology professor explains that even the country's Indigenous populations migrated from other areas of the country. She is fascinated by this idea, because she realizes that even the most long-standing ethnic categories in Mexico, like her own family, came from somewhere else. This fact compels her to dedicate her life to studying Mexican archaeology, eventually going on to become an archaeologist of pre-Columbian Mexico.

Novia que te vea depicts a shared marginalization between Indigenous and Jewish communities in Mexico through Rifke's shifted research focus from pre-Columbian cultures to other Jewish groups in Mexico. At the end of the film, Rifke tells Oshi excitedly that she has begun a third book on a group of Jews whose ancestors arrived in Mexico in the fifteenth century. Curiously, she does not tell Oshi that this group was Sephardic (which a group of Jews that arrived to Mexico in the fifteenth century most certainly would have been, as virtually all Jewish immigrants to Latin America at that time were). She does tell Oshi that the group was completely isolated for centuries and "they are still Jewish." Rifke's use of the word "still" suggests the belief that patterns of assimilation over time would make Jewish practices obsolete, a recurrent theme in the film as Rifke and Oshi struggle to maintain friendships with non-Jews while holding on to their Jewish identities. This recalls the discussion in chapter 2 of the idea in the film *Hacer patria* that many Jewish immigrants to Argentina eventually forgot that they were Jewish. To Rifke's delight, however, this Jewish enclave has been preserved.

The looming presence of Mexican muralism is integral to the visual mise-en-scène of *Novia que te vea*, reminding viewers of the relationship between Jewish and Mexican self-understandings. Mexican muralism usually alludes to the murals created in the 1920s by Diego Rivera (1886–1957), David Alfaro Siqueiros (1896–1974), and José Clemente Orozco (1883–1949). They all had strong social and political preoccupations in their efforts to educate people on national history and foster Mexican identity. The majority of Rifke and Oshi's time together takes place either in the university they are both attending or in the Hashomer group of which they are both members. In the interior shots of the university setting, Schyfter often shows the main characters in the courtyard or on staircases surrounded by works from Mexico's muralist movement. In one scene Rifke and Saavedra are together on a staircase as he asks her to join him for coffee, to which she responds that she cannot and leaves him there as she rushes off. A mural looms over his head, making him visually associated with the Mexican national project. Immediately before this brief exchange with Rifke, Saavedra and some classmates had been talking about a meeting to discuss Karl Marx's *Das Kapital*. Saavedra's character is thus strongly equated with socialism and nationalism. In contrast, Rifke is positioned as more peripheral to these discourses, as she exits the frame and Saavedra remains in it, superimposed onto the mural. The visual composition of this sequence underscores Rifke's struggle to be seen as integral to the national project. The murals depicting Mexican history that surround Rifke and Saavedra in their school day accentuate the importance of their relationship as an interfaith and inter-ethnic foundational story. Rifke and Saavedra's relationship brings to mind Doris Sommer's *Foundational Fictions: The National Romances of Latin America* in which Sommer explores heterosexual, interethnic love relationships as etiologies of national identity. Sommer focuses on Jewishness in her analysis of the Colombian novel *María* (1867) by Jorge Isaacs, who like the novel's male protagonist Efraín, was the son of a Jewish family that converted to Catholicism. As Sommer states of Efraín and the Jewish María's love relationship, "Both lovers are apparently white, if

Jews can be legitimately white in a nineteenth-century code that generally equates ethnicity with race, or in any other code for that matter" (186).[2] In this way *Novia que te vea* creates its own cultural model of a Jewish-mestizo "foundational fiction." Indeed, as I show below, existing critical considerations of the film have discussed how it rewrites foundational myths of Mexican national identity.

These characters' bodies – clearly codified as *mestizo* or Jewish – are visually equated with icons of national identity, as Schyfter frames their encounters within images of Mexican history. Saavedra and Rifke's relationship creates a new model of ethnic and cultural hybridity in Mexico. Within the broader framework of the film's treatment of icons of Mexican identity, this union recalls the relationship between Spanish conquistador Hernán Cortés and La Malinche, the Indigenous woman with whom he had a love affair that, legend has it, resulted in the first mestizo Mexican child, Martín Cortés. Such seminal understandings of Mexican identity as Octavio Paz's "The Sons of la Malinche," one of the essays in his 1950 book *The Labyrinth of Solitude* (*El laberinto de la soledad*) have thus conceptualized La Malinche as the mother of all Mexicans. In her book *Women Filmmakers in Mexico*, Elissa Rashkin states, "[Saavedra and Rifke's] sexual union is itself an historically significant act, one with the potential to replace the ambivalent heritage of Cortés and Malinche with a new *foundational* myth of Mexican identity based on acceptance rather than violence" (160, my emphasis). In addition to Rashkin's crucial distinction between violence and acceptance, the other salient difference between Saavedra and Rifke's union and that of Cortés and La Malinche is that Saavedra is mestizo rather than European or Indigenous. La Malinche is also understood to be a traitor to Indigenous culture because of her acquiescence to Cortés's advances. Rifke and Saavedra's relationship is based on "acceptance rather than violence," and it does not involve betrayal of one's own culture (as Mexicans have imputed to La Malinche) through the couple's agreement to raise their children Jewish. *Novia que te vea* complicates thinking about assimilation and racial hybridity in its insistence on maintaining minority culture rather than absorbing it into a racial "melting pot," a point to which I return presently in my discussion of José Vasconcelos (1882–1959), the "cultural caudillo" of the Mexican Revolution.

Rifke's interest in archaeology, I submit, is part and parcel of the film's consideration of the complex negotiations between assimilation and the preservation of difference. Her desire to know about archaeology underscores that her self-understanding as a Mexican citizen is largely informed by her knowledge of national history. This character's interest also reminds viewers that a model of Jewish Mexican citizenship must take into account pre-Columbian – and specifically Indigenous – identities because of these groups' conditions of marginalization. As in her marriage to and procreation with Saavedra, *mestizaje* comes to be seen as an integral component of Rifke's consideration of her own Mexicanness. As Rashkin notes in her reading of *Novia que te vea*, "Mexico's Jewish population has been largely invisible and overwhelmingly excluded from the *foundational* ideology of Mexico as a mestizo nation, part indigenous and part Spanish" (142, my emphasis). In perhaps a more positive vein, Teresa Alfaro-Velcamp interprets *Novia que te vea* to show that "*mexicanidad* is a flexible, dynamic concept that allows ethnically 'other' individuals to join the Mexican nation" (262). Likewise, Joanne Hershfield submits, "Schyfter's 1993 film challenges this notion of a singular Mexican national identity by taking into account differences in ancestry, ethnicity, and gender. In doing so, the film enlarges an understanding of Mexican national identity" (71). And so, through her study of pre-Columbian Mexican cultures, the film's protagonist Rifke finds points in common between her own Jewish family and Mexican identity. She is thus more able to find both a sense of belonging in Mexico and a purpose in life as a budding archaeologist.

Mexican mestizo identity includes Jewish identities, articulating a point often missed by earlier critics of *Novia que te vea*. As the Jewish Mexican author and critic Ilan Stavans has pointed out, Latin American societies are "homogeneously mestizo" in such a way that "the particular is continually being devoured by the monstrous whole [and] the Jews are ... part of that particular" ("Introduction" to *Tropical Synagogues* 1). Although never named explicitly in *Novia que te vea*, considerations of ethnicity and its relationship to national identity in Mexico evoke José Vasconcelos's 1925 concept of *raza cósmica* (the cosmic race), which has been shown to have salient implications regarding the role of the body vis-à-vis the Mexican Revolution.[3] Within this cultural paradigm, *mestizaje* is not only an ethnic category, but also a spiritual and nationalistic concept. Vasconcelos makes direct reference to Jews in his utopic, eugenicist essay, stating, "Judaic striae can be seen that have hidden themselves in Castilian blood since the days of the cruel expulsion; the Arab's melancholies are a trace of the sickly Muslim sensuality; who among us doesn't have some or all of that or doesn't desire to have it?" (17). Jewishness has thus been shown to undergird ethnic understandings of national identity stemming all the way back to Iberia before the Jews were expelled.

It is necessary to consider Vasconcelos's image of "Jewish striae" in Castilian blood in order to inscribe Jewish ethnicity within cultural and critical models of Mexican ethnic identities. In this way, Jews are not entirely outsiders to the ethnic categories that have configured existing

Figure 3.1. MAPAM flag at Hanukkah meeting in *Novia que te vea.*

understandings of Mexican identities. Upon learning that everyone in Mexico immigrated from somewhere else, Rifke develops a deep interest in archaeology. Yet, there is a problematic model of national ethnic identity that takes Jewishness into account but in a way that does not recognize or allow for Jewish difference, as Vasconcelos does with other categories of ethnic difference. Furthermore, the Judaic striae of which Vasconcelos speaks are Sephardic, not Ashkenazi, such that the consideration of Jews within his model is not wholly inclusive of Jews. Yet, there is a degree to which, albeit partially and problematically, the Jewish body has been included within hegemonic cultural models of Mexican national identity. My reading of *Novia que te vea* in dialogue with Vasconcelos sheds light on elements that have "hidden themselves" in the Castilian blood that forms part of mestizo identity, just as Jewishness has remained largely "hidden" in critical understandings of the construction of race and nationalism. In turn, I contest prevailing conceptualizations of centre and periphery by bringing Jewishness to the fore in discussions on national identities.

Israel, Zionism, and 1960s Student Movements

In her efforts to reconfigure national identity in *Novia que te vea,* Guita Schyfter foregrounds national, regional, and local politics in Mexico. The director has asserted her deliberate choice in setting the film in the 1960s so as to explore the characters' involvement in revolutionary groups that were largely inspired by the success of the Cuban Revolution in 1959. As in other Latin American countries, Mexico's progressive young people found themselves swept up in the revolutionary and socialist fervour of political movements in the 1960s. Rifke is shown in the courtyard of her university helping to paint signs that say, "Yes to Cuba, No to Yankees," in solidarity with Castro's regime and in opposition to US imperialist forces. To repress dissent, the Mexican government sought out communist youths and arrested them in the days leading up to President Kennedy's 1962 visit to Mexico City. Saavedra is one of these young Communist Party members who are arrested. As Ilene S. Goldman has noted, *Novia que te vea* "uses Kennedy's visit and the Mexican government's show of anti-Cuba, pro-U.S. behavior to highlight the tumultuous historical circumstances in which Rifke and Oshi must reconcile their identities" (loc. 2457–60). The film's representation of political struggles may be understood as both uniquely Jewish and as facilitating solidarity between Jews and non-Jews. In the case of Mexico, the 1960s have a poignant meaning for student movements in light of the 2 October 1968 Tlatelolco massacre. On the heels of months of ever larger demonstrations protesting the 1968 Olympics in Mexico City, just days before they were to start, armed forces opened fire on some ten thousand unarmed university and high school students and labour union workers gathered in peaceful protest in the Plaza de las Tres Culturas in the Tlatelolco section of Mexico City; well over a thousand people were arrested and hundreds of people were killed. Rashkin writes, "The fact that *Novia* unfolds prior to the [Tlatelolco] massacre of 1968 allows it to depict the ideals of its characters without bitterness, as wellsprings of hope and personal empowerment" (146). Rashkin's mention of "wellsprings of hope" again evokes Schyfter's avowed emphasis on the "effervescence" of revolutionary culture and beliefs.

For Oshi and Rifke, the experience of participating in Hashomer Hatzair (or Shomer) is integral to political orientations, recalling the importance of this organization as discussed in the introductory chapter. As Alfaro-Velcamp points out, "In the film, Shomer... celebrates Israel and encourages spending time on a kibbutz uniting Mexican Jews. This group allows Oshi and Rifke to explore their Jewishness with other Jewish Mexicans" (275). In the scene in which Rifke and Oshi first meet each other, the camera pans across each of their faces as another member of the group discusses the importance of the Maccabees and Jewish resistance against repression. Behind him is a menorah in the shape of the Star of David and, farther in the background, a flag of Israel's United Workers Party, the leftist party with which Hashomer Hatzair merged. The visual composition of this shot, coupled with the dialogue discussing the Maccabees, equates allegiance with socialist Zionism with the Maccabean Jews' struggle against repression. *Novia que te vea*

Figure 3.2. Painting pro-Cuba signs in *Novia que te vea*.

thus visually equates the observance of Hanukkah – commemorating the Maccabean Revolt – with the tradition of Jewish resistance as well as with 1960s political activism. Again, as in the superimposition of characters' bodies onto the muralists' works, Jewish bodies are visually equated with icons of resistance.

Schyfter crafts a depiction of the Hashomer Hatzair group that accepts multifaceted and contradictory Jewish identities. Through this nuanced portrayal of Hashomer Hatzair, the director reminds audiences that even within a group of Jewish socialist Zionists, cultural and ideological differences abound. *Novia que te vea* thus further complicates cultural understandings of how Jewish identities and politics inform one another. During a camping trip with members of Hashomer, Oshi tells a Polish and presumably Ashkenazi peer of hers that her parents want her to drop out of Hashomer so that she can marry, prompting another Hashomer member to ask her whether she wants to study. She tells him that she wants to study painting but that her parents will not allow her to do so. Oshi goes on to explain that her parents are from Turkey and speak Ladino at home, to which her friend responds, "It's incredible how different our Jewish communities are. Each one has its own synagogue, its own school, and its own pantheon. It's absurd." Even within this group of ideologically aligned young Jews, differences between Jewish communities are made explicit.

Through underscoring such differences Schyfter is able to debunk understandings that Jews' political beliefs are monolithic, which she also conveys through her Jewish characters' differing stances on Israel. In the 1960s, the Israeli-Palestinian conflict had effects on Jewish communities worldwide. The contrasts between the lack of overt interest in Zionism among Oshi's family members and the heated debates about Zionism that go on in Rifke's home may be a function of differences surrounding the topic between Sephardic and Ashkenazi Jews. Ashkenazi Jews, on the whole, were more likely to be aligned with Zionism, while Sephardic Jews were largely less interested in the Israeli-Palestinian debate than their Ashkenazi counterparts. In Oshi's home there are no conversations about Israel, whereas Rifke's family constantly debates Zionism. For Alfaro-Velcamp, these differences may be attributed to the shifting geopolitics surrounding the Israeli-Palestinian conflict over the course of the 1960s: "Until the first Arab-Israeli war, Middle Eastern Jews had very limited affinity with Zionism, a creation of Central and Eastern European Jews" (275). Not all Ashkenazi Jews at this time were Zionist, as Rifke's Uncle Meyer reminds viewers. Yet, that the conversations surrounding Zionism take place within the Ashkenazi family's home and are absent from the Sephardic characters' conversations recalls these broader trends in global Jewish politics.

Like the films discussed in the previous chapter, *Novia que te vea* nuances cultural understandings of Jewish political beliefs by presenting Jews who ascribe to a wide array of stances on Zionism. Oshi's family does not discuss the State of Israel, but she is present at Rifke's family's dinner table for the conversation between Rifke's uncle and father regarding Israel. Within their parents' generation, however, while heated debates surrounding the State of Israel abound, these characters are depicted as being removed from national politics. Rifke's father asserts, "A Jewish state was and is necessary to normalize the idea of Jewish life" in response to her Uncle Meyer's challenge to him that if he is so Zionist, why then did he not immigrate with his family to Israel. Despite her father's insistence that a Jewish state is necessary in order to normalize Jewish life, he asserts that he was correct in bringing his family to Mexico because the country welcomed them with open arms. This exchange elucidates two key debates in which Schyfter seeks to intervene: on the one hand, variations within Jewish communities – even within one family – regarding the State of Israel and, on the other, the importance of Mexico as a place of refuge for Jews. Rifke's father speaks of Mexico with a similar passion and fervour with which he speaks of Israel. Rifke's father thus illustrates Jewish feelings of belonging and citizenship in Mexico, as opposed to the more hostile acts of Othering elsewhere in the film. Uncle Meyer continues to suffer from trauma experienced during the Holocaust. Despite his outspokenness at times regarding his political activities, Meyer is shown to have lost faith, declining to go to Temple on the Holy Days. Rifke's father attempts to cajole him by celebrating the recent arrest in Argentina of Adolf Eichmann, one of the major organizers of the Holocaust, an arrest he celebrates as "the first time Jews will have the opportunity to bring one of their murderers to justice."

Novia que te vea addresses Zionism in relation to broader questions of inclusion and belonging. When Rifke's father comments that the State of Israel is important for unification, Meyer quips that unification does not matter. Rather, difference is what matters. In his words, "Differences are treasures." As he makes this statement, Schyfter shows their dinner guest, Oshi, smiling as she listens intently. The scene's juxtaposition of Uncle Meyer's affirmation that differences are richness with the image of Oshi – who is different from them on the basis of her Sephardic identity – implicitly equates a non-Zionist stance with the acceptance of difference. Meyer's presence serves to debunk monolithic conceptualizations of Jewish political affinities, even within a single family. Schyfter explains her depiction of Meyer in the following terms: "I discussed the most important moments in history: Uncle Meyer, those old socialists who didn't believe in the state of Israel; the father who is the Zionist that all the Jews needed, etc. I wanted to give a picture of that whole socialist world that people don't know" (qtd. In Rashkin 154). The inclusion of this character is integral to Schyfter's emphasis on the multivalent political affinities among Mexico's Jewish communities.

Beyond the Marriage Plot?

Insofar as the film's treatment of Oshi's and Rifke's choices to pursue their own careers and love interests despite their families' wishes goes, *Novia que te vea* has its characters move beyond stereotypical expectations of Jewish women. The film does not, however, present its protagonists' life trajectories in opposition to their Jewish identities. Oshi does not marry the Sephardic man whom her parents hope she will marry and Rifke does marry a non-Jew (Saavedra) who agrees to raising their children Jewish. Both, unlike their mothers, establish careers outside the household. The film does not show Saavedra and Rifke's wedding, despite including their son's bar mitzvah. Indeed, the film never shows a bride despite its title *Novia que te vea*. Rather, Rifke and Saavedra's union is depicted visually through a lovemaking scene set in Guadalajara during their college years, where they have escaped together after Saavedra's brief detention. Schyfter is highlighting Rifke's corporeality. The film moves away from the idea of Jewish women's corporeal passivity that I discussed at the beginning of this chapter and foregrounds the body rather than a spiritual rite in what the director chooses to show of their relationship. In Nissán's novel, the non-Jewish love interest converts to Judaism and undergoes a circumcision in order to marry the Jewish woman. Schyfter's film adaptation, in comparison with the novel, eschews questions of how males embody Jewishness. Neither Oshi nor Rifke disavows her Jewish identity despite going against some of the traditions that their parents present as inseparable from Jewish identity. The film's final scenes, set years after the film's main setting during the early 1960s, portray a meeting between Oshi and Rifke occasioned by the bar mitzvah of Rifke and Saavedra's son. In this sense, the film frames the relationship between the two friends over multiple decades in their shared Judaism. At the same time, both protagonists have fostered their respective interests – in archaeology and in painting – and have thrived in their endeavours.

Gender is shown to bear on these characters' political actions. Rifke admires Saavedra for his political commitment. Hashomer Hatzair was not a militant group and differed from the communist student movement of which Saavedra forms part. Hashomer Hatzair did not adopt the same "poner el cuerpo" practices, so it makes sense that its members would not have risked their bodies for their political beliefs. The Jewish female characters, however, despite sharing many of the same political affinities as Saavedra, are not arrested for their beliefs. Political affinities and allegiances occupy a central focus of these characters' lives during their student days, but discussions of politics do not figure in their final conversation as adults. Yet, if the struggles of 1960s Mexico's political climate do not continue to occupy their minds on a regular basis once they have grown up, their commitment in their youth to these causes nonetheless bears on who they have become as adults.

Throughout *Novia que te vea* Schyfter creates a picture of Mexican Jewish female identities that resists any monolithic characterization of these identities individually or taken as a whole. Rather, Rifke's and Oshi's life stories show that there are many ways to be a Jew, to be a woman, and to be a Mexican. Insofar as the Jewish female characters do not militate as adamantly as do other characters such as Saavedra, and there are significant obstacles that they must overcome in order to actualize their beliefs and aspirations, *Novia que te vea* is, in a way, rather conservative. As Luna rightly asks in concluding her analysis of this film, "Where did the idealism go? The radical politics?" (161). Schyfter frames her retrospective consideration of Jewish life for Mexican women in the context of massive student movements, and she has them meet through Hashomer Hatzair. This is because, as my reading of *Novia que te vea* has underscored, even for Jewish Mexican women who may ultimately lead seemingly conventional or traditional lives, 1960s leftist politics were a watershed moment in their life trajectories and served as the backdrop against which they negotiated their identities as Jews, women, and Mexican citizens. Through their respective life choices, these women found ways to be more than just brides and more than just an additional "flavour," in the words of Saavedra's father, in the country.

El amigo alemán

During a heated argument in Jeanine Meerapfel's 2012 film *El amigo alemán*, title character Friedrich Burg decides to return from Germany, where he is currently a student, to his homeland of Argentina. With a dramatic gesture, he throws his Borges books into the trash. Then he proclaims to his love interest Sulamit Loewenstein that Borges – whom they had lovingly read together as children in Buenos Aires – is "no longer his Borges," ever since that writer publicly shook the hand of Juan Carlos Onganía, the brutal dictator and de facto president of Argentina from 1966 to 1970, a presidency marked by the repression of dissidence. Both Friedrich and Sulamit are children of immigrants from Germany, although Sulamit is Jewish and Friedrich is not.

Here, in the wake of the 1960s student movements in Europe, Friedrich declares that he can accomplish more for liberation struggles from within a Latin American country than from Europe. Through Friedrich's act of casting aside his Borges books *El amigo alemán* stoked memories of the debates regarding Argentine-born Jorge Luis Borges (1899–1986) as a writer vis-à-vis Latin American revolutionary culture. Among these debates perhaps the most widely known is Cuban Roberto Fernández Retamar's 1971 essay "Calibán," which indicts Borges as a bourgeois colonialist. In 1950s Argentina two intellectual leaders who were fundamental for 1960s and 1970s revolutionary movements, Juan José Hernández Arregui and Jorge Abelardo Ramos, criticized Borges by analysing his "elitist" readings of the gaucho poem *Martín Fierro*. Ramos states, "As the working class has become the leader of national revolution [...] Borges has taken to revile the very idea of the nation" (137), while Hernández Arregui concludes his contribution to *Contra Borges* with "Borges-ism is the shallow stained-glass window that reflects the frivolity of the elite" (111). Similarly, Adolfo Prieto dismissed Borges's literary criticism as "*prescindible* (dispensable, unnecessary)" (62) and repeatedly defined him as "a writer without literature." David Viñas, writing in *Antiborges*, defended Prieto's stance.[4] The place of this iconic writer relative to 1960s and 1970s revolutionary culture – as well as within present-day understandings of that culture – was such a point of contention that denouncing Borges, as Friedrich Burg does here, serves as shorthand to mark an individual as belonging to these revolutionary movements. *El amigo alemán* reveals the complexities of global liberation movements vis-à-vis relationships between Jews and non-Jews, a topic that has barely figured in Jewish Latin American cinematic production. Friedrich, who has vacillated between self-identification as German and self-identification as Argentine, proclaims to Sulamit that he is "*latinoamericano*," furthering his identification with global liberation movements rather than as either German or Argentine. In this climactic scene, Sulamit's place as a political subject is, in contrast, more uncertain than Friedrich's fervent identification with decolonization politics.

The film's diegesis spans forty years of Argentina's history. *El amigo alemán* begins with Friedrich and Sulamit's childhood years, which were spent in a wealthy suburban area of Buenos Aires. The children befriend each other, but shortly thereafter Sulamit's father falls ill and dies. Sulamit and her mother move to a more modest neighbourhood of the city, while about this time Friedrich, the son of German immigrants, discovers that his father was a high-ranking SS (Schutzstaffel) officer. Friedrich informs Sulamit of his plans to go to Germany to study and to learn more about his father's Nazi past. After some time Sulamit joins him there, and the two enter into a romantic relationship. This relationship is impeded, however, by Friedrich's passionate focus on social justice and liberation movements in the midst of the student protests. He returns to Argentina to fight for the revolution, but Sulamit stays in Germany to study and to teach. During the dictatorship Friedrich is imprisoned. Upon his release from prison he moves to a remote village inhabited by Mapuche, a group of Indigenous inhabitants of south-central Chile and southwestern Argentina including parts of present-day Patagonia. Years later he writes to Sulamit to invite her to come back to Argentina.

My examination of *El amigo alemán* begins with the historical context of the film's opening scenes, which depict the coexistence of Nazis and Jews in post–Second World Peronist Argentina, a situation from which anti-Semitism and Nazi sympathizing in Argentina are inextricable.[5] From there I explore questions of the family, assimilation, and hegemony in both a Jewish and non-Jewish context. My specific focus is on how these processes of assimilation and interpellation prefigure and facilitate individuals' political beliefs and identifications with political movements, both nationally and internationally. These political identifications reach a point where they impede interpersonal identifications. Ultimately, I argue that the protagonists' return to Argentina after many years away facilitates reconciliation with both self and Other that finally allows the characters to sustain a relationship with each other.

Throughout *El amigo alemán*, war, politics, friendship, and religious affiliation are in constant tension. Friendship and enmity are repeatedly shown to be determinants of individuals' political orientations. Expanding on my earlier discussion of Gabriella Slomp's reading of Carl Schmitt's *The Concept of the Political*, Slomp describes the "global revolutionary": "This type of person is willing to kill and die for abstractions, be they ideals or people. For Schmitt, ideologies such as Leninism or religious fundamentalism have to some extent contributed to the development of absolute enmity and its counterpart: abstract friendship" (206). Such "abstract friendship" impedes specific interpersonal relationships, including the friendship between Sulamit and Friedrich ("real" or "existential" friendship in Schmitt's terms). It is only after he moves past his fervent commitment to global revolutionary causes and the absolute enmity therein that Friedrich at last is able to re-establish a relationship with his childhood friend. The historical, political, and social weight of the Holocaust and international politics after the Second World War at times serves to facilitate and, at others, to block the friendship between the two main protagonists in *El amigo alemán*. This is the context and provides the backdrop for the meeting of these two individuals and for their affinity for one another that develops over decades; however, the increasingly passionate political identifications of Friedrich, the film's title character, impede the realization of their friendship and their subsequent love relationship.

Like in *Novia que te vea*, the Holocaust and Nazism are depicted in *El amigo alemán* not as the main focus, but as a context in which ethnic and ideological identifications orient the self-understanding of younger generations as national citizens. In *El amigo alemán*, the children – whether of Nazis or of Holocaust victims and survivors – have to reckon with Nazism and anti-Semitism as they assimilate into mainstream Argentine culture and form their own political affinities. Daniela Goldfine points out in her article "Acts of Memory in the Jewish Argentine Cinematic Present" that both the Holocaust and the country's latest military dictatorship have been common topics for filmmakers of Meerapfel's generation. The lingering effects of Holocaust memory in *El amigo alemán* bring to mind Marianne Hirsch's model of postmemory. She writes, "'Postmemory' describes the relationship that the 'generation after' bears to the personal, collective, and cultural trauma of those who came before – to experiences they 'remember' only by means of the stories, images, and behaviours among which they grew up" ("An Interview with Marianne Hirsch"). Sulamit's childhood is similarly pervaded by reminders of the Holocaust. Throughout the film, she wears a ring that used to belong to her great aunt, whom she never knew but for whom

Figure 3.3. Mr. Loewenstein and the Burgs in *El amigo alemán*.

Sulamit is named, and who died in the Holocaust. As Patricia Nuriel makes explicit in her review of *El amigo alemán*, "The Shoah is the underlying current that spans the length of the story" (108). Meerapfel differs from other filmmakers of her generation who depict Jewish culture in twentieth-century Argentina. Indeed, *El amigo alemán* expands on topics presented more subtly in her own previous productions, such as *La amiga* (1988), about a couple whose son is taken by the military regime and the wife's childhood friend, a Jewish woman of German ancestry, uses her social connections as a successful actress to help find the son. *El amigo alemán* is original for how explicitly it treats the intersections of religious-ethnic categories, politics, and interpersonal relationships.

Peronist Argentina and the Coexistence of Nazis and Jews

Jeanine Meerapfel situates *El amigo alemán* within the particular political climate of 1950s Argentina that allowed for the coexistence of both Jews and Nazis, as revealed in the film's beginning. Sulamit and her father are driving through their wealthy suburban neighbourhood in Buenos Aires. Mr. Loewenstein stops his convertible in front of the kosher store and tells his daughter to wait in the car while he goes in. On the sidewalk he coldly acknowledges Friedrich's parents, his across-the-street neighbours, in German, and they respond politely, though not effusively. Plastered to both the sides of the kosher butcher's storefront and the storefront of the business across the street – which the Burgs then enter – are posters of Juan Domingo Perón (b. 1895), president of Argentina from 1946 to 1955, and again in 1973 until his death in 1974.[6] In this shot, Mr. Loewenstein, the Burgs, and Perón's face all fill the frame, reminding viewers of Perón's ambiguous and controversial policies regarding the Axis powers during the Second World War and especially, following the war, the immigration of Nazis into Argentina. The visual composition is this frame has a similar effect to the posters of Charles Lindbergh at the beginning of *Novia que te vea*. The Loewensteins' opinions of Perón's leadership are never discussed in *El amigo alemán*. However, the repeated mentions of Perón not only orient the audience chronologically, but also remind viewers that Peronism had a direct bearing on the protagonists' ideological affinities and their life trajectories, as I discussed in the case of David Blaustein's film *Botín de Guerra*, in chapter 2.

Sulamit's early youth is punctuated by Perón being forced to leave the country in 1955. As her ailing father is taken to the hospital, the ambulance drives out of sight from in front of the Loewensteins' home and a vehicle broadcasting Peronist propaganda enters the frame. No sooner is her father in the hospital than a group of hospital workers rush out of the building, informing Sulamit and her mother that Perón has been ousted and the military has taken over the country. The film thus signals a move from the domestic realm of family to the public realm of politics, a tension that will frequently arise in the lives of the main protagonists in *El amigo alemán*. Sulamit is shown at her father's funeral – the only time she is shown in a synagogue. She bemoans to her mother that they are relegated to the balcony (as is the custom for Orthodox Jews) when, to her mind, they should be up close for her father's funeral. This sequence depicts a trajectory in which politics enter into Sulamit's life (through the vehicle spewing propaganda) immediately followed by a moment that makes her take issue with the gendered distinctions of Judaism. Here Meerapfel is signalling the tensions between gender, religious identification, and politics. Specifically, this tension arises surrounding the ways in which Sulamit's body is expected to occupy space as a young Jewish woman.

The film portrays Sulamit risking her safety and putting her body on the line for causes in which she believes from an early age, such as the fight against Nazism and anti-Semitism. After her father's death, she begins attending a public school, where she and fellow members of the school newspaper write about Eichmann. She shows the story to her friend Friedrich, who tells her that in his school they would not be allowed to publish the political cartoon they drew because at his German preparatory school it is not seemly to speak of Nazis. After the piece is published, Sulamit is beaten in the streets by a group of boys as they call her "fucking Jew." Her mother meets with the school director who assures her that the boys will be expelled, to which her response is to ask if the boys come from German families. Again, as *El amigo alemán* suggests through Mr. Loewenstein's encounter with the Burgs at the beginning of the film, Sulamit's family is depicted as being wary of other Germans out of a suspicion that they may be Nazis. Given Sulamit's age at the time, this incident at school most likely occurs during Argentina's period of democratic rule (1958–1965).

Family and Generational Gaps

Although the differences between families of different religious and ethnic backgrounds are underscored, tensions within families are also brought to the fore in *El amigo alemán* – most notably in Friedrich's rejection of his family's Nazi past, but also through Sulamit's interactions with her own family. In the film, the family unit is shown to be a mechanism by which beliefs are determined and crystallized, but also as a force against which children rebel in forming their own beliefs distinct from those of their parents. As with friendship, the film shows family to be the locus of a sustained tension between self and Other, between like and unlike.

The generational gaps between both Friedrich and Sulamit and their respective parents illustrate the complexities of immigration as well as of the political and historical circumstances of Argentina in the 1950s and 1960s. Meerapfel highlights these generational gaps through the different linguistic registers that characterize the respective generations of the families that appear in the film. In the homes of both the Loewensteins and the Burgs, the parents speak in German while their children answer them in Spanish. The mother tongue is used to unite parents and children insofar as the children understand what their parents are saying to them, yet at the same time, there is a linguistic divide created by their children's refusal to answer in the same language. In their 2004 study *Lazos de familia: Herencias, cuerpos, ficciones* (Family ties: Inheritances, bodies, fictions), Ana Amado and Nora Domínguez focus on the family and specifically on family "ties" and what these necessarily connote: the ability to both connect two things and to cut them loose from one another. "Ties" and their necessary contradictions are present in Meerapfel's film through the staggering generational gaps between parents and children.

The generational gap between Friedrich and his parents reaches such a point that he ceases to have any contact with them, whereas Sulamit and her mother quarrel – with the mother shouting in German and Sulamit shouting back in Spanish – but they always reconcile. Shortly after she arrives in Germany, Sulamit asks Friedrich how his mother is, only to learn that she has died. Friedrich explains to Sulamit that he had not told her about his mother's passing because he disavowed his family upon learning the truth about his father's Nazi past. Then Friedrich shows an uncomfortable, yet disinterested Sulamit photographs of his father's Nazi friends. He explains that one of them had been responsible for Eichmann's immigration into Argentina and that another had been in charge of smuggling into Argentina monies that the Third Reich stole from Holocaust victims. As he becomes increasingly agitated, Friedrich proclaims, "I am the son of that man, do you see?" Sulamit, in contrast, remains calm and tells him that she, too, is the child of her parents. Sulamit and Friedrich's friendship is thus complicated not by the fact that Friedrich's parents were Nazis, but by Friedrich's consuming need to compensate for his parents' past. In contrast, Sulamit is repeatedly depicted as being aware of her family's past sufferings and grievances, but she is eager to shed the burdens of the past. Sulamit, unlike Friedrich, chooses not to take on the burdens of the past, while Friedrich, consumed by his father's involvement in acts of atrocity, decides to stake his life in the struggle against oppression to try to make up for them.

Generational gaps in the Jewish community in 1960s Argentina are understood to be connected with the younger generation's political and revolutionary commitment. The historian Beatrice Gurwitz analyses linguistic divides between Jewish youths and their parents within Argentina's Jewish community of the late 1960s, and she writes, "The youth found the older generation, despite its efforts to adapt, fundamentally incapable of grasping the nuances of what a revolutionary community in Argentina should look like" (259–60). Discrepancies between young people and their parents are related to individual processes of forming and expressing political allegiances.

Assimilation and Peronist Hegemony

Assimilation is figured in *El amigo alemán* as a process of moving out of one's own family circle and into a broader Argentine community as an opposing force to family bonds. The protagonists' assimilation is related to their subsequent identification with revolutionary politics as part of their identification with a broader national community. In most circumstances, this broader community may be understood in terms of "cultural hegemony," defined in Antonio Gramsci's terms, as glossed in the introductory chapter to this book. Over the course of their adolescence,

Friedrich and Sulamit assimilate into Argentina's 1950s and 1960s mainstream culture. For each of them, the process of assimilation is marked by a displacement from their upper-class neighbourhood and lifestyle into middle- or working-class sectors. Meerapfel's film reveals the prevalence of the hegemonic culture not among the upper class – for the upper-class milieu here is an immigrant group often depicted as not being interpellated into hegemonic practices – but rather, among the popular classes, where nationalism and assimilation are the norm. Here, the film illustrates the functions of working-class hegemony in Peronist Argentina, as discussed in the previous chapter. Assimilation processes pave the way in *El amigo alemán* for the protagonists' later encounters with revolutionary politics in Germany and Argentina.

Sulamit is presented as assimilating into the Christian community by celebrating Christmas with the Burgs rather than Hanukkah with her own family. Yet, her family continues to conserve its Jewish identity. The film thus depicts a growing generational, cultural, and linguistic divide between Sulamit and her mother. Additionally, her parents continually refer to Friedrich and his family as "the Germans," treating him and his family as Others because, unlike them, they are not Jewish. This way of referring to Friedrich – from which the very title of the film derives – also draws attention to the Loewensteins' own difficulty in identifying themselves as German in view of the atrocities of the Holocaust. The family continues to speak German at home, while showing a reluctant assimilation into non-German or non-Jewish Argentine culture. At the same time that the life trajectories of *El amigo alemán*'s protagonists evoke global issues of the Holocaust, Cold War politics, and revolutionary movements, Friedrich and Sulamit's story is distinctly Argentine. In addition to the coexistence of both Jews and Nazis, the historical moment in which they grew up also called for assimilation into hegemonic Catholic or lay culture.

After her father dies, Sulamit begins to attend a public school rather than the French private school she had previously been attending and to which affluent families sent their children: she is now assimilating into middle-class Buenos Aires culture outside the German immigrant community. After Sulamit has changed schools the film shows her mother ironing her white apron – a stark juxtaposition with the rich, dark tones of the cardigan and plaid skirt she had worn at the French school – which they then fumble to put on properly. Sulamit is shown assembled with the other students at her public school, singing the national anthem as the flag is raised on the pole, a ritual observed every morning at public schools in Argentina but not at her previous school or at Friedrich's German school. Sulamit's change of schools is squarely presented as her insertion into the Argentine national project that is visually sustained by the lack of contrast between the students' white aprons against the pale grey of the schoolyard. This image of Sulamit interpellated into the national project contests the pervasive "myth of dual loyalty" that has questioned national loyalty among the Jewish communities in Argentina at the time. Raising the flag in the schoolyard is a prevalent trope in Argentine films that depict recent history. Benjamín Ávila's 2011 film *Infancia clandestina* includes a scene in which its protagonist, Juan (son of Montoneros), refuses to raise the flag at school because he has been taught that the national flag is a war flag. The iconic 1986 film *La historia oficial* begins with its protagonist, history teacher Alicia, with her students in the schoolyard as they sing the national anthem while the flag is raised.

Assimilation is also seen as facilitating personal relationships. Whereas in her French school Sulamit is shown as an outsider (through a scene in which the teacher informs her that her ethics class, which she attends while her companions have religion class, has been cancelled for the day), at the public school Sulamit and a female classmate innocently and contentedly take each other's hand. In this whitewashed space of the schoolyard, their holding hands shows that within this middle-class hegemony Sulamit is able to find her niche more easily than she could in her previous, elite school.

Friedrich also assimilates into non-German Buenos Aires. He leaves home after discovering his father's SS documents and moves to a shantytown in a different part of the city to live among the people there. For the first time in the film he is referred to not as Friedrich but as "Federico." Friedrich's leaving home prefigures his later identification with liberation movements. At the same time, both Friedrich and Sulamit are depicted as having cast off their upper-class backgrounds as well as their German and/or Jewish identities. *El amigo alemán* thus highlights the connections between social class and ethnicity. In moving away from the upper classes of Buenos Aires society, both Friedrich and Sulamit become less German and more Argentine as they assimilate into middle-class life.

Jews, Non-Jews, German Argentines, and Germany 1968

In *El amigo alemán* the two main characters' German identities, as I have shown here, complicate their self-understandings as Argentine and also serve as another entry point to political activism, as they become embroiled in political happenings as students in 1960s Germany. The shared German identities of the Loewensteins and the Burgs are often depicted as a point of division rather than of identification. Early in the film Sulamit returns home from spending time with Friedrich, and her father asks if she was with the Germans, to which she responds in the negative, explaining that Friedrich is Argentine, like her. Her response to her father signals the hope that her generation held for friendships and filial connections that would transcend the divisiveness that marked the generation before them. Mr. Loewenstein reacts to her assertion that she and Friedrich are both Argentine by shaking his head and lowering his eyes sadly.

An affinity for Germany is paradoxically juxtaposed in the film with Sulamit's linguistic and cultural assimilation into non-German and non-Jewish Buenos Aires youth culture of the 1960s. Her mother interprets her decision to go to Germany as a facet of her teenage rebellion and as part and parcel of belonging to mainstream youth culture. Nonetheless, Sulamit informs her mother that she is interested in going to study in a country where they at least know how to pronounce her last name. The first words in the film are Sulamit's voiceover telling the audience that, when her parents officially named her as an infant, the civil servant informed them that the name did not exist in Argentina. The film thus underscores Sulamit's conflicted identification as German and Argentine: she is aware that she does not fully fit into either category. Once in Germany, she struggles to master the German language but ultimately makes a career of teaching German-Spanish translation courses. In addition, the film shows her return to Argentina multiple times. Her identity lies somewhere in between being Argentine and being German.

The film's use of Germany as the country to which the characters travel from Argentina facilitates a consideration of the effects of the student movements in Europe in the 1960s, in which Friedrich becomes increasingly entrenched. Paradoxically, Friedrich's fervent commitment to issues of liberation and social justice – figured as a byproduct of his friendship with Sulamit – reaches such an extreme that his friendship with Sulamit is no longer possible. Here I return to my earlier consideration of Slomp's "abstract friendship," as opposed to real friendship and born of global revolutionary commitment. When Sulamit first arrives in Germany to study, she is overwhelmed and exhausted as she tries to follow Friedrich's incessant tirades on revolution and liberation struggles. As their relationship takes on a sexual valence, their once lighthearted friendship is overtaken by politics. Sulamit grows increasingly impatient and worn out by Friedrich's obsession with revolution and armed struggle. As Meerapfel explains in the interviews for the release of the DVD of *El amigo alemán,* Friedrich's storyline is one with which she was familiar from both her own time in Argentina and after she moved to

Europe. In Germany Meerapfel met students whose parents were Nazis and who joined in the revolutionary fervour of the 1960s in part as a way to rebel against their parents. In Argentina she knew individuals who took up arms and participated in violent guerrilla struggles. Friedrich's life trajectory – and particularly Meerapfel's explanation of it – elucidates tensions among global revolutionary struggles at the same time that they are positioned as inexorably linked to one another.

El amigo alemán depicts Sulamit in a position of having to choose between the militant fighter Friedrich and a more passive, academic love interest. In one scene, Sulamit is seated at a table in a university common space while Friedrich argues for the necessity of guerrilla tactics. As she sits silently, Michael, a young professor, remarks to her that moderation is key in the struggle. She smiles, and the two grow closer after she tells him she can no longer bear to attend Friedrich and his friends' meetings about revolution. After arguing with Friedrich over his stubbornness and inability to talk about anything other than revolution, Sulamit and Michael begin a love relationship. Whereas the film rarely shows Sulamit and Friedrich caressing each other, Michael is portrayed as affectionate and doting towards Sulamit. Unlike Friedrich, who is constantly consumed by his political passions, Michael is uninterested in the liberation struggles. During their time in Germany, Friedrich comments to Sulamit, "Maybe that's why I love you so much," to which she responds with a blank stare. He goes on, "Because you're Jewish," evincing an affinity towards her motivated by an identification with her on the lines of minority identities. Friedrich's affinity towards Sulamit, motivated by his feelings of guilt and complicity over his father's Nazi background, is the basis for their friendship and it is also part of his commitment to social justice.

In light of the film's treatment of Jewish identity and 1960s political movements, the omission of any mention of Israel or Zionism in *El amigo alemán* is striking, particularly when considered alongside *Novia que te vea*. If many Jews disavowed their religious and ethnic identities in order to assimilate to the broader ethos of revolutionary movements in the late 1960s and 1970s, in Meerapfel's film one observes the inverse of the same phenomenon. Friedrich identifies with Sulamit and the Jewish community's hardships, and this identification serves as the basis for his passionate affiliation with global liberation movements. The film's eschewing Zionism or Israel, I maintain, can be attributed to the contradictions between self-identification as Jewish and revolutionary, historical and ideological tensions that remain unresolved. Furthermore, as Amalia Ran submits (and as I explore further in the next chapter's discussion of *El abrazo partido*), Israel and Zionism have been a difficult subject to treat for cultural agents of Meerapfel's generation. A younger generation of Jewish filmmakers and authors, however, is treating Israel in a more distanced, disinterested way.

Abstract Friendship and Real Friendship

El amigo alemán reveals the apex of Friedrich's revolutionary fervour as a moment that precludes real, interpersonal affinity and simultaneously facilitates casual sexual encounters. Once Friedrich returns to Argentina, Meerapfel shows him in an organizational meeting with an armed guerrilla group. In this meeting he is with a woman whom he kisses and who latches on to him but who barely speaks, a stock character depicted as an accessory to Friedrich just as his weapon is an accessory for the guerrilla fighter. Their passion for each other is figured as but a facet of revolutionary commitment. The scene recalls common attitudes of sex as a part of the fast-paced and passionate lifestyle of young revolutionaries who may lose their lives for the cause at any moment. Nicolás Casullo, a well-known Argentine revolutionary, has remarked, "The revolution was also made in bed: the more orgasms you had, the more revolutionary you were, and the more revolutionary you were, the more orgasms you had" (qtd. in Anguita and Caparrós 795). Like Slomp's category of the global revolutionary's "abstract friendship," many revolutionaries exhibited promiscuity as part the revolutionary ethos. This facet of revolutionary culture, however, contradicted avowed principles of chastity and fidelity that were integral to groups such as Montoneros and especially to the Ejército Revolucionario del Pueblo (People's Revolutionary Army).

Sulamit does put her body on the line to try to track down Friedrich once he has returned to Argentina and the country's military dictatorship begins in 1976, with the overthrowing of President Isabel Perón. From Germany she phones a family friend of Friedrich's parents only to have him hang up on her at the mention of Friedrich's name, for Friedrich has been excommunicated from his family after his falling out with his father. Concerned for Friedrich, Sulamit travels back to Argentina and goes to meet with some women associated with Madres de la Plaza de Mayo, a movement of Argentine mothers who campaigned for their children "disappeared" during the military dictatorship. Meerapfel shows Sulamit on a quiet street in the middle of the day, walking cautiously past a door and then doubling back once a slow-moving Ford sedan has gone by. Through the use of this vehicle, the so-called "icon of state terror" (Reati) in which paramilitary forces notoriously kidnapped political prisoners, the film introduces the possibility of Sulamit's arrest. Madres de la Plaza de Mayo figure prominently in Meerapfel's *La amiga*; indeed, Christian Gundermann interprets that film as a fictional testimonial of the history of Madres de la Plaza de Mayo (see *Actos melancólicos*). In her efforts to ascertain Friedrich's whereabouts and ensure his safety, Sulamit puts her body on the line and runs the risk of being kidnapped and tortured herself, exemplifying the notion of poner el cuerpo discussed earlier in this chapter. When Sulamit goes to visit Friedrich in prison she is disappointed to see that he registers little emotional reaction on seeing her; he speaks only of his plans to help the Mapuche recover their land once he is released from prison. Again, Friedrich identifies with an abstract concept of camaraderie and solidarity while being unable to reciprocate specific interpersonal affinity.

The film's circular diegesis is bookmarked visually by sweeping takes of the Patagonian landscape. The film begins *in media res* with Sulamit on the Tren Patagónico as she is travelling to see Friedrich. During the first three minutes of *El amigo alemán*, Meerapfel includes images of the clouds rising through the Andes as the train cuts through the countryside. At the end of the film, Meerapfel returns to this train trip and to Patagonia, where Friedrich now lives among the Mapuche. Although the film's narrative vacillates between Germany and Argentina, there are no similar visual representations of Germany, simply domestic spaces and some city street shots. Meerapfel thus visually emphasizes a strong connection to the Argentine landscape. The shots of the Andes are distinctly Argentine and Latin American. These images coalesce with Friedrich's self-definition as *latinoamericano* and his desire to help the Mapuche people recover their land.

El amigo alemán underscores a diachronic consideration of the legacy of revolutionary struggles in the years after Argentina's dictatorship. Once he is released from prison, Friedrich travels to a remote Mapuche village and declares to a man there that he has come to help them in their struggle for liberation, to which the gentleman replies that at the moment they are harvesting potatoes, and he is welcome to help them. Friedrich's principles are thus immediately – and comically – revealed as anachronistic and out of place. After spending a while working among the Mapuche and establishing personal relationships with individuals there, Friedrich changes. He becomes less rigid, and eventually he writes to Sulamit to invite her to come to visit him. In her apartment in Germany, Sulamit reads the letter at her desk as Meerapfel shows in the background a framed "Venceremos (We shall overcome)" poster of Salvador Allende that Friedrich's roommate had given her before leaving Germany to go back to Chile, following Allende's election in

1970. The framing of the poster visually depicts revolutionary politics as something Sulamit supports. Yet, unlike the Chilean who had the poster on his wall, as he was more actively involved in progressive politics in the early 1970s, hers is a framed – and temporally distanced – support for the movement. Meerapfel reminds viewers that Sulamit, in comparison with the Chilean who goes back to his country, does not fully put her body on the line for the cause.

In this same shot Meerapfel visually equates Sulamit's Jewish background with her political affinities. Superimposed onto the poster in the background is a menorah, one of the few clues to adult Sulamit's religious identifications. The visual equation here between the menorah and the Allende poster suggests that Sulamit holds for both a certain reverence and that they are both somehow parts of her past that inform her present. This visual composition of this frame is akin to the superimposition of the menorah in the shape of the Star of David onto the MAPAM flag in Schyfter's film *Novia que te vea*. Akin to the reminder in that scene of the significance of the menorah for the Maccabean Jews' resistance, here, the menorah and an icon of resistance – Allende – are likewise visually coupled.

In these later scenes of *El amigo alemán*, Friedrich retains a commitment to social justice and equity but in a less fervent way than in his youth. In Patagonia, he has established a lifestyle that offers him justice and contentment on a smaller scale, despite the failure of his previous quests for global liberation and justice. Sulamit asks Friedrich if the young man whom she meets outside his house is his son and is informed that it is the son of a Nazi friend of his father's who, like Friedrich, has stopped speaking to his own father and come to live with Friedrich. However, unlike in his previous diatribes vilifying his father, here Friedrich simply states with slight resignation that the young boy has come there to live. His righteous indignation over his parents' Nazi past has given way to openness and compassion. Knowing that he will never be able to correct the world's injustices, Friedrich has begun to do what is within his own power to make the world a slightly better place.

Friedrich's changing focus to the land and to a connection with his fellow man is his impetus for writing Sulamit to ask her to come to visit him. Returning to categories of friendship and enmity in her readings of Schmitt, Gabriella Slomp affirms, "What sets the revolutionary apart from the autochthonous or telluric partisan is the lack of a special bond to a particular land" (203). Meerapfel remarks that she chose the opening and closing locale of the "casa de los cóndores" because of its significance as the place to which condors return each year after travelling thousands of kilometres. This space thus serves as a visual metaphor

Figure 3.4. "Venceremos (We Shall Overcome)" poster and the menorah, *El amigo alemán*.

for the trajectories of Sulamit's and Friedrich's lives. After decades of living in different hemispheres and divided by political struggles, they have returned to each other and to their shared country of birth.

The film ends with Friedrich asking Sulamit if she plans to stay there with him, to which she responds by asking if he will come with her. The film's central question of whether its protagonists are German or Argentine will probably never be resolved. Their identities as second-generation immigrants will always be imbued with the stories of Germany that predate their existence and that have influenced the trajectories of their lives. In the interior of Argentina, and in the far reaches of Patagonia, the protagonists are able to find an existence that is less bogged down in the wars of their parents, the weight of their own past (both shared and apart), and the seemingly irresolvable causes that have consumed most of their lives.

In the penultimate scene of *El amigo alemán* Friedrich and Sulamit are lying in bed together, and he quotes a line from a poem. Sulamit responds by asking him, "Did you finish your war with our poet?" Friedrich answers her, "I think I've finished all of my wars." This moment of nostalgic and sentimental identification through making love and reciting poetry is made possible through Friedrich's letting go of all of his wars. Friedrich's absolute enmity has given way to a more specific connection to the land and to the possibility of real friendship (which, for its part, has made way for romantic love), remitting Slomp's categories of enmity. Whereas Friedrich was previously capable only of abstract friendship and sexual relationships as part of his revolutionary commitment, he is now able to engage in specific interpersonal relationships. His earlier denouncement of Borges evokes an entire generation's political ethos, while his final identification with Sulamit on the basis of his having "finished his war" with their beloved poet's questionable politics posits the possibility of moving beyond the categories of friendship and enmity perpetuated by an unchanging commitment to past political categories.

Conclusions

The films *Novia que te vea* and *El amigo alemán* represent the complexities of Jewish women's identities as they relate to Mexican and Argentine national identities and negotiations with feminism, Zionism, and leftist movements. Jeanine Meerapfel strongly suggests an optimistic future for her protagonists' romantic lives, and her film's open ending with a childless, single woman is certainly more amenable to feminist sensibilities than Guita Schyfter's coupled-off protagonists. Considering that these films were produced two decades apart from one another, the more conservative model of Jewish femininity in *Novia que te vea* makes sense within the context of 1990s conservatism in Mexico and in other parts of Latin America. Yet, it bears repeating, the protagonists of *Novia que te vea* also have fulfilling careers. In sum, these films have Jewish women use their bodies to express their agency. In this regard, the films contest the idea of Jewish women's physical passivity.

Meerapfel shows Friedrich, her protagonist, first identifying with Sulamit's plight because, as he tells her, she is Jewish, and yet later, he goes on to avow solidarity with the Mapuche in their struggles to recover their land. In this regard, Meerapfel's film suggests an equation between Jewish and Indigenous suffering. Because Sulamit does not become a mother before the film ends, *El amigo alemán* does not posit the same type of foundational fiction narrative as does *Novia que te vea* of a Jewish-mestizo family. This difference evokes Argentina's narratives of racial whitening that have long underscored the country's notions of ethnic identities. Unlike Mexico's myth of the *raza cósmica*, which erases racial difference through mixing, Argentina's long history of self-identification as a nation of European immigrants is visible through much of its filmic production. As George Reid Andrews argues, by the 1880s, "Argentina was becoming rapidly differentiated from her sister South American republics, which, with the exception of Uruguay, remained numerically dominated by a racially mixed population of Afro-Indio-Europeans" (106). Since the nineteenth century, Argentina has defined itself as unique among Latin American nations for being whiter and more European, quite unlike the model of the cosmic race discussed in relation to *Novia que te vea*.

The interpersonal relationships depicted in these films are mediated through conversations surrounding revolutionary and radical politics. Both *Novia que te vea* and *El amigo alemán* may be interpreted as somewhat conservative insofar as their Jewish female protagonists choose not to *poner el cuerpo* in social movements, and in the case of Schyfter's protagonists, marry and start families. At the same time, they underscore the central role that revolutionary and student movements played in Jewish life in twentieth-century Latin America, even for individuals who did not explicitly join part of full-on militant movements or participate in urban guerrilla groups.

Chapter Four

Lost Embraces: Jewish Parent-Child Relationships and 1970s Politics

In recent years representations of childhood and adolescence have become increasingly ubiquitous in Latin American cultural productions.[1] Intergenerational negotiations as a topic have provided writers and filmmakers alike a platform from which to explore personal and family stories as well as broader political paradigms. Film has used childhood experiences to question the points of contact between individual identities, interpersonal relationships, and political affinities within the context of insurgent political movements and subsequent moments of state conflict in 1960s and 1970s Latin America. Examples of such films include *Voces inocentes* (*Innocent Voices*, dir. Luis Mandoki, Mexico/El Salvador, 2004), *Machuca* (dir. Andrés Wood, Chile, 2004), *Infancia clandestina* (*Clandestine Childhood*, dir. Benjamín Ávila, Argentina, 2011), and *Los rubios* (dir. Albertina Carri, Argentina, 2003), all of which were popular and well received by critics.

For younger Jewish filmmakers, a focus on coming of age and on vexed parent-child relationships may be understood in relation to the directors' experiences of coming into their own as filmmakers. Carolina Rocha has analysed this coming of age of Jewish Latin American directors, including Burman, Hamburger, and others of their generation. She argues that, in addition to marking the experiences of the filmic characters with religious rites of passages, "the use of *Bildung* may also be related to cinematic exposure (or lack thereof) of these young directors" ("Jewish Cinematic Self-Representations" 42). The coming of age portrayals of the characters in their films stake the directors' claim for Jewish stories within a broader framework of contemporary Latin American cinema. Burman and Hamburger are between fifteen and thirty years younger than Schyfter and Meerapfel; they are part of a new generation of Jewish filmmakers from Latin America. Yet, these younger directors, too, take up the political conflicts of the 1960s and early 1970s that directly affected the generation before them. The political climate of the 1960s and 1970s continues to inform Jewish subjectivities and self-representations.

Filmic narrations of child-parent relationships have gone so far as to present children as political subjects, contesting common conceptions that childhood is an apolitical experience. Instead, childhood is portrayed as a stage in which political identifications are negotiated. Films turn their attention to the experiences of childhood to show how these experiences affect the relationships that children have with their parents as well as with the broader public spheres of the nations to which they belong. Childhood experiences orient the ethnic and religious self-identifications of individuals. In examining two films here in considerable detail, my particular focus is on how the protagonists' experiences with gendered rites of passage in Judaism, namely, the bris and the bar mitzvah, serve as guideposts in their processes of coming of age prompting them to grapple with both gender and ethno-religious identifications.

The two films address memories of childhood in a patently politicized key. The Brazilian director Cao Hamburger's *O ano em que meus pais saíram de férias* (*The Year My Parents Went on Vacation*, 2006) is about the child subject Mauro Stein, while the Argentine director Daniel Burman's *El abrazo partido* (*Lost Embrace*, 2004) centres on twenty-something Ariel Makaroff and his fraught relationship with the father who left him when he was an infant. Discussions of Ariel's childhood and his relationship with his parents pervade the film, although throughout *El abrazo partido* Ariel is an adult. The way both films emphasize childhood memories brings to mind Marianne Hirsch's model of postmemory and the transmission of experience – or, indeed, at times, a breakdown in the transmission of memory as these films bring out. They feature stories that older generations have passed on to the protagonists. Childhood memories are bound up in the political struggles with which the parents of the protagonists claimed solidarity. Geoffrey Maguire takes up this issue in his book *The Politics of Postmemory* when he calls for "a politics not simply of memory, but one which also encompasses generational identity, [and] historical representation" (3). In Maguire's estimation, memory, intergenerational dynamics, and politics are intimately linked to questions of historical representation. Drawing from Maguire, and building on my discussion of postmemory in chapter 2, I argue that for Jews, as shown in these films, Jewishness is central to the intergenerational transfer of political identifications. Jewishness and politics converge to inform the protagonists' coming of age because the mechanisms for the transfer of memory, established in these families through Holocaust and post-Holocaust experiences, allow for the later intergenerational transfer of memory in the context of Latin American state violence.

In this chapter my interest lies in the ways in which Jewish parent-child relationships facilitate the transfer of memory and political affinities. In her model of postmemory, Hirsch focuses on the Holocaust. Meanwhile, postmemory has also been taken up in non-Jewish contexts in analyses of recent cultural productions. Indeed, postmemory has become ubiquitous in discussions on postdictatorship in Latin America. As I posited in earlier chapters, postmemory is particularly relevant to Jewish experiences with political struggles and state violence, and it has been the subject of critical considerations of Jewish experiences during this same historical context (see, e.g., Levinson). Postmemory is both patently political, as Maguire argues, and enmeshed with the experiences of many Jewish families in the intergenerational transmission of their memories of the Holocaust.

Bridging generational conversations with my focus in the previous chapter on how Jewishness is constructed in a gendered context, I consider how the characters in two films examined here come to identify (or not) as young Jewish males. Both films depict young subjects who witness – but do not participate – in all of the gendered rites of passage associated with Judaism. These liminal positions allow for a broad exploration of gender and religious identifications, prompting me to return to my earlier consideration of Kathryn Bond Stockton's idea of childhood as an essentially queer experience. As she states in *The Queer Child,* childhood is not so much a question of "growing up," as one of "growing sideways." That is, the experiences of childhood constitute not a linear trajectory, but rather a stage in which subjects have the latitude to explore gender non-conformity. In *El abrazo partido* and *O ano em que meus pais saíram de férias,* one observes a tacitly queer depiction of family models insofar as the protagonists in both films are depicted as coming of age outside the norms of nuclear family models – and this, in large part, as a result of their parents' political decisions. The characters negotiate their gender identifications as well as their Jewish identities within these non-normative and possibly queer matrices. The construction of gendered identifications suggests an array of relationships to political empowerment that differs from the conventional romantic plots of *Novia que te vea* and *El amigo alemán.* As in my discussion of gendered embodiment, here I consider how gender, politics, and Jewishness converge in the experiences of childhood to orient individuals' negotiations of various facets of their identities.

In both films that are about to be examined here, the protagonists' parents leave them to go and fight for causes to which they are committed.

At the beginning of *O ano em que meus pais saíram de férias,* Mauro Stein's parents leave him with his grandfather in São Paolo's Bom Retiro neighbourhood, while they go underground during the insurgency against Brazil's dictatorship. Viewers never learn for certain where Mauro's parents go. When he was a child, director Hamburger's own parents were arrested by the military regime for a while; thus, perhaps recalling his own perceptions when he was a child, he uses young Mauro's innocence to preclude the audience from knowing the parents' whereabouts. In *El abrazo partido,* Ariel Makaroff's father has left him as an infant in Buenos Aires to fight for Israel in the 1973 Arab-Israeli War. National politics and Jewish identities complicate these protagonists' relationships with their parents. The urban spaces represented in these films – Once (as well as Villa Crespo) in Buenos Aires and Bom Retiro in São Paolo – are nuclei of Jewish life in these respective cities in the early 1970s and into the twenty-first century. Once and Bom Retiro, in a sense, themselves become characters in these films, to some extent taking the place of missing parents to inculcate Jewish customs and culture in the young protagonists. This role is evocative of the histories of these Jewish neighbourhoods. Both Once and Bom Retiro changed significantly over the decades between the early 1970s and the early 2000s when these films were made, namely, a significant contingent of their respective Jewish communities dispersed to other areas of the cities and to the suburbs, not unlike the case of Barrio Reus in *El barrio de los judíos,* as discussed in chapter 2. The films offer a diachronic consideration of Jewish communities' belonging in these urban spaces and in their nations more broadly.

Emphasis on Jewish communities provides the protagonists in both of this chapter's films with extra-familial models of Jewish identifications in contrast to their own families' fraught relationships to Judaism and Jewishness. The transfer of memory and Jewish urban centres orient these characters' processes of negotiating their Jewishness and political affinities. Moreover, in these neighbourhoods, Jews coexist alongside other immigrant groups together with Afro-Latin Americans and Indigenous populations. Moving beyond the idea of the proverbial "melting pot," these films underscore Jewish encounters with racial Others in a way that questions understandings of citizenship along racial and ethnic lines. The films' attention to categories of difference, coupled with their focus on the legacies of political struggles, show that relations to other ethnic categories are integral to belonging and citizenship for both Jews and non-Jews alike within the broader context of political conflict: national, religious, and gender identifications are negotiated through intergenerational exchanges within urban spaces tacitly coded as Jewish.

El abrazo partido

Centred on its treatment of Jewish identities and Israel, the film *El abrazo partido* received considerable critical attention. Existing scholarship has not interpreted this film in the context of 1970s politics in Argentina, yet I argue that *El abrazo partido* cannot be understood outside the framework of the pervasive revolutionary politics that characterized that country in 1973 – the year that Ariel's father Elías left for Israel. *El abrazo partido* can be viewed as complementary to *El amigo alemán*, where the former wrestles with commitment to the State of Israel, while revolutionary politics (both regional and global) are important matters in the latter film. Meerapfel foregoes discussing Israel and Zionism in favour of focusing on solidarity with revolutionary politics in Latin America, and Argentina specifically, with some attention to student protests in Europe. Burman's story is of a man who leaves Argentina to fight for Israel. This complementarity between *El amigo alemán* and *El abrazo partido* brings to mind León Rozitchner's assertion, "Our confronting the Israeli problem is simply a means of putting off our own confrontation with the national Argentine reality" (*Ser judío* 95).[2] For Rozitchner, commitment to national politics and a preoccupation with Israel disrupt one another. In *El amigo alemán* and *El abrazo partido* Jewish Argentine characters either express solidarity with Latin American revolutionary movements or fight for the State of Israel. In this light, the lack of any mention whatsoever to what was happening in Argentina itself in 1973 in *El abrazo partido* perpetuates the line of thinking that Rozitchner traces whereby one takes up either the issue of Israel or the issue of Argentine national politics. To elide national politics in a film focused on childhood in the 1970s is especially noteworthy within the broader panorama of Argentine cinematic production in the early 2000s, when films about childhood experiences marked by revolutionary politics abounded.

El abrazo partido was Argentina's official entry for the 2004 Oscar for Best Foreign Language Film, and it is the second film in what has come to be known as the "Once trilogy." In the loose trilogy, the Once neighbourhood of Buenos Aires is presented as the epicentre of Jewish Argentina. All three films – *Esperando al mesías* (2000), *El abrazo partido* (2004), and *Derecho de familia* (2006) – are about a protagonist named Ariel, portrayed by Uruguayan actor Daniel Hendler, who each time is a slightly different character with a different surname. In 2016 Burman returned to Once and to the character of Ariel in a fourth film, *El rey del Once*, although this time Ariel was portrayed by another actor, Alan Sabbagh. In the three earlier films Ariel is depicted in a state of arrested development and as a typical schlemiel. Unlike the other films, however, *El abrazo partido* is set entirely within the Once neighbourhood and thus at times gives the impression of an ethnographic documentary of Once and its inhabitants.

In chronicling daily life in one of Argentina's most quintessentially Jewish neighbourhoods, the formal aspects of *El abrazo partido* blend elements of documentary and fiction film. This engagement with a variety of generic forms resonates with Cynthia Tompkins's recent book on experimental cinema in Latin America, discussed in the introduction. Elements such as the shaky camera showing the streets of Once coupled with Ariel's voiceover and the inclusion of home video recordings of Ariel's *bris* emphasize non-conventional forms of self-representation to portray specifically Jewish experiences. Burman blends cinematic forms foregrounding audiovisual storytelling specifically related to Jewish identities. Such innovation is typical of Burman's cohort of filmmakers, who are collectively known as New Argentine Cinema – most critical accounts mark the beginning of this wave of filmmaking with the release of the experimental and widely acclaimed film *Pizza, birra, faso* (*Pizza, Beer, and Smokes*, dir. Israel Adrián Caetano and Bruno Stagnaro, 1998).

In its treatment of Buenos Aires urban spaces, *Pizza, birra, faso* focuses on aimless adolescents, introducing a cultural model of abandoned youth. The emergence of New Argentine Cinema has itself been articulated in terms of parent-child relationships. Childhood experiences coupled with intergenerational tensions are its central preoccupations. Sergio Wolf submits that his generation of filmmakers were orphaned, meaning that they had to reinvent new cinematic forms in the absence of a thriving cinematic culture in the country in the mid- to late 1990s (Francisco Márquez). His fellow Argentine filmmaker Nicolás Prividera, however, counters Wolf's characterization pointing out that many filmmakers of their generation were *literally* orphaned by having parents who were disappeared or exiled during the country's dictatorship (ibid.). *El abrazo partido*'s sustained attention on the protagonist's fraught relationship with his father can thus be understood as an engagement with themes of intergenerational tensions that functions simultaneously on multiple narrative levels. With Latin American politics as its backdrop, the film's formal perspective parallels the director's subjectivity concerning the representation of postmemory and the formation of a masculine-oriented identity through Jewish rites of passage.

Generational gaps frame the film's treatment of Israel. *El abrazo partido* is the only film in the Once trilogy to be co-written by Argentine author Marcelo Birmajer, well known among Jewish Argentine intellectuals and politicians for his somewhat conservative stances on

Argentine and global politics. He is especially outspoken in his defence of Israel and at times a scornful critic of Argentina's revolutionary movements. Birmajer is the author of *Los tres mosqueteros* (2001). This novel is about the return to Argentina of a Jewish man once active in Montoneros in the 1970s who then settles in Israel – both for protection from the Argentine military dictatorship and as an act of making *aliyah*, or returning to Israel. This basic tenet of Zionism is also relevant to *El abrazo partido*. In his fictional works and in his essays, Birmajer displays a strong interest in the intersections between Latin American and Jewish political affinities. His essay "Ser judío en el siglo XXI" takes up these issues in reference to members of Uruguayan Tupamaros, a left-wing urban guerrilla group in the 1960s, who that supported Israel. Birmajer rather cynically editorializes this seemingly paradoxical phenomenon as "one of those fast and absurd pirouettes that only two identities as backward as the Jewish and the Latin American could allow" (9). *El abrazo partido* treats similar issues through Elías's involvement in the 1973 Arab-Israeli War, although the film makes no explicit reference to the 1960s and 1970s revolutionary involvements in Argentina or elsewhere. Given Birmajer's stated interest in the contradictions between support of Israel and revolutionary commitment, this omission becomes the more noteworthy.

El abrazo partido is set in the present, in the early 2000s. Yet, 1973, the year of Ariel's birth and his father's departure for Israel, looms in the background and is repeatedly mentioned. The film's retrospective focus on childhood recalls Stockton, when she writes, "The child is precisely who we are not and, in fact, never were. It is the act of adults looking back ... [and] the very moves to free the child from density – to make it distant from adulthood – have only made it stranger, more fundamentally foreign, to adults" (5). These ambiguities of childhood, which Stockton articulates as a form of queerness, are manifest in *El abrazo partido* through Ariel's fraught masculinity and his questioning of his identity as a Jew and an Argentine.

In recent years, Argentine film directors have been making innovative use of scant resources because of a lack of funding, resulting in a boom of experimentation and critical success. After years of hyperinflation and economic instability, in December 2001 Argentina experienced a crash, worse than the stock market crash of 1929, leading to a run on the banks, rioting, and political instability that culminated in a succession of five presidents within a two-week period. This economic instability is central in *El abrazo partido*. As Joanna Page argues, "Cinema has registered, and indeed helped to construct, certain modes of subjectivity relating to Argentina's experience of capitalism, neoliberalism, and economic crisis" (3). The impending economic crisis prompts an identity crisis in Ariel as an Argentine, as a Jew, and as a man.

Ariel's anxieties surrounding masculinity rooted in his childhood experiences dovetail with Stockton's model of the child not as a person in his or her own right, but as "the act of adults looking back." Ariel is presented as an itinerant subject whose identity is in negotiation, his childhood to be understood as this act of looking back. *El abrazo partido* facilitates a diachronic consideration of Argentine politics and engages explicitly with the reality of the economic crisis and its implications for Argentine citizens. Throughout the film, Ariel is attempting to recover aspects of his Polish ancestry as he prepares to travel to Europe because he has few prospects in Buenos Aires. Ultimately, he does not leave the country, and near the end of the film, his father returns from Israel. As with many Argentine films produced in the first decade or two of the twenty-first-century, the economic crisis provides a contextual backdrop against which to consider issues of citizenship, sovereignty, and identity. These themes all take on special significance in the case of the protagonist's relationship to his Jewishness.

"Creaciones Elías"

Despite his desire to flee the country, Ariel is squarely inscribed within the Argentine national project and in the Jewish neighbourhood of Once in Buenos Aires. *El abrazo partido* begins with a voiceover through which Ariel offers the audience an exhaustive inventory of the spaces and people in his neighbourhood. He introduces the various businesses in the galleria, the small shopping mall space that houses his family's store, "Creaciones Elías." Ariel muses that, given that name, a casual observer might suspect that his father is a shopkeeper who has just stepped out to run an errand or to look for another size in the storeroom, when, in fact, Elías has been gone for decades and has left behind nothing but his name. The name Elías creates a subtle continuity with the first film in the Once trilogy, *Esperando al mesías* (*Waiting for the Messiah*), insofar as the prophet Elías is promised to precede the messiah.[3] In this sense, the name of the family business further ironically underscores the absence of the father.

Yet, the name of the shop also connotes the legacy that Elías has indelibly left behind in the galleria, in the Once neighbourhood, and in Ariel's life. The establishment of Jewish businesses in Buenos Aires has long been a fundamental component of Jewish Argentine life. To this day, the Once neighbourhood continues to bustle with generations-old Jewish family enterprises. These storefronts bear witness to decades of family life, national history, and the global geopolitical debates that have affected immigrant communities. At the beginning of *El abrazo partido*, Ariel's voiceover states that the galleria may appear to be just a collection of small businesses, but he goes on to say that the stories of the people there are worth telling. As Tamara Falicov writes, in *El abrazo partido* there is an emphasis on "the daily on-goings in the galleria – a mall-like arcade – with all of the shopkeepers' daily lives keeping the frame abuzz and the various business transactions and interactions amongst themselves and their clientele" (135). Ariel asserts, "But we know that we are much more than just our businesses." The protagonist's understanding of the importance of family enterprises recalls my point in previous chapters that establishing businesses was a way in which Jewish communities inscribed themselves in their respective nations. Burman's use of voiceover here serves as an audiovisual method of projecting the place of Jewish communities in national history, urban centres, and the film industry itself.

As the audience quickly becomes aware, Ariel's relationship with his father is deeply fraught due to the many unresolved tensions between them. The title evokes Ariel's loss of his father's embrace in his childhood and into his adult life. The title also refers to Elías's lost arm, for the phrase "el abrazo partido" or lost embrace is also a pun on Elías's missing arm, "el brazo partido," which Ariel assumes he lost fighting in the 1973 war. This double entendre couples Elías's commitment to fight for Israel with Ariel's sense of abandonment, highlighting the enmeshment of the two. As Ariel will comment sardonically to his mother, he resents his father for having gone to Israel so that he could "save all the world's Jews except for one." The film thus poses an opposition between family and commitment to one's principles. Specifically, *El abrazo partido* explores the effects of this tension on parent-child relationships.

Through this opposition, *El abrazo partido* evokes comparisons with films about revolutionary commitment. In recent years stories of complicated relationships between children and their parents who fought in revolutionary causes have pervaded Argentine cinematic production, as in the examples mentioned at the beginning of this chapter. *El abrazo partido* differs from these other films in its focus on the State of Israel. Carri's *Los Rubios* and Ávila's *Infancia clandestina* deal with children of Montoneros, as indeed, Carri and Ávila themselves were children of Montoneros. Unlike their films, however, *El abrazo partido* pays no attention to the political tensions that abounded within Argentina during Ariel's childhood and at the time when his father left the country to fight in the Arab-Israeli War. In light of this omission, Elías's choice to fight for Israel brings to mind the tensions for Jews between being pro-Israel and being aligned with liberation movements – such as Montoneros – that positioned themselves *against* Israel. Given the attention to Ariel's early childhood, this omission is especially glaring because 1973 was a year marked by huge political activity and conflict within Argentina. The most tumultuous political event of that tumultuous year was the return of Juan Domingo Perón after eighteen years of exile. Upon his arrival, on 20 June 1973, Perón was met by thousands of supporters at Ezeiza Airport in Buenos Aires in a rally that turned violent, resulting in thirteen deaths of left-leaning supporters and hundreds of injured at the hands of the paramilitary forces. The Ezeiza Massacre, as it has come to be called, was a watershed moment for Argentina's revolutionary movements. In view of these historic events at home, Elías's departure for Israel that same autumn cannot help but evoke the still unresolved tensions between espousing a commitment to the State of Israel and solidarity with national liberation movements. The film presents commitment to Israel in line with Rozitchner's assertion that the Israeli-Palestinian conflict distracted from the political upheaval that characterized Argentina at the time.

The emphasis in *El abrazo partido* on Ariel's disappointment with his father is similar to other Argentine authors and filmmakers of Burman's generation who reckon explicitly with their parents' political decisions and the political and economic situation that they inherited from them. In Ariel's case, these negotiations necessarily involved his father's relationship to the State of Israel. Aside from his anger over his father's departure, Ariel never articulates any opinions or beliefs of his own regarding Israel. In "'Israel': An Abstract Concept or Concrete Reality," Amalia Ran characterizes Birmajer and other writers of his vintage, arguing that "Zionism, Israel, Hebrew, or Yiddish, along with the memories of the past, are connected to a new type of sensibility: they form an integral part of the Jewish identity of the younger generation without ever provoking a crisis. This new tendency generates a type of *cool* Judaism, secular and amusing" (35, original emphasis). As I stated earlier, *El abrazo partido* complements Meerapfel's *El amigo alemán*, insofar as the former focuses on Israel in 1973 but not on Argentine politics, while the latter focuses on Argentine revolutionary politics and makes no mention of the conflict in Israel or of Israel as an issue. In light of Ran's characterization, the contrast between the two films may be attributed to generational differences between filmmakers and writers of Birmajer and Burman's generation, on the one hand, and Meerapfel's, on the other. The respective foci and elisions – or, indeed omissions – in each of these films bring into relief a paradigm in which solidarity with Israel and militancy for national liberation struggles within Argentina remain too difficult to reconcile with one another within the present-day cultural imaginary. Through the differences between the father Elías and the son Ariel, *El abrazo partido* suggests that support of the State of Israel is a generational issue.

Once: The Jewish Neighbourhood

The treatment of the Once neighbourhood in *El abrazo partido* allows for a depiction of everyday Jewish life in Buenos Aires that is intrinsically linked to both Argentine national politics and Jewish identities. As Pablo Suárez writes, "The film's narrative structure appears to be simplicity itself, but beneath the surface its workings are intricate and complex ... Burman presents daily experience as fundamentally unpredictable" (56). In Burman's film, depiction of this Jewish neighbourhood and the everyday life therein is steeped in both cultural practices integral to Jewish communities and the spectral presence of global conflicts that affect the Jewish community, specifically the 1973 Arab-Israeli War. The director himself has stated that his portrayal of collective memory in this space takes on political significance: "I think my job as a filmmaker is to record the collective memory of a certain community, rather than focus on a [sic] personal lives and experiences. Ariel is an individual, but his dilemma and way of thinking is always political and a common one among the people of his community and generation" (qtd. in Shoji). The circumstances with which Ariel grapples in *El abrazo partido* are part and parcel of both the particular experiences of his Jewish neighbourhood and family and the political reality of early twentieth-century Argentina.

In portraying this neighbourhood and Ariel's family, *El abrazo partido* includes more frequent reminders of the Jewishness of its characters than do most of the other films I explore in this book. Burman shows characters wearing yarmulkes in the street and in their businesses in the galleria. Menorahs are usually to be seen in the interior shots of characters' homes. One day, Ariel goes to the synagogue to speak with the rabbi. These typically Jewish aspects of the film's mise-en-scène become ironic as it becomes clearer that Ariel, in fact, has few connections to Judaism. Nonetheless, Ariel is surrounded by images connected to Jewish culture. Nadia Lie argues, "While Sonia Makaroff [Ariel's mother] seems quite at ease with her Jewish-Argentine life, Ariel, on the contrary, is portrayed as a young man in his 20s who continuously seems dissatisfied with life and tries to escape from it" (579). The insularity of the galleria space and the Once neighbourhood, which Burman conveys through tight framings and claustrophobia-inducing camera shots, underscore Ariel's dissatisfaction with his current reality and lack of opportunity.

The galleria offers a cross-section of Jewish life in Argentina and the stories of people therein. As Ariel's voiceover underscores, immigrant families from other origins, for example, Koreans and Italians, run businesses all in the same space. This portrayal of solidarity among different immigrant groups in Latin America is similar to what Lesser explores in his "How the Jews Became Japanese," which I mentioned in chapter 2. To recapitulate, Lesser shows that cultural stereotypes and critical concepts alike often conflate varying ethnic groups in Brazil because of a prominent narrative in which "normative 'Brazil' cannot include ethnicity that differs from nationality" (10). The climax of the film's simple plot is a footrace with hand trucks between the galleria in which the Makaroff family business is located and the galleria next door. Although all of the business owners in the galleria are of immigrant families, they recruit the galleria deliveryman, a Bolivian immigrant named Ramón, to compete in the race. Ramón's function as "right-hand man" to Ariel's brother Joseph is in line with common depictions of Indigenous (often Bolivian and Paraguayan) immigrants in Argentine films in roles as domestic workers. The racial difference between Ramón and the predominantly Jewish business owners whom he is representing in this competition is significant for considering Jewish citizenship vis-à-vis the broader national project. Whereas this element has a relatively minor role in Burman's film, I address in the second half of this chapter the racial differences that are vital for Hamburger's representation of Jewishness and national ethnic identifications in Brazil in his film *O ano em que meus pais saíram de férias*. The character Ramón is significant here insofar as the galleria is a cross-section of ethnic minorities in Argentina, and the film *El abrazo partido* thus prompts a consideration of the place of another ethnic-religious minority therein: Burman portrays a community of immigrants that is welcoming to Bolivian (Indigenous) immigrants but in which Ramón, nevertheless, is relegated to a different role from the Jewish, Asian, and Italian immigrants.

Through its depiction of characters who wish to leave the country in search of better prospects elsewhere, *El abrazo partido* emphasizes the effects of Argentina's economic crisis on the Once neighbourhood in particular. As Carolina Rocha shows, this film "reflects on the effects of neoliberalism and globalization and their impact on Buenos Aires citizens" ("Cine despolitizado" 337). Now, at the dawn of the new century, Ariel faces few opportunities due to the economic crisis. Like Ariel, the rabbi of his local synagogue is also planning to leave Argentina to lead a congregation in Miami, Florida. In this way, Ariel's desire to leave his country provides him with a connection to his Jewishness. As happened with many Argentines during the economic crisis of the early 2000s, the rabbi himself has grown tired of the struggles of everyday life and he, too, seeks to emigrate. Ariel's voiceover informs the audience that this same rabbi performed his bris many years earlier. Yet, as the film makes clear, Ariel is no longer active in the synagogue. The film poignantly evokes not only the shared itinerancy of the rabbi and Ariel as proverbial wandering Jews, but also the lack of stability within the Jewish communities in Buenos Aires at this time. Thecharacter of the rabbi serves as a somewhat vestigial presence of a religious connection that has largely lapsed; even a ceremonial presence of Ariel's connection to Judaism is no longer available to him, since the rabbi is on the verge of leaving the country.

The characters' desire to leave Argentina is undeniably symptomatic of the country's economic troubles. At the same time, the idea of leaving, motivated largely by the economic crisis stemming from the political upheaval in Argentina, also evokes exile and the particular role that exile plays in Jewish life. In his essay "Being Jewish," the French writer Maurice Blanchot (1907–2003) states, "The words exodus and exile indicate a positive relation with exteriority, whose exigency invites us not to be content with what is proper to us (that is, with our power to assimilate everything, to identify everything, to bring everything back to our I)" (*The Infinite Conversation* 127). The characters' impending exiles, even though Ariel ultimately does not leave, are circumstantial effects of Argentina's current economic and political instability and, at the same time, may be understood as part of the Jewish condition.

Family, Childhood, and Memory

Although *El abrazo partido* takes place during Ariel's adult years, references to his childhood pervade the film's dialogue. Ariel often tires of hearing his mother Sonia recount the story of what she terms the "ancestral scream" that he made as a young child when he was lost on the beach. Interestingly, Burman stated in an interview with Carolina Rocha that this element of the film was autobiographical (Rocha, "Judaismo e identidad masculina"). Sonia ascribes a meaning to this scream and names it in such a way that evokes the tensions of intergenerational relations through Ariel's dismissive reaction to her anecdote. When Ariel goes to visit the rabbi to make sure that his birth certificate will be valid, he expresses concern that a corner of it has been snipped, to which the rabbi responds assuring him that the document is indeed valid. Ariel quips, "Oh, so it's like the circumcision." Burman also includes footage of a bris, along with Ariel's voiceover stating that this footage is the only image he has of himself with his father. Here again, as in Jodorowsky's surrealistic film, circumcision serves as a marker of Jewish identity as well as of father-son relationships. Like in *La danza de la realidad*, here, too, circumcision emphasizes an estranged relationship between father and son and takes on an ironic valence. In both films, circumcision is treated in a way that underscores distance between generations, which becomes ironic since the circumcision is meant to connect Jewish males. Additionally, circumcision becomes related to nationality through Ariel's comparison between his bris and his nicked birth certificate.

Intergenerational relationships have an important role in the transmission of memory. Postmemory has a strong presence in *El abrazo partido* in Ariel's relationships with his parents and with his grandmother. These relationships are mediated through stories that Ariel repeats but does not fully know because he did not live them. This aspect of the film resonates with Hirsch's description of postmemory, when she writes, "To grow up with such overwhelming inherited memories, to be dominated by narratives that preceded one's birth or one's consciousness, is to risk having one's own stories and experiences displaced, even evacuated, by those of a previous generation" ("The Generation of Postmemory" 107). Much of what Ariel narrates about his family stems from moments he is too young to be able to recall firsthand. He has relatively few memories or experiences of his own to offer through his voiceovers. With regard to his father, he relies on stories he has been told by his mother and other members of the galleria community. Ariel's voiceover introduces the galleria's sandwich shop and states that he never eats there because his father was once served a sandwich with rotten mayonnaise and he threw the mayonnaise jar across the premises. Ariel adds that this anecdote is not a great story, but that he likes to tell it anyway because it is one of the few stories he knows about his father. For her part, Ariel's grandmother refuses to discuss Poland; his knowledge of his grandmother's relationship to Poland consists exclusively of what others have told him. Yet, as the plot develops, Burman shows that much of what Ariel thinks he knows about his father is, in fact, erroneous. In this way, the film reveals the complexities that arise from the intergenerational transmission of memory.

Hirsch's model of displacement may be likened to Stockton's notion that the function of childhood in the cultural imaginary has more to do with adults looking back and imagining a self that never was than with childhood itself. Both memory and childhood are conceptually moving targets rather than fixed referents. In keeping with Stockton, the polyvalence of childhood also problematizes fixed notions of gender identification. Masculinity and honour are operative in Elías's choice between fighting for Israel and being a father to his son. This choice contrasts starkly with Ariel's arrested development as he flounders into his twenties. Carolina Rocha has stated, "Effectively, the paternal figure who first is depicted as a war hero who leaves for Israel to fight in the Yom Kippur War (1973) implies a type of traditional masculinity in the public sphere but at the expense of his private role within the family" ("Judaísmo e identidad masculina" 31). *El abrazo partido* presents an opposition between one's ideological causes and familial commitment as part and parcel of masculinity in an intergenerational context. The film's diachronic treatment of present-day Argentina and Argentina in 1973 problematizes the dynamic between family and politics.

Fiction is shown as important to the family's understanding of how family and politics converge. When Ariel bemoans his father's absence his mother Sonia often recounts the plot of the famous 1970 Italian film *I girasoli* (*The Sunflowers*, dir. Vittorio De Sica). *I girasoli* portrays an Italian man who is conscripted and has to leave his wife, whom he married in the first place in an attempt to delay being deployed to fight in the Second World War, and he never returns to her, choosing instead to start a new life in Russia. Sonia extrapolates from the film: "War changes people." For decades she has tried to convince her son that his father, like the protagonist of *I girasoli*, left to fight a worthwhile war and that his experience in this war left him forever changed. Sonia tells her son that his father did the noble thing by leaving his family to fight. The film's use of a Second World World War love story as an intertext underscores the fact that the characters in *El abrazo partido* continue to struggle with their Jewish identities within a sociopolitical context that remains inflected by the Holocaust and the aftermath of the Second World War. *El abrazo partido* subtly links *I girasoli* and the Second World War with Elías's allegiance to Israel in the Arab-Israeli War. Burman and Birmajer remind viewers of the ways in which twentieth-century geopolitics have oriented Jewish identities.

Before long, however, *El abrazo partido* informs its audience that the 1973 Arab-Israeli War was not, in fact, the only reason for Elías's departure. Rather, Elías left Argentina because his wife had had an affair with the shopkeeper next door, a transgression for which Elías could not bring himself to forgive her. Ariel also learns that his parents divorced before the 1973 war, a few months before he was born. *El abrazo partido* questions the points of contact between interpersonal connections and political causes by showing that an action originally presented as a religious-political motivation, that is, Elías's departure for Israel, was actually prompted by his disillusionment with his family situation. For much of the film, the audience is led to believe that Elías has abandoned his family to fight for the Israeli cause, sacrificing family for his political convictions. Then it turns out that his reasons for sacrificing his kinship bonds are in part because of injury to those very bonds. Once the film reveals this truth much of what Ariel and his mother have said about their family history is no longer reliable.

Ariel has spent his whole life believing, and bemoaning, that his father left him "to save all the world's Jews except for one." The strains on the father-son relationship are akin to the tensions between Sulamit and Friedrich in *El amigo alemán* and Slomp's notion that political categories of enmity may impede interpersonal identifications. The truths that *El abrazo partido* reveal about Elías's motivations to leave his family problematize conceptions about the points of contact between personal and political convictions, particularly in the case of Jewish individuals. His leaving is, in a sense, an aliyah or an act of allegiance to Israel, but personal motivations that had little to do with religious beliefs were also very much a factor. Once Ariel learns this fact, and his father returns from Israel, he is more open to considering reconciliation.

From Argentine to Polish and Back Again

Like his knowledge of his father's past, Ariel's understanding of his grandmother's Polish roots changes over the course of the film. The first section of *El abrazo partido* is titled "Ser polaco (Being Polish)" in reference to Ariel's attempts to access his grandmother's documents from Poland so that he can obtain his visa, which he clarifies is to travel to Europe, not to Poland. His impetus for doing so is not motivated by a family connection, for the intergenerational transmission of memory is truncated here just as it has been in the case of Ariel's relationship with his father. Rather, Ariel's desire to travel to Europe stems from the lack of opportunities for work that he finds in Argentina due to the economic crisis.

Ariel shows a fundamental lack of understanding of the Holocaust and the pogroms that his grandmother escaped when she immigrated to Argentina. He comments that his grandmother is reluctant to discuss Poland because, in his words, she has "a crazy idea that in Poland Jews are being pursued." Such remarks add to the humorous tone of the film. Ariel's dismissal of his grandmother's fear of persecution also highlights breakdowns in the transmission of memory at the same time that Ariel does, literally, acknowledge the hardships that previous generations in his family suffered. His grandmother's only remaining connection to Poland is through song.

Ariel's encounters with his grandmother are confounded by the complexities of memory. She refuses to engage with her memories of Poland because she was traumatized by the Holocaust. The one instance in which she does acknowledge her Polish roots is through singing a song in Yiddish, "Amol iz Geven a Yid (There Once Was a Jew)." The title line, "There Once Was a Jew" functions as an invocation to call Ariel into being as her grandson and as an Argentine citizen. The song, performed by the Warsaw-born singer Rosita Londner (1923–2014) who portrays Ariel's grandmother, is superimposed onto the visual movement of Ariel through the streets of Once. This scene's audiovisual juxtaposition thus equates the recovery of the grandmother's own memory – in this case, a happy memory of a time of innocence in Poland before she was forced to leave – and Ariel's acceptance of his Polish roots, his Argentineness, and his Jewishness. This affective moment of his grandmother's song that recovers her Polish past both parallels Ariel's coming to terms with his Argentine nationality and, at the same time, shows that being Polish and Jewish is an integral part of what it means for him to be Argentine. I use the term "affective moment" here to gloss the spontaneous, emotion-filled event in which the grandmother unexpectedly bursts into song as a moment that fosters an interpersonal bond and also evokes sociocultural phenomena of belonging and citizenship. Inela Selimoviç takes into account such instants in recent Argentine cinema in her recent book *Affective Moments in the Films of Martel, Carri, and Puenzo* (2018).

Similarly, by the end of the film, the last title to introduce a section of the diegesis is "Being Argentine," creating a chiasm with the film's first section title "Being Polish." Like his grandmother who journeyed decades earlier from being Polish to being Argentine, Ariel is presented as going from being Polish (or aspiring to be Polish) to being Argentine. The film projects a trajectory that recalls the shifting interpellations of previous generations from being citizens of their countries of origin to Argentine citizens. Yet, even someone such as Ariel who has a minimal understanding of his Polish ancestry cannot feel a sense of his belonging as an Argentine without first gaining a connection (through his grandmother's singing) with his Polish identity.

The grandmother's song, in Yiddish, serves to root Ariel in the Once neighbourhood. Unlike Jewish religious rites (e.g., Ariel's glib discussion of circumcision) or a connection to the State of Israel (which he duly dismisses), it is a more secular, depoliticized aspect of Jewish culture – his grandmother's song – that Burman juxtaposes with his movement through Once. The film retains its central tensions between assimilation and difference rather than having Ariel come to identify

Figure 4.1. Ariel and Elías embrace in *El abrazo Partido.*

with any homogeneous or monolithic citizenship or identification for himself, but includes a sentimental recuperation of his Polish ancestry as part of what the film depicts as "being Argentine."

At the end of the film, Elías has returned. Although he and Ariel have not spoken to one another openly, the film suggests through Ariel's conversations with his mother that he has decided to forgive his father for leaving him.[4] In the film's final shot, as they walk down the street in Once, Ariel reconciles with his father and the two embrace, thus visually inscribing the father-son pair within this urban space. The tensions between "being Polish" and "being Argentine" continue to characterize Jewish-Argentine experiences into the twenty-first century and in second-generation immigrants. Ariel has not engaged with his father about his actions, despite his objections throughout the film. Yet, through this embrace on the streets of Buenos Aires, *El abrazo partido* portrays reconciliation within the family and with the current national reality despite the troubles at home both in 1973 and in the early 2000s. In his relationships with both his grandmother and his father, it is through coming to terms with the stories and experiences of older generations that Ariel is able to move past his objection to his father's commitment to Israel over fatherhood and past his own reluctance to make a life for himself in Argentina.

O ano em que meus pais saíram de férias

Released in 2006 to considerable critical acclaim, *O ano em que meus pais saíram de férias* (*The Year My Parents Went on Vacation*) was Brazil's entry for the Oscar for Best Foreign Language film. Director Cao Hamburger crafts a depiction of São Paolo's Jewish community in which religion and revolutionary politics are, at first glance, seemingly far removed from one another. The film's protagonist Mauro Stein, like Hamburger himself, is the son of a Jewish man and a non-Jewish woman. He has been raised non-Jewish, and his parents are part of the socialist insurgent movement against Brazil's dictatorship. Mauro's exposure to Jewish life and to the political events in his country prompts him to contront possibilities for self-identification, particularly as he forays into the patently gendered aspects of Jewish rites.

O ano em que meus pais saíram de férias shares thematic affinity with the Argentine works Maguire analyses whose protagonists are children of militants. In examining the "politics of postmemory," Maguire argues that, whereas children are usually considered to be apolitical, "recent narratives ... have revealed the extent and intensity of the politicization of the childhood experience during the dictatorship period in Argentina, forcing us, as a result, not only to reassess ... left-wing militancy, but also to reconsider our understanding of the nature and challenges of childhood itself and its relationship to the political" (133–4). Hamburger's film underscores the process that Mauro undergoes in becoming a political subject. In doing so the director revisits Brazil's insurgent politics in 1970 to show how childhood is affected by children's lived experiences with political activism. In this film these experiences are often oblique or subtle.

Immediately before the June 1970 World Cup games, Mauro's parents drop him off at his paternal grandfather's apartment building in Bom Retiro, the Jewish neighbourhood of São Paolo. Once he enters the building, with his parents already gone, Mauro discovers that his grandfather has passed away. Reluctantly, an elderly neighbour Shlomo takes Mauro in, and the young boy lives among the inhabitants of this apartment building for weeks as he awaits the return of his parents. At the end of the film Mauro's mother comes back but without his father, who has died, and the two go into exile. Unlike the other films I discuss in this book – the majority of which focus on revolutionary movements during the tenure of democratically elected governments – *O ano em que meus pais saíram de férias* takes place during Brazil's dictatorship, which began in 1964 and lasted until 1985. The repression of dissidence was especially brutal during the five-year presidency of General Emílio

Garrastazu Médici, which ended in 1974; these are commonly known as the "lead years." Mauro's parents leave him during this period, so that he will be safe.

From Mauro's perspective both Jewishness and politics are mysterious. Yet, both come to bear indelibly on his coming of age. Carolina Rocha writes, "[Mauro's] orphanhood deflects the importance of politics and focuses on his survival in an unfamiliar place" ("Children's View of State-Sponsored Violence" 91), the "unfamiliar place" being the Jewish community in his deceased grandfather's apartment building in Bom Retiro. Rocha's and my readings of *O ano em que meus pais saíram de férias* are not as far apart from one another as they might seem insofar as we both acknowledge that the film presents a stark dichotomy between Jewishness and politics. However, I argue that Mauro's experience in the apartment building in which his parents leave him is inflected with traces of his parents' militancy (often manifest through silences or euphemisms) and, over the course of the film, the two separate spheres that Mauro and his parents inhabit – Jewishness and political militancy – come into increasing contact with one another.

Mauro's exile at the end of the film makes him a patently politicized subject, even if an unwilling one. As, for example, in *El abrazo partido*, exile has been represented as a quintessential component of the Jewish condition and a mode through which Jews in particular experience political conflict. *O ano em que meus pais saíram de férias* ends with Mauro's voiceover asserting: "I ended up being what's called an exile, which I think means having a father who is always late and never makes it back home." Here, Mauro becomes a political subject insofar as he himself becomes an exile, which he describes in the same characteristically euphemistic tenor that he uses in his narration. As do Ariel's voiceovers in *El abrazo partido*, Mauro's voiceovers reveal how little he knows about his father.

Bom Retiro

São Paolo's Bom Retiro, much like the Once neighbourhood in *El abrazo partido*, serves as a haven of quintessentially Jewish life and a backdrop against which Mauro negotiates his identity. Throughout *O ano em que meus pais saíram de férias*, Bom Retiro has a crucial role. With the exception of a few minutes at the beginning of the film, the entire diegesis is circumscribed by this neighbourhood, which here becomes a synecdoche of Jewish São Paolo. The retrospective narrative, in addition to the importance of focusing on the particular political climate of Brazil in 1970, is crucial in its return to a moment when Bom Retiro was still the cultural centre of Jewish life that it was in its heyday. Hamburger's film foregrounds the legacy of this urban space for Jewish Brazil. The specificity of the setting Bom Retiro contrasts with the film's cosmopolitan themes and international distribution. Akin to the exoticized elements of Chamecki's *Danken got*, discussed in chapter 2, A.O. Scott, in his review of the film, emphasizes the "seductive" elements of its setting: "*The Year My Parents Went on Vacation* is most seductive when it focuses on the details of daily life in the lower-middle-class São Paolo neighborhood Bom Retiro. The rhythms of commerce, worship and domesticity – the sounds of apartment house courtyards, synagogues, and shops – frequently overshadow what turns out to be a fairly conventional and sentimental story." The review notes that the milieu is "for most viewers, novel," in contrast to what Scott interprets as a disappointingly conventional storyline. Such reviews, particularly when published in the *New York Times*, speak to the complexities of the distribution and reception of a film that is deliberately rooted in a specific space – Bom Retiro – yet is also patently cosmopolitan in its treatment of Jewishness and exile. Scott's review highlights the ways in which *O ano em que meus pais saíram de férias* bridges local and global aspects of Jewish life, even if or perhaps because the storyline is "fairly conventional and sentimental."

As has happened in many neighbourhoods in cities throughout the Americas in which Jews established themselves, the Jewish families who once inhabited Bom Retiro have now largely left the neighbourhood. The anthropologist Misha Klein notes that Bom Retiro – often referred to as *plétzale*, or "plaza" – was "the starting point for a new life and a new identity as paulistano and as Brazilian, a familiar place within the vast and growing city" (54). But for Mauro the space is entirely new and unfamiliar. Hamburger includes some images of large monuments in São Paolo reflected in the car windows as Mauro's parents drive him into town to his grandfather's home. From this point on, though, the entirety of the film takes place within a few blocks in Bom Retiro and through Mauro's gaze. Unlike in *El abrazo partido*, the protagonist's voice does not orient the audience within the Bom Retiro space, because Mauro is not familiar with it. The film thereby emphasizes that Mauro is an outsider to this neighbourhood and to Jewish life more generally. At the same time, the insularity of São Paolo's Jewish community comes into sharp relief through the external gaze of an outsider. The film creates an analogous relationship between its geographical and thematic aspects.

Hamburger sets his film in Bom Retiro as a way of reminding his audience of the importance of this neighbourhood for Brazil's Jewish communities, and he then shows how the revolutionary insurgency in which the protagonist's parents are involved becomes integral to Jewish Brazilian identity.

Jewishness vs. Politics

On the face of it, Jewishness and politics occupy separate spheres in the narrative of *O ano em que meus pais saíram de férias*. Yet, the intergenerational transmission of both political and religious beliefs – from Mauro's parents, their militant peers, and the Jews in the grandfather's building – orient Mauro's understanding of the world around him. Through their ongoing contact with one another, Shlomo becomes more involved in politics and Mauro learns Jewish customs. In contrast to the political involvement of Mauro's parents, the Jewish community is explicitly coded as non-political to a great extent out of fear of repression in the circumstances of Brazil's current dictatorship. Shlomo, who discovers Mauro and eventually takes him in, tells people at a synagogue meeting that he suspects Mauro's parents are "involved in politics" and that the community, therefore, should not need to take responsibility for him. Someone counters that the parents' political involvement should not matter, as Mauro's father is "one of their own" since he is a Jew. As the congregation members' opposition between Jewishness and politics here underscores, Mauro has moved from the politicized environment of his parents' household to the seemingly apolitical space of his late grandfather's apartment building.

The residents of the building begin to call Mauro "Moishele," a nickname that at first he scoffs at but later comes to accept. His identity – at the most basic level of the names by which others call him – changes almost immediately once he arrives in this new, unfamiliar space. Not only does this nickname make him more a part of the community, but it also recalls the practice of giving a Jewish name to children in connection with religious rites of passage, such as the bris and bar mitzvah. This renaming functions to interpellate Mauro as a Jew and as part of the community. "Moishele" is significant, too, for its literal meaning of "to pull out" in the original Hebrew found in Exodus 2:10, where the pharaoh's daughter pulls the infant Moses out of the Nile River and the royal family adopts him. Like Moses, Mauro is a child who has been uprooted from his home and living among a surrogate family comprised of his deceased grandfather's neighbours.

O ano em que meus pais saíram de férias emphasizes Mauro's status as an outsider to Jewishness during his time in the Bom Retiro building. His lack of familiarity with Jewish rites underscores his condition as an outsider to Jewish life. In a comical scene near the beginning of the film,

Mauro's embodied difference is made evident: Desperate for a place to relieve himself while Shlomo is in the shower with the bathroom door locked, Mauro urinates in a planter inside the apartment. When Shlomo comes out of the bathroom, rather than scold him, he simply laughs and exclaims, "You are not Jewish!" upon seeing Mauro's uncircumcised penis. As in Jodorowsky's and Burman's films, circumcision (in Mauro's case, the lack thereof) highlights ruptures in the Jewish lineage (because Mauro's father is Jewish but his mother is not and the parents have chosen not to raise him Jewish). Shlomo's levity here suggests that he understands Mauro and is willing to be more lenient with him knowing that he has not been raised Jewish and empathizing with his outsider status. The patently gendered aspects of Jewishness underscore embodied difference and the complexities of a child's negotiations of his identity formation as male identifying (possibly) Jewish, and Brazilian.

Hamburger's representations of assimilation into Jewish practices are intimately linked to the gendered intergenerational transmission of memory. These intergenerational relationships are complicated by the fact that both Mauro's father and his grandfather die during the film's diegesis. Moreover, there are no maternal figures to pass down Jewish practices or beliefs, since Mauro's mother is not Jewish and his paternal (Jewish) grandmother is no longer living. In the grandfather's building, the women joyously introduce Mauro to the more fun aspects of Jewish life, while Shlomo is portrayed in relation to the more properly religious components of Jewishness. Mauro's initiation into Jewish life is clearly gendered. Hamburger includes a montage of large meals with Jewish grandmothers telling him, "Eat more! You're too skinny," juxtaposed with the soundtrack of "Chiribim Chiribom" by the Barry Sisters playing on a record player. Mauro's voiceover tells the audience that lunchtime with different neighbours was his favourite time of day. Here, Mauro's relationship to Jewishness is mediated through food and a popular Yiddish recording. The film's montage set to this upbeat song is similar to *El abrazo partido*'s shots of Ariel walking through Once with his grandmother singing in Yiddish. As Mauro makes his way through his grandfather's building, he is adopted for the day by different Jewish grandmothers, emphasizing the centrality of the intergenerational transfer of Jewish practices.

In *O ano em que meus pais saíram de férias*, male characters are more closely linked to Jewish religious rites, as opposed to women's connections with exuberant, secularized aspects of Jewish life. Over the course of the film, Mauro changes to become increasingly familiar with Judaism, specifically with the gendered elements thereof. At his grandfather's burial near the beginning of the film, Shlomo places a yarmulke on Mauro's head, and it sits awkwardly before falling several times. As Shawn Stein submits in his review, "After Shlomo attempts to adjust it for [Mauro] the yarmulke falls from his head, leaving the spectator with an image that, although it may be funny, tacitly portrays Mauro's complicated state as an outsider" (259). Specifically, Stein notes in his reading of this scene that Mauro's mother is not Jewish. Gendered elements of Judaism (e.g., the matrilineal transmission of Judaism and the wearing of a yarmulke) preclude Mauro from belonging at this ceremony even though it is his own grandfather's burial. Later, Mauro wraps himself in Shlomo's prayer shawl as he runs through the hallway dribbling his soccer ball, for which Shlomo chides him. Mauro does not know the significance of the cloth (or its gendered distinctions). The requisite vestments of Judaism are both foreign to Mauro and patently gendered. This taboo here also evokes gendered elements of Judaism.

O ano em que meus pais saíram de férias explicitly treats gender distinctions between Jewish adolescents. Towards the end of his time in the Bom Retiro apartment building, Mauro attends a bar mitzvah where he blends in with the young Jewish children there, as opposed to his earlier faux pas fumbling with his yarmulke at his grandfather's funeral. His attendance at another boy's bar mitzvah underscores that he is not having his own bar mitzvah. Hanna, Mauro's new friend from the apartment building, is relegated to the women's balcony during the ceremony, and Mauro takes note of this. At the reception, however, the film reminds viewers of these characters' somewhat unconventional gender identifications. Mauro is first dancing with another girl, but then he looks over at Hanna sitting alone and brings her out onto the dance floor and they begin to dance more wildly among a group of children, rather than as couples. Hanna and Mauro's friendship at times suggests a budding childhood romance, but more often it suggests a lack of conformity with heterosexual identifications, even in spaces in which traditional gender roles are strictly codified, such as the bar mitzvah. For much of the film Hanna is portrayed as a typical tomboy; she makes money by charging young boys to look through a hole that peers into the dressing room of her mother's shop as ladies try on clothes. Hanna's entrepreneurship reads as homosocial as she facilitates adolescent males' desire. The dynamic between Mauro and Hanna – particularly the dance scene at the bar mitzvah in which they dance as friends along with others rather than as a couple – strongly evokes Stockton's notion of "growing sideways" rather than growing up.

Judaism, gender, and political strife are brought together in this scene when the bar mitzvah reception is interrupted by military repression in the street after Brazil wins the FIFA World Cup in 1970. In this moment,

Figure 4.2. Mauro and Ítalo in *O ano em que meus pais saíram de férias.*

Mauro takes on his parents' struggle. One of the people injured is Ítalo, a communist companion of Mauro's parents. He previously had introduced himself to Mauro at the café run by the Greek family as a friend of his father. Shlomo takes Mauro to go try to enquire about his father's whereabouts from this man. According to Tzvi Tal, here "the audience discovers that Shlomo collaborates with the opponent student activist Ítalo, thus contradicting the Marxist axiom of religion as a block to revolutionary change" ("Jewish Puberty" 151–2). The military operatives begin to suspect Shlomo and bring him in for questioning because he met with Ítalo and because he visited Mauro's home. At the same time, Mauro brings Ítalo into Shlomo's apartment. Mauro's compassion for Ítalo evokes questions of loyalty among militant peers and in a Jewish context. The child knows instinctively to take care of Ítalo, I submit, because Ítalo is his parents' companion in the insurgent struggle (although openly Mauro only states that he is an acquaintance of his parents). Alternatively, Stein has discussed the film's portrayal of Mauro caring for Ítalo within the context of the parallels between state repression against communists in the film, on the one hand, and the repression of Jews during various pogroms throughout history, on the other (260). Here, I pause to bring together Stein's suggestion that Mauro's solidarity towards Ítalo has to do with Jewish experiences of repression and my interpretation that Mauro takes care of Ítalo because he is his parents' companion in the insurgency. Taken together these two interpretations evoke the connections between anti-Semitism and state repression during Latin American dictatorships. Mauro's solidarity and kindness towards Ítalo may be attributed both to the solidarity he learned from his parents' political commitment and to his initiation into Jewish life that has taken place during his time in his grandfather's apartment building in the neighbourhood of the Bom Retiro.

Soccer in *o pais do futebol*

O ano em que meus pais saíram de férias represents soccer as closely related to both Jewishness and politics. It comes as little surprise that a film about childhood in *o pais do futebol* (the country of soccer) should focus on the role soccer plays in its protagonist's coming of age during a moment rife with political struggles. As this byname connotes, soccer has long been integral to national identity in Brazil. The backdrop of the 1970 FIFA World Cup is effective as shorthand to orient the film's narrative, particularly in light of both the brutal repression that took place in response to the country's victory and the use of the win by the military regime to gain popular support. But soccer serves a much more important function than simply reminding the film's audience of the temporal setting and the brutality of the dictatorship. Throughout soccer serves as a multivalent metaphor of father-son relations, insurgent tactics, community, and friendship. Moreover, the sport is inexorably linked to the particular political situation in which Brazil found itself in 1970, as well as to the shifting dominant narratives of national identity that had characterized the previous decades of Brazil's history. In discussing the film, Alejandro Meter has noted, "The recovery of [Mauro's] Jewish roots and his (perhaps unconscious) affirmation of his Jewishness are directly linked to his passion for football" (93). Soccer has the role of bringing Mauro together with the other residents of his grandfather's apartment building and the Jewish neighbourhood Bom Retiro and of initiating him into Jewish life. At the same time, soccer orients Mauro as a burgeoning political subject.

Indeed, Mauro understands the world around him through soccer. In the film's opening scene, his voiceover states that his father used to say to him that in soccer anyone might make a mistake except for the goalie. The goalkeeper, he asserts, is special and stands alone to protect everyone. Near the end of the film, Mauro is playing soccer with Hanna as his voiceover reflects that perhaps his father always knew Mauro would play soccer into his adult life and for that reason told him these lessons about soccer. His father's description of the goalie as standing alone with a singular mission also serves as a metaphor of his parents' political activity and of his father's sacrifice of his own life for his political beliefs.

As the film follows Mauro's gaze, while often he himself is unaware of the particularities of his parents' actions, objects related to soccer fill in the gaps of the narrative. Shlomo leaves Mauro to go in search of his parents, but he does not tell Mauro where he is going. Before he leaves Mauro asks him where he is going and he says nothing, mirroring their first encounter in which Mauro remains silent when Shlomo asks him where his parents are. In both conversations the other one knows or at least suspects the answer but does not want to confirm it. After Shlomo returns Mauro finds two of his soccer action figures from home and knows that Shlomo has visited his house. Here the objects remind Mauro of his home and are a trace of his parents' absence. They also highlight the mutual understanding between Shlomo and Mauro. In this sense soccer paraphernalia fulfil a complementary function to the Jewish objects, such as the yarmulke and the prayer shawl from earlier moments in Shlomo and Mauro's relationship. Soccer-related objects also mediate Mauro's relationship to Hanna. She brings him the missing Pelé card for his album of World Cup players and tells him "Happy birthday," to which he responds that it is not his birthday. Later, as he is leaving with his mother at the end of the film, Mauro gives Hanna his soccer ball and tells her "Happy birthday," although it is not her birthday. Mauro's most significant relationships in the film are mediated through objects related to soccer.

Soccer has a particular significance for the Bom Retiro neighbourhood's immigrant communities, as the film emphasizes. For Carolina Rocha, Bom Retiro is "portrayed as the home of Jewish, Italian, and Greek immigrants who coexist side by side, united (or divided) by the very Brazilian passion for soccer" ("Children's View" 93). Soccer brings together the different ethnic groups that comprise the neighbourhood. Similarly, Shawn Stein notes, "The excitement of the World Cup and the possibility of Brazil's third victory captured the imagination of the immigrant residents in Bom Retiro, eliminating religious and ethnic barriers and putting off, at least during the three weeks of the championship, people's attention to the armed violence that was taking place in various urban centers" (257). As with the galleria space in *El abrazo partido*, the portrayal of soccer in *O ano em que pais saíram de férias* underscores affinities between immigrant groups, an important component of cultural and critical understandings of Jewish Latin America. In addition to uniting these Jewish, Italian, and Greek immigrants of whom Rocha speaks, Hamburger's representation of soccer in Bom Retiro introduces the possibility of new, more inclusive models of racial and ethnic relations in Brazil, specifically between Jews and Afro-Brazilians.

Futebol mulato and *Democracia racial*

Soccer becomes a way of engaging with salient themes of race relations between Jews and Afro-Brazilians in *O ano em que meus pais saíram de férias*. In a moment that emphasizes the tight-knit community in Bom Retiro, Mauro attends a soccer match between the neighbourhood's Jewish and Italian residents. Mauro informs viewers through his voiceover from the bleachers that the Jews had a secret weapon: Edgar, the Afro-Brazilian boyfriend of the Greek woman whose family runs a local coffee shop. Edgar is already mesmerizing to Mauro and the other young boys in the neighbourhood because they are envious that he is dating the attractive Greek woman. After seeing the soccer match, Mauro's fascination grows and his voiceover tells viewers, "I wanted to be black and to fly." Rocha points out that Mauro's reaction to Edgar's soccer skills "betrays his previous colorblindness" ("Children's View" 93). Indeed, a great deal of Mauro's coming of age has to do precisely with encountering ethnic differences as he is immersed in a Jewish community for the first time in his life. In turn, he is becoming more race-conscious.

Mauro's assertion of wanting to be black and to fly speaks to societal preoccupations with race in connection with soccer common throughout Brazil at the time. As the historian Roger Kittleson has noted, "The Brazilian modernity of the 1950s to the 1970s was generally an African-descended identity. The roots of this identity lay in the 1930s and '40s, in notions of a mixed-race culture. In sporting terms, this meant the concept of a Brazilian 'mulatto football,' which grew from its early formulations in the work of Gilberto Freyre and Mário Filho into a distinctively Brazilian *futebol-arte*" (54). The sociologist Gilberto Freyre's *democracia racial* underscores cultural understandings of Brazilian national identity at this time and duly undergirds popular understandings of soccer in the *pais do futebol*. "Racial democracy" has commonly been used to refer to the idea that Brazilians did not perceive racial tensions and differences as acutely as other societies have. Peter Wade maintains, however, that regarding *democracia racial* "some of this ... was very optimistic – indeed naïve – stuff when applied to the realities of Brazilian social structure and culture" (34). Beginning with work by the historian Thomas Skidmore in the 1960s, the term "racial democracy" has for years been criticized for the whitewashing inherent to it. This is akin in some ways to Vasconcelos's "raza cósmica" and within it the fraught place of Jews, which I discussed in the previous chapter. Kittleson considers how "racial democracy" converged with soccer, noting that the idea of "mulatto football" also became increasingly fraught due to the obvious contradictions of the ruling classes' co-opting of ethnic identities. Through the 1950s and 1960s, however, this narrative of mulatto football remained largely en vogue.

In this regard Mauro's comment that he wants to be black and to fly is typical of widespread attitudes regarding soccer in Brazil at the time. Here I pause to consider what "wanting to be black" means in the specific case of a child who is half-Jewish and, at this point in the film *O ano em que meus pais saíram de férias*, is becoming more aware of his own ethnicity. During the riots after Brazil's 1970 FIFA World Cup victory, Edgar spots Mauro in the crowd and picks him up to take him home on his motorcycle, evidence of a special affinity between these two characters. Shawn Stein considers the way the film's depiction of the Jewish child dialogues with Freyre's model of racial democracy. Stein proposes that Hamburger's film "could have been about Japanese Brazilians, Syrian Brazilians, or Lebanese Brazilians (the big groups of immigrants not considered white) but Hamburger chooses to focus on his own roots to reflect on the role of Jews within the topic of Brazilianness" (259). Stein offers an equation between immigrant groups – yet, crucially, not between immigrants and racially Indigenous or African sectors of society – as a way of considering whether Hamburger's film ultimately propagates or demystifies the notion of racial democracy. As Stein concludes, "*O ano em que meus pais saíram de férias* draws on multiculturalism to suggest to the spectator the dream of a more inclusive and tolerant future" (262). I submit, however, that the film's treatment of Mauro's astonishment over this Afro-Brazilian character, coupled with the special care that Edgar displays for Mauro, implies Mauro's story could *only* have been about an ethnic group not considered to be white. Rather, through Mauro's proclamation that the Jews "had a secret weapon" and his desire to emulate his "ability to fly," the film depicts a specific identification between Jews and Afro-Brazilians. Edgar – like Ítalo, Shlomo, and the older women in the apartment building – serves as a surrogate parent to Mauro in his parents' absence. Mauro's shifting understanding of his identity and his place in the world are guided by his encounters with Jews, a militant activist, and an Afro-Brazilian man. *O ano em que meus pais saíram de férias* underscores the centrality of racial and ethnic identifications for the protagonist in the absence of his own parents. These themes become even more significant in light of the importance of national identity for Mauro and the other inhabitants of Bom Retiro during the World Cup that is taking place at this time.

Given the importance of race for conceptualizations of politics and national identity for *democracia racial*, Mauro's preoccupation with race must also be taken into consideration within the context of the film's broader treatment of his parents' militancy. At different points in the film, several characters insist that Jewishness is incompatible with active political participation. Mauro does not speak directly of his parents' political activity, but his exile at the end of the film makes him a specific sort of political subject. At the same time, he has come to learn more about his Jewishness. In addition to the optimistic vision of future inclusion that Stein reads in *O ano em que meus pais saíram de férias*, the film introduces the possibility that the protagonist may be able to be a Jewish Brazilian – without political participation and Jewishness being in tension with one another.

Conclusions

Throughout the two films discussed in this chapter, Jewish parent-child relationships lend themselves as a thematic lens through which racial identifications, intergenerational conversations, gender, and exile converge to inform the protagonists' self-understandings as Jews and as citizens of Argentina and Brazil, respectively. Although neither film's protagonist overtly articulates a strong understanding of or interest in his parents' political struggle, their lives have nonetheless been indelibly marked by the causes with which their parents aligned themselves. Moreover, Burman and Hamburger both emphasize the complexities of the intergenerational transmission of Judaism and politics in such a way that the two bear on one another. The films' use of quintessentially Jewish neighbourhoods as epicentres of Jewish Argentina and Jewish Brazil serve to guide their subjects' processes of identifications with national and global political movements as well as with the national project. Here, I maintain, is where the ethnic and racial differences that characterize each of these urban spaces, Once and Bom Retiro, become of fundamental importance, for ethnicity and political subjectivities are co-constitutive. This symbiosis bears directly on Jewish subjectivities as well as on ethnic identifications and belonging more broadly.

Epilogue

What Sort of Affinity? Conclusions and Areas for Future Study

Participation in Latin American revolutionary movements was often an incomplete process for Jews. Personal experiences of the Jewish condition, including exile, migration, and assimilation, strongly informed their encounters with the political sphere in their respective countries, as did religious elements of both their own Jewish and the prevailing hegemonic Christian culture. Jewishness is ever present in their processes of identification and participation in revolutionary politics, yet it is almost never presented as a determining principle. Nevertheless, as we have seen in this book, for many individual men and women leftist political leanings and self-identifications as Jews were co-constitutive of one another despite the inherent conflicts therein.

In my detailed readings of recent Latin American films, I have traced a persistent determination among filmmakers to return to 1960s and 1970s revolutionary politics in their efforts to examine and portray what this epoch meant – and continues to mean – for Jewish Latin Americans. Filmmaking has become a site of exploration for what Emmanuel Levinas, in his essay "Being Jewish," terms a "sort of affinity," that is, the interstitial spaces between Judaism and the "non-religious manifestations of the world." In projecting onto the screen their communities' pasts and presents, filmmakers have forwarded models of how Jews negotiated places for themselves in the political sphere. In the opening lines of this book I cited the director Guita Schyfter explaining why she made her 1993 film *Novia que te vea*: Schyfter's avowed mission was to return to what she terms "that great effervescence" of the 1960s in Latin America, which lasted into the 1970s, to show this historical period as integral to Jewish life and how in later cinema it finds echoes throughout Latin America.

I return now to the question that I have tried to answer all along: How is film used to project for a mainstream audience self-representations of the place of Latin American Jews and Jewish communities in the revolutionary politics of the 1960s and 1970s? Through a variety of aesthetic and thematic approaches, Jewish filmmakers have centred their communities in the political life of their respective countries. Jewish identification with leftist revolutionary movements in Latin America is represented as being, to some extent, a natural progression of the political affinities long understood to be part and parcel of Jewishness, such as responses to Zionism, the Russian Revolution, and the Holocaust. In contrast, the extreme nature of many of these activist groups (particularly the armed movements), the embrace of Palestine, and the heavily Catholic concepts of martyrdom and the New Man created a conflict for some Jews and thus a barrier to their full identification with revolutionary politics. Jewishness and Catholicism both informed political subjectivities. The films examined here enable viewers to experience the different ways Jews involved themselves with leftist movements in Latin America in their efforts to synthesize their long-held religious and political beliefs with the disparate tenets of revolutionary political organizations.

Since the mid-1990s Latin American filmmakers have been charting a history of Jewish communities in this region, where family histories of immigration and assimilation have given way to complex moments of reckoning as they came into contact with leftist politics. Some directors, for example, Guita Schyfter and Jeanine Meerapfel, chronicle their own generation's history and their own processes of reconciling Jewishness with revolutionary politics, while for directors Daniel Burman and Cao Hamburger the encounters of the generations before them with the complicated geopolitics of the 1970s loom large in their self-identifications as Jews. In all of these films, the experiences of previous generations of Jews in immigrating to Latin America and becoming part of the political sphere of their respective countries remain central to their characters' sense of collective identity.

I have sought to reveal not only *that* Jews participated in leftist politics in twentieth-century Latin America, but more precisely, *how* they did so, and how they "came to feel for themselves a place" (Levinas) in these movements. My specific aim has been to uncover the extent to which Jews have been portrayed as participating in revolutionary politics *as Jews*. Jewishness certainly facilitated a "sort of affinity" between religious identifications and the secular world, in this case, politics. Yet, by and large, in the films discussed here participating fully in revolutionary politics as a Jew is presented as a difficult, if possible, endeavour. The complexities regarding Jewish participation in these movements reveal that Jewishness informs political affinities in a variety of ways: at times fostering affinities within and among communities and, at others, causing divisions within and among groups, families, and indeed, generations.

Areas for Future Directions of Study

Much remains to be discussed regarding gender and Judaism in film. Gender is inexorably linked to cultural questions surrounding the Jewish body. Through such acts as circumcision, the codification of the Jewish body – as several of these films explore – takes on a politicized valence through the directors' treatment of questions of inclusion and exclusion vis-à-vis the national project. How gender and Judaism come to bear on political identifications is an area of enquiry ripe for further consideration, in both a Latin American and a global context. Ilana Dann Luna addresses these issues compellingly in the context of Mexican film, and Daniela Goldfine has done important work on gender and Judaism in Argentine film and literature, as I have cited in previous chapters.[1] Neverthess, the points of contact between Judaism, gender, and political subjectivities remain complicated and beg for further critical attention. Many of these films subtly suggest the gendered (often perceived by Jewish characters as sexist) traditions within Judaism. Elsewhere, there are other, more optimistic cultural examples of the place of women in Judaism in Latin America.[2]

In the area of gender and Latin American cinema, there have been two particularly significant recent contributions: the Chilean director Sebastián Lelio's film *Disobedience* (2017, US-UK co-production) and Damián Szifrón's *Relatos salvajes* (*Wild Tales*, 2015, Argentina-Spain co-production). These critically acclaimed, commercially successful films offer groundbreaking representations of Jewish femininity and sexuality. *Relatos salvajes* consists of short films, the last of which features a Jewish wedding reception where the bride realizes that the groom has been cheating on her for months. After a meltdown, she escapes to the balcony of the ballroom and has sex with a hotel worker. She re-enters the celebrations, and the short ends with her and the groom having sex in the reception hall. This short film is rife with affectively charged instants of embodied rage and lust. Szifrón's films often portray characters with Semitic surnames and make passing references to Jewish roots, as is the case with the majority of the shorts in *Relatos salvajes*, but the last short in that film is his only work that centres on an overtly Jewish event. *Disobedience* is about two women in an Orthodox Jewish community who enter into a lesbian affair with one another. Not only in its depiction of their sexual encounters, but throughout the film, Lelio emphasizes the embodiment of Orthodox Jewish femininity, most notably, through his focus on wearing wigs. A review of the film in Argentina's *Página/12* carried the headline "A Film about Bodies" (Broderson). Lelio is not Jewish but is a pioneer of queer cinema; he won the Oscar in 2018 for *Una mujer fantástica*. Although neither of these films considers the role of Jewish women as political subjects, their shared focus on corporality certainly nuances cultural understandings of Jewish women's bodies and sexualities (particularly in Orthodox communities).

Questions of Jewishness and gender appear to be ever more pervasive in recent media around the world. The 2016 Israeli comedy *The Women's Balcony* tells the story of a synagogue in which the women's balcony collapses, leading the women in the congregation to claim the women's balcony as their space in response to a conservative elder's reluctance to replace it. I would be remiss not to mention also the popular Amazon shows *Transparent* and *The Marvelous Mrs. Maisel*. Time and again, *Transparent* explores the convergences and divergences between Jewishness, trans and queer activism, and leftist sensibilities. *The Marvelous Mrs. Maisel*'s questioning of the stereotypical "Jewish princess" and her foray into late 1960s counterculture gestures towards civil rights movements and women's liberation, for which the show's protagonist avows support. More recently, Netflix released the limited series *Unorthodox* in 2020 to rave reviews. Similar to *Disobedience* this series depicts Orthodox communities' emphases on women's bodies. Like the film *Novia que te vea*, the series *Unorthodox* underscores the pressures placed on protagonist Esty to marry and have children. Not one but two films about Ruth Bader Ginsburg were released in 2018: the CNN Films documentary *RBG* and the feature film *On the Basis of Sex*. Neither focuses much on the justice's Jewish identity. For Ruth Bader Ginsburg, being excluded from the minyan after her mother's death led her to distance herself from organized Judaism (not unlike Sulamit's complaints at her father's funeral in *El amigo alemán*). Nevertheless, Ginsburg has the Deuteronomy verse 16:20 "Justice, justice shall you pursue" in Hebrew placed throughout her chambers, and has stated that this Jewish principle has undergirded her life's work. Such visibility – in global, critically acclaimed media – of Jewish femininity and sexuality foretells compelling critical conversations surrounding these topics in the years to come.

By all indications politically inflected Jewish filmmaking from Latin America continues to flourish. The 2011 Mexican-Argentine co-production *El premio* (dir. and scr. Paula Markovitch) centres on seven-year-old protagonist Cecilia Edelstein as she and her mother are in hiding during the dictatorship and after her father has been killed by the soldiers; save her surname, there is no mention of Jewishness in the film. Similarly, the Uruguayan director Álvaro Brechner's film *La noche de doce años*

(*The Night that Lasted Twelve Years*), a co-production between Spain and Uruguay, premiered in 2018 to immediate critical praise and to a Netflix distribution agreement. The film is an adaptation of *Memorias del calabozo* (*Prison Memories*), the autobiographical account by Mauricio Rosencof, Jewish playwright and leader of the Tupamaros National Liberation Movement, of his imprisonment during Uruguay's dictatorship.[3] The film eschews Rosencof's Jewish identity and his political militancy in depicting his twelve years as a political prisoner. *La noche de doce años* focuses also on Rosencof's companion, fellow Tupamaro José Mujica, who later became the president of Uruguay (2005–2010), during which time he staunchly aligned himself with Bolivia's President Evo Morales and other leaders of the Pink Tide. This filmic portrayal of Jewish memory of political imprisonment raises questions of postmemory that I have explored throughout this book.

The Israeli-Palestinian conflict continues to occupy a central place in global filmmaking. Sameh Zoabi's 2018 film *Tel Aviv on Fire* has received overwhelming critical acclaim, ranging from Best Screenplay and Best Film at the Haifa Film Festival to the Golden Space Needle audience award in the 2019 Seattle International Film Festival. Set in the West Bank, the film centres on scriptwriters who are working on a soap opera about the 1967 Arab-Israeli War. Zoabi's parodic, and ingenious use of the soap opera form allows for a comedic exploration of the legacy of this conflict for present-day Jews and Arabs. In fact, the characters debate what different possible tones and plotlines in the series would mean in the context of present-day Israeli-Palestinian relations. Both the soap opera within the film and the film itself conclude that media cannot suggest reconciliation or harmony (i.e., there can be no happy ending to the soap opera) since the weight of the conflict is so heavy. Nonetheless, film and other media can prompt conversations that promote mutual understanding. As in various films I have discussed in this book, *Tel Aviv on Fire* underscores the significance of audiovisual aesthetics – specifically, the ways in which 1960s Jewish-Arab geopolitics are portrayed – for media production and politics today.

The Israeli-Palestinian conflict has lent itself to myriad conversations in which Palestine, as a colonized space, is aligned with other colonized or previously colonized spaces, many of which now comprise what has come to be considered the Global South. These points of ideological solidarity are crucial for understanding Jewish solidarity with decolonization movements. Santiago Slabodsky addresses this topic in his *Decolonial Judaism: Triumphal Failures of Barbaric Thinking* (2014). Slabodsky explores such issues as the resistance with which Levinas was met by liberation theologians in Latin America in 1970 over his views regarding Palestine. As I have explored elsewhere, the solidarity of Latin American Jews with Palestine has been presented in terms of a shared affinity along geographical lines.[4] León Rozitchner couches his exploration of Jewishness and Zionism within the Tricontinental Conference's affirmation of support of Palestine; and as Anne Garland Mahler has shown in *From the Tricontinental to the Global South: Race, Radicalism, and Transnational Solidarity*, Tricontinentalism is key for understanding radical thought in the Americas and in the Global South. Further readings of the points of contact between Jewishness and political affinities would benefit greatly from engaging in such conversations on the Global South.

How Jews do or do not fit into categories of race and ethnicity merits more critical consideration than I have been able to give it here. Questions of how race and difference relate to hegemonic, aggregate models of ethnic nationalism are present in virtually all of the films I have discussed. As I have shown, these themes are part and parcel of the phenomena of Jewish citizenship and political participation. Further, these questions may shed light on broader issues of how race and ethnicity inform or determine citizenship and belonging. Stephen Silverstein's book *The Merchant of Havana: The Jew in the Abolitionist Archive* provides much needed insight into the relations between Afro-Cuban and Jewish identities in nineteenth-century Cuba. In turn, scholarly enquiry may begin to address how these dynamics manifest themselves in later years in many parts of Latin America, where Jewish communities have often been considered in one of three ways: as an analogue for white populations writ large, in an insular fashion focused on Jewishness exclusively, or alongside other immigrant groups such as Italians, Arabs, and/or Asians. Although I have briefly explored relationships between Jews, Afro-Brazilians, and Indigenous populations, much work remains to be done on this topic. The connective threads between ethnic identifications and political tendencies are shown to be many, yet they can never be taken for granted. In this sense, we are reminded of the discussion of "*ruso*," an imprecise term that continues in use to describe anyone who is Jewish in (Spanish-speaking) Latin America and, as we have seen, connotes a specific ideological tendency towards solidarity with the Russian Revolution – whether actually present or not. Future studies may examine how the relationships between Jewish ethno-religious identification and expressions of political affinities interact with these same relationships in other ethnic groups.

Final Thoughts: Affinities of All Sorts

In a variety of registers and contexts, Jews are often portrayed in a liminal position in the face of leftist politics. In this regard, my consideration of how Jewish identities come to bear on revolutionary politics in Latin America, and vice versa, finds conceptual affinity with present-day conversations worldwide. One may think, for example, of the debate over whether *Wonder Woman* could truly be considered a feminist film because Israeli actress Gal Gadot espouses Zionist beliefs. Especially for many Arab women, the choice to cast Gadot means that the film is not feminist in an intersectional sense. Although *Wonder Woman* is a perhaps somewhat trivial depiction, these objections to the film are relevant to my consideration of representation insofar as many women feel that a "white woman" (as many of the think pieces referred to Gadot) who has been in the Israeli army and sworn support for Israel could not possibly represent them, and therefore the film is a failure for feminism.

Elsewhere, some Jews have felt they are forced to eschew their Jewish identities in order to participate in social justice movements. We may consider the debacle that unfolded when protesters were ejected for waving pride flags with the Star of David on them at the 2017 Chicago Dyke March. There was debate over whether the flag in question was an Israeli flag with a rainbow superimposed on it, as the organizers suggested, or a "Jewish pride flag," a rainbow flag with the Star of David on it. The protesters asserted that their dismissal from the march was anti-Semitic, while March organizers maintained that it was in line with the movement's anti-Zionist stance. Both the Anti-Defamation League and the Human Rights Campaign condemned the organizers' decision. The 2018 and 2019 iterations of the Dyke March again banned pride flags with the Star of David on the ground that they too closely resemble the Israeli flag.

At the heart of this dispute is the meaning of the Star of David: for those wielding the flags, the Star of David was a symbol of their Jewish faith, whereas for the event officials it represented Zionism (and, in their view, imperialism). Yael Horowitz and Rae Gaines, two of the organizers of the 2019 event in Washington, DC, sought to disentangle this enmeshment between Jewish pride and Zionism in an opinion piece they released in advance of the event: "We are angry that Israel has taken Jewish symbols and converted them into symbols of nationalism and xenophobia ... We are angry that it exploits Queers and Pride to pinkwash the occupation and settler colonial violence. We are sad that Zionism has stolen vibrant Diasporic and diverse Jewish identities from us." In the estimation of these organizers, it is incumbent upon

Jewish activists to unmoor symbols of Jewishness and Judaism from the Zionist connotation with which many readily interpret these symbols. Not doing so, they find, steals from them a part of their vibrant Jewish identities. From the perspectives of Jewish queer folks wanting to display their Jewish pride through rainbow flags with the Star of David on them, Dyke March organizers were saying that Jews were not to participate in this manifestation of progressive politics *as Jews*. According to those ejected from the 2017 demonstration, they were forced to abjure a part of their identity – their Jewishness – if they were to form part of this movement. On the other end of the spectrum, one thinks of Judith Butler's cancelled speech at the New York Jewish Museum after she openly supported Boycott, Divestment and Sanctions (BDS) movements. Butler was not acceptable as a scholar of Jewish thought because her politics were perceived as too anti-Zionist.

More recently, in the summer of 2018, New York State Senate hopeful Julia Salazar came under scrutiny for describing herself as a "Jew of Color from Colombia." Salazar has affirmed that she converted to Reform Judaism in college after wondering about her surname's Sephardic origins. She has also stated that her Jewish faith strongly informs her political stances as a member of the Democratic Socialists of America. Detractors have claimed that Salazar uses her Jewish identity opportunistically to advocate for BDS policies. A series of perspectives on the issue appeared in late August 2018 in the magazine *Forward*, where Ilan Stavans weighed in to assert that to accuse Julia Salazar of "not being Jewish enough" is to write off all Latin American Jews since the history of the Inquisition, and "Crypto-Jews" makes Latin American Jewish identities less clearly defined. As Stavans puts it, "Salazar's amorphous Jewish identity is not untypical of Jews from Latin America, who see themselves not in the 'standard' ways of American Jews with their stable, organizational affiliations" ("Think Julia Salazar Isn't Jewish Enough?"). Similarly, Liana Petruzzi's contribution, "Julia Salazar Is a Cautionary Tale: Question Israel and Your Jewishness Will Be Questioned," compares having a surname that is not Ashkenazi to questioning Israel, since both will make others question an individual's Jewishness. As these responses show, the points of contact between Jewish identities (and specifically in a Latin[x]-American context) and political beliefs remain fraught, calling into question, yet again, what it means to participate actively in political movements *as a Jew*.

These recent dilemmas highlight the vexed points of contact between Jewish identities, leftist anti-Zionist politics, and gender/sexuality. Progressive politics continue to create situations in which Jews must grapple with their Jewishness – and often eschew outward markers of this element of their identities, such as the Star of David – in order to be fully accepted as members of such political movements. These ongoing debates help explain why filmmakers feel compelled to revisit the complexities of Jewish participation in leftist political movements that characterized their nations' recent pasts. We also come to see why so many cinematic depictions of Jewish life in Latin America should choose to focus on groups such as Hashomer Hatzair that served to introduce young Jews to progressive politics. Indeed, the ubiquity with which this organization is treated emphasizes the importance of groups that bridge religious practices with political ones. Yet, this same group's Zionist stance complicated Jewish identifications with revolutionary political groups because the majority of these tended to align themselves with Palestine. All we can conclude from these depictions is that there is, indeed, an affinity between Jewishness and politics, and that perhaps we should think not of a "sort of affinity" as Levinas posits, but rather of "affinities of all sorts" between the religious and the political facets of Jewish life.

Notes

Introduction

1 This and all translations from Spanish and Portuguese are my own.

2 The Spanish *judío* and Portuguese *judeu* are both the adjective and noun, "Jewish" and "Jew." Cynthia Baker's 2015 book *Jew* clarifies that *Jewish* as opposed to *Jew* "seems often to carry a far more circumscribed charge than does the noun form" (xiii). Baker includes the term "Jew" in italics throughout her book, "as signifying a word, figure, person, allegory, metaphor, phantasm, caricature, synecdoche, image, stereotype, identity, persona, and the like" (xii).

3 Mignolo takes as a point of departure six premises (drawing from Arturo Escobar) as his rationale for his critical model of Latin America as "an idea." Mignolo states: "1. There is no modernity without coloniality, because coloniality is constitutive of modernity. 2. The modern/colonial world (and the colonial matrix of power) originates in the sixteenth century, and the discovery/invention of America is the colonial component of modernity whose visible face is the European Renaissance. 3. The Enlightenment and the Industrial Revolution are derivative historical moments consisting in the transformation of the colonial matrix of power. 4. Modernity is the name for the historical process in which Europe began its progress towards world hegemony. It carries a darker side, coloniality. 5. Capitalism, as we know it today, is the essence for both the conception of modernity and its darker side, coloniality. 6. Capitalism and modernity/coloniality had a second historical moment of transformation after World War II when the US took the imperial leadership previously enjoyed at different times by both Spain and England" (xiii).

4 Buenos Aires has been the focus of a seemingly disproportionate amount of critical attention for logical reasons. The city has the sixth-largest population of Jews of any city in the world, at around 250,000. It is also home to the world's only kosher McDonald's outside of Israel; while this

anecdote is perhaps trivial, it is evidence of the city's thriving Jewish life. Buenos Aires has also received a considerable amount of critical attention within the realm of Jewish studies (both globally and in Latin America) following the 1994 bombing of the Asociación Mutua Israelita Argentina, a Jewish community centre in the Once neighbourhood, the deadliest terrorist attack in the Americas before September 11, 2001. Nearly twenty-five years later, the case remains unresolved. Mirna Vohnsen's excellent monograph, *Portrayals of Jews in Contemporary Argentine Cinema: Rethinking Argentinidad* (2019) discusses the ways in which Argentine cinema has foregrounded Jews in national history and identity.

5 Graff Zivin's *The Wandering Signifier* uses "Jewishness" exclusively within scare quotes throughout the monograph in which it is treated as a rhetorical device.

6 For more on the significance of the ordering of "Jewish–Latin American" vs. "Latin American–Jewish," see Raanan Rein's *Argentine Jews or Jewish Argentines?*

7 See Judith Elkin.

8 My emphasis on Levinas's "feeling for oneself a place" may, for some readers, bring to mind the ubiquitous current conversations on affect in Latin American film. Whereas Fredric Jameson in his *The Ideology of Theory* famously posited the "waning of affect" in the 1980s, later critical publications in Latin American cultural studies have strongly argued otherwise and have compellingly placed affect at the fore of critical considerations of film and other cultural productions. Although I have not sought to foreground affect as a theoretical approach to my readings of the films examined here, in a sense my theoretical approach does draw from Beasley-Murray's suggestion that there is not a clear distinction between affect and the political, but rather that affect may be considered to constitute the borderline between the political and the infrapolitical. Beasley-Murray posits: "There is no politics without infrapolitics, in that this latter provides the affective preconditions or conditions of possibility for the political, which in turn shapes and sets limits to the infrapolitical habitus" ("Life During Wartime" 5). I read this distinction that Beasley-Murray makes as an analogue for Levinas's concept (to which I will be returning) of a "sort of affinity" between separate spheres of human life, and specifically in the case of Jews.

9 Although other work (including Graff Zivin's) has focused on Levinas's critical model of ethics and Otherness as they relate to Jewishness, my focus here is on Levinas's specific consideration of what it means to be Jewish.

10 Ronaldo Munck and Pablo Pozzi recently submitted, "Anti-Semitism was answered by an increasing and deepening commitment to the Zionist cause" (6).

11 Butler's critique of Zionism engages with Levinas's ethics of the Other and his exploration of the "Thou Shalt Not Kill" maxim but not "Être juif." As Rebecca Stein's review of Butler's book underscores, Butler's subsequent emergence as a strong supporter of the Boycott, Divestment and Sanctions (BDS) movement meant that *Parting Ways* took on new implications, not the least of which were calls for Butler to remove herself from scheduled speeches such as one on Kafka at the New York Jewish Museum in 2014, which she ultimately cancelled.

12 For more, see Raphael Gross's *Carl Schmitt and the Jews: The "Jewish Question," the Holocaust, and German Legal Theory* in which Gross concludes that, despite the many justifiable objections to Schmitt, his theories continue to flourish throughout cultural and critical thought.

13 For more on the reception of Benjamin in Argentina, see Graciela Wamba Gaviña (1993) and Beatriz Sarlo (2000, 2006). Benjamin's "messianic time" can also be considered in relation to a focus on Christian tropes in revolution. Nelly Richard's *La insubordinación de los signos* (*The Insubordination of Signs*) (1994) discusses Benjamin and postdictatorship memory in Chile. Ricardo Forster's *El exilio de la palabra: En torno a lo judío* (*The Exile of the Word: Concerning Jewishness*) (1998) focuses on the Jewish aspects of Benjaminian thought but not in relation to memory politics in Argentina.

14 Andrew Rajca discusses the religious beliefs that undergirded the "Never Again" – Nunca Más and Nunca Mais – human rights commissions' reports in Argentina and Brazil, respectively.

15 Novels that deal with 1960s and 1970s revolutionary movements include but are not limited to the following: Martín Kohan's *Museo de la revolución* (2006), Laura Alcoba's *La casa de los conejos* (2008), Carlos Gamerro's *Un yuppie en la columna del Che Guevara* (2011), Patricio Pron's *El espíritu de mis padres sigue subiendo en la lluvia* (2011), and Roberto Bolaño's *Amuleto* (1999).

16 During this time, several prominent filmmakers throughout the region penned manifestos that proposed revolutionary theories as the necessary praxis of filmmaking. In Brazil, films such as Nelson Pereira dos Santos's 1963 *Vidas secas* and Glauber Rocha's 1964 *Deus e o diabo na terra do sol* began to focus on the poverty and strife that plagued lower-class life in the country, with the purpose of fomenting solidarity with the working class. In Argentina, directors Fernando "Pino" Solanas and Octavio Getino – founders of the group Cine Liberación – published their manifesto, *Hacia un tercer cine* (*Toward a Third Cinema*), put into practice by their cinematic *ars poetica, La hora de los hornos* between 1967 and 1968. Much more than a mere depiction of revolutionary culture, the film is a call to arms as outlined in their manifesto. Similarly, in Cuba, the film director Julio García Espinosa advocated for "an imperfect cinema," while fellow Cuban filmmaker Tomás Gutiérrez Alea directed his 1968 masterpiece, *Memorias del*

subdesarrollo, to combat imperialist ideas and to think through revolutionary praxis and beliefs.

17 The celebrated Mexican director Alejandro González Iñárritu's first feature-length film, *Amores perros* (2000), although set in the present, incorporates character El Chivo's involvement in guerrilla violence in the 1960s. Ignacio Sánchez Prado has stated that the film "transmits the failure of the utopian and revolutionary discourse of the generation of the 1960s" ("*Amores perros*" 42). Similarly, Dierdra Reber points out that the "rise and fall of revolutionary violence ... serves as the ... film's only history of which to speak" and goes on to say that *Amores perros* "draws an arc between the revolutionary 1960s and the neoliberal present" ("Love as Politics" 282). In this sense, the legacies of revolutionary movements pervade the narrative of a film set in the late 1990s and whose plot has been broadly interpreted as being fundamentally conservative.

18 Eisenstein's sexual orientation has also been shown to be of significance to his filmic imagining of postrevolutionary Mexico in *¡Que viva México!*, another aspect in which identities are brought to bear on filmmaking (see Salazkina).

19 Similarly, Raymond Williams defines "structure of feeling" as a set of experiences "still in process, often indeed not yet recognized as social but taken to be private, idiosyncratic, and even isolating, but which in analysis (though rarely otherwise) has its emergent, connecting, and dominant characteristics, indeed its specific hierarchies" (132). Put another way, private feelings of belonging inform how individuals engage with and understand themselves in relation to mainstream hegemony.

20 I explore this issue further in my article "Exposing Mechanisms of Truth and Memory" (2016).

1 Saintly Politics

1 A note about terminology: I use "Christian" where referring to beliefs and "Catholic" as a modifier for culture. In Latin America in the 1960s and 1970s, Protestant churches had but a very minor presence, although in recent decades they have enjoyed a significant rise in the numbers of their followers. There was, notably, an evangelical variation of liberation theology, most notably through the *misión integral*, which focused on evangelism and social responsibility and was popularized in Latin America through René Padilla in Ecuador, Samuel Escobar in Peru, and Orlando Costas in Puerto Rico. However, this contingent was not a central component of revolutionary culture at the time, whereas Catholicism was; nor has it been shown to have much of an impact on the present-day legacy of revolutionary culture. Megachurches have gained popularity throughout the region, particularly in rural areas. A 2014 PEW research poll found that while 90 per cent of Latin Americans

had identified as Catholic throughout most of the twentieth century, only 69 per cent now self-identify as Catholic. Specifically, the survey focused on what religion people were raised in as opposed to the religion with which they now self-identify. Although 80 per cent of respondents reported being raised Catholic, only 69 per cent reported currently self-identifying as Catholic, whereas only 9 per cent reported being raised Protestant and 19 per cent now identify as Protestant ("Religion in Latin America").

2 I introduce the fraught term "Judeo-Christian" with an intent, as I address further, of problematizing what is taken for granted by that term in such a way that eschews the differences between Judeo, Christian, and Judeo-Christian. "Judeo-Christian" is often used to signify a hegemonizing force that absorbs Judaism within dominant Christian practices; however, I grapple with the term here precisely in order to signal the way in which Jewishness often sits uncomfortably within this hegemony. In particular, I focus on how secular politics adopts a vague aggregate so-called Judeo-Christian religious model in a way that comes across to Jews as sometimes Christian and sometimes lay.

3 In *Christian Prophecy: The Post-Biblical Tradition*, Niels Christian Hvidt argues that "prophecy, as known in ancient Israel, continued in Christianity as an inherent and continuous feature and charism in the life of the church and that prophets have a vital role to play in the new covenant" (4).

4 The same eschatological world views have also been shown to line up with the rationale for dictatorial regimes, as Chilean anthropologist Osvaldo Torres Gutiérrez argues in his consideration of the Movimiento de Izquierda Revolucionaria (MIR) in the 1960s and the politicians who betrayed them. Catholic doctrine is used in upholding political positions that are diametrically opposed. In this regard, one's belief in a specific faith does not wholly determine political identification, although the two inform one another. In Chile specifically, unlike in Colombia or Argentina, the MIR and other revolutionary movements focused less on Church doctrine, likely because of the momentum that the socialist movement was gaining over the course of the 1960s and into Allende's presidency. As I argue in my discussion of the film *Machuca*, however, left-leaning priests have come to play a central role in the cultural imaginary surrounding socialist movements in Chile during this period.

5 See Valeria Manzano (2014) and also my article "Metamorphoses of 1968" (2019).

6 As Harold Ditmanson notes, "The gospel of Jesus Christ presupposes the Torah and the Prophets. In both Testaments the same God of grace and justice is speaking. In both faiths the true God is present and active. Christianity does not enjoy this unique relationship with Buddhism, Hinduism, Confucianism, nor even with Islam. There is for the Christian,

as for Jesus, no other God than the God of Abraham, Isaac, and Jacob" (192). The role of prophecy uniquely links Christianity and Judaism to one another. Elsewhere, James Carroll posits that prophecy plays a part in anti-Semitic beliefs among early Christians, who supplanted "prophecy historicized" for "history remembered," which came to form the basis of a troubling quantity of anti-Semitic beliefs.

7 "Perón told us: for you all, no armed struggle. I need you to be the rear-guard" (Cuchetti 99).

8 Raanan Rein explores the role of Jews in Peronist movements in *Los muchachos peronistas judíos* (2015).

9 For purposes of discussing del Barco's use of Levinas, I use "immanence" here to refer to the general idea of a divine presence as manifested in something that resides in all human spirits.

10 *El Ojo Mocho* is a political and cultural journal published in Argentina that often focuses on issues related to recent history.

11 Here, del Barco does not name Rozitchner, but this direct response to other responses to the letter is included in the same volume as Rozitchner's response to del Barco, so it is highly likely that he did, in fact, read Rozitchner.

12 Paul writes, "For it is by grace you have been saved, through faith" (New International Version [of the Bible] (hereafter *NIV*), Ephesians 2:8).

13 In his response published in *Journal of Latin American Cultural Studies*, del Barco clarifies that his reference to Juan Gelman and salvation comes from a 2004 interview of Gelman published in *El País*. Del Barco makes direct reference to Gelman's comment here, "The way is not to seal off … because that is a cancer that constantly beats beneath civic memory and prevents the construction of anything healing" (156). Del Barco does not explicate how he is reading Gelman's assertion in line with salvation, but Gelman's mention of "the way" does resonate strongly with "I am the way and the truth and the life" (*NIV* John 14:6). This interpretation would make particular sense insofar as the interview with Gelman focuses on the idea of truth. Yet, later in the same interview that del Barco references, Gelman refutes poetry as a way of changing the world: "The messianic idea of poetry as a way of changing the world is not true (Lo contrario del olvido no es la memoria, sino la verdad)." Interestingly, del Barco makes no reference to this other mention that Gelman makes to a "way" or to his rejection of the "messianic idea of poetry." Del Barco's invocation of salvation, regardless of how he derives it from Gelman's words, is patently secular and related to ideas of truth, memory, and justice.

14 The trajectory from revolutionary solidarity to religious commitment has been analysed in the case of Chilean militant Luz Arce, a member of Chile's *Grupo de Amigos del Presidente* (Group of Friends of the President

[Allende]) who, as she avows in her testimony *El infierno*, became a born-again Christian. Liliana Heker's 1996 novel *El fin de la historia* similarly recounts the life story of a Montonera, Leonora Ordaz, who begins to collaborate with the military regime in Argentina and baptizes her daughter while she is held captive as a political prisoner.

15 Vidal also invokes Church doctrine in his discussion of *jus ad bellum* and *jus in bellum*. His explanation of the latter, which he presents in line with Catholic doctrine, is not historicized or contextualized within a broader framework of the Church in Latin America at this time. He does, however, mention the role of the Catholic Church during Chile's transition to democracy in the 1990s.

16 The other common myth associated with the revolutionary left in Latin America is that of a phoenix rising from the ashes. As León Rozitchner notes, "The Left's traits exhibit all of the signs of both collective and individual social pathology: getting rid of blame and death was fundamental. We have reason to be ashamed, we say, and nevertheless, each of use rises again like the Phoenix from the ashes, this time foreign, in which we again find the warmth that reinvigorates us" (*Acerca de la derrota* 30).

17 By "neocolonialism," I am referring to the phenomenon also termed "informal empire" and "economic imperialism" to designate the economic power that the US and other global markets (now China) have come to wield over Latin America that, if not not wholly "colonial" in the sense of military power, nonetheless function in a similar way to colonialism. Jean-Paul Sartre used the term in 1964 in *Colonialism and Neo-Colonialism* to condemn France's presence in Algeria and to argue that France remove itself from Algeria.

18 "Now when you hear the sound of the horn, flute, zither, lyre, harp, pipe and all kinds of music, if you are ready to fall down and worship the image I made, very good. But if you do not worship it, you will be thrown down immediately into a burning furnace. Then what god will be able to rescue you from my hands?" (*NIV* Daniel 3:15).

19 Laura Podalsky reads the "sensorial dynamics" in *La hora de los hornos* to focus on the way in which affect functions in this film so as to contest long-standing interpretations of the film as eschewing emotion in favour of politics.

20 This model of exemplarity recalls Catherine Sanok's analysis of female saints in which "saints were understood to mediate between Christ and ordinary Christians, not only as intercessors but as ethical models: the saint imitates Christ typologically and in turn provides a tropological (that is, moral) exemplar to those who read or hear her story" (2). As I show in my discussion of the film *San Ernesto nace en La Higuera*, this model serves to consecrate Che Guevara as a secular saint of the revolutionary cause.

21 As Lillian Guerra has noted of the Castro government's response to the protests of Catholic activists, "The government immediately engaged individual Catholic priests in rituals of prayer and promoted the idea that being a true disciple of Fidel made one a true disciple of Christ" (146). This is another instance of the secularization of religion for revolutionary politics.

22 Gutiérrez Alea's 1968 film *Memorias del subdesarrollo* introduces protagonist Sergio, the "New Man" of the Cuban Revolution, in the context of the Bay of Pigs crisis. Sergio has three love interests in the film, a Jewish German woman, a Catholic woman, and a born-again Christian. His 1976 film *La última cena* is set in nineteenth-century Cuba and recreates the Last Supper with slaves on a sugar cane plantation. His 1994 film *Fresa y chocolate,* an adaptation of the Senel Paz novella *El lobo, el bosque y el hombre nuevo,* explores the tensions between the staunchly revolutionary character Diego and the devoutly religious characters with whom he comes into contact.

23 Horne's song begins:

If those historic gentlemen came back today
Jefferson, Washington and Lincoln
And Walter Cronkite put them on channel 2
To find out what they were thinkin'
I'm sure they'd say
Thanks for quoting us so much
But we don't want to take a bow
Enough with the quoting
Put those actions into words
And we mean now.

24 The Catholic Church responded in vastly different ways to dictatorships throughout different countries and over time. The Church was often complicit. Nevertheless, there are salient exceptions such as the Vicaría de la Solidaridad in Santiago, Chile, which helped families and friends to find information about *desaparecidos,* and the Santa Cruz Church in Buenos Aires that served as a meeting space for the Madres de la Plaza de Mayo. Santa Cruz is also significant for having served as a refuge for French nuns who were kidnapped and killed by the military regime for their efforts to help the Madres de la Plaza de Mayo.

25 From 1976 onward, the organization, under the auspices of the Archdiocese of Santiago and with the support of Pope Paul VI, helped resist the kidnappings and tortures that took place during Pinochet's rule. After the transition to democracy, the Vicariate became an invaluable resource for the defence of human rights and justice efforts in the country.

26 In a sense, Father McEnroe's actions anticipate a controversy sparked almost immediately after Jorge Mario Bergoglio was named to become Pope Francis in 2013. A photo surfaced and went viral on social media of a

priest who, from behind, could have been identified as Bergoglio and was offering communion to Jorge Rafael Videla during Argentina's dictatorship. It was later revealed that the priest who was offering communion to Videla was, in fact, someone else. Journalist Horacio Verbitsky explores the complicity of the Catholic Church, including Pope Francis VI, at length in his 2005 book *El silencio: De Paulo VI a Bergoglio. Las relaciones secretas de la iglesia con la ESMA*. The controversy that continues to shroud the Catholic Church in Argentina in the context of postdictatorship further calls into question the role of religion within present-day memory politics.

27 The relationship between the Old Testament and the New Testament lends itself to particular hermeneutics insofar as much of the Old Testament anticipates parts of the New Testament.

28 Bruno Bauer asks: "What is the nature of the Jew who is to be emancipated, and the nature of the Christian state which is to emancipate him?" to which Marx responds that the question that must be asked is not this one that Bauer proposes, but rather, "What kind of emancipation?" and states that "it is because you can be emancipated politically, without renouncing Judaism completely and absolutely, that political emancipation itself is not human emancipation."

2 Here We Are to Build a Nation

1 This assertion may, for some readers, invite an allegorical interpretation of the film in line with Fredric Jameson's now rather infamous model of Third World allegory put forth in "Third-World Literature in the Era of Multinational Capitalism." Jameson explains there the postmodern affinity for allegory in its capacity to celebrate discontinuities: "The allegorical spirit is profoundly discontinuous, a matter of breaks and heterogeneities, of the multiple polysemia of the dream rather than the homogeneous representation of the symbol" (73).This idea of allegory's discontinuity in Jameson in particular has appealed to Nelly Richard and Idelber Avelar. An intellectual affinity with Jameson is to be expected from postdictatorial thinkers, insofar as Jameson – contemporaneously with postdictatorial critics – found himself lamenting the defeat of leftism at the hands of the neoliberal machine, also perceived to be a totalizing, hegemonic circumstance against which rupture and discontinuity may be deployed as a contestatory strategy. I avoid this critical approach because of the problems that many responses to Jameson have evoked in doing so (most notably Aijaz Ahmad).

Jean Franco responded to Jameson stating that "not only is 'the nation' a complex and much contested term, but in contemporary Latin American criticism it is no longer the inevitable framework for either political or cultural products" (130). Additionally, as Robert Tally recapitulates in a reference entry in *Global South Studies*, "Jameson's intent, if not necessarily his outcome, was to grapple with the emergence of a Global South that could maintain itself as qualitatively different from the metropolitan powers of the age of imperialism in the context of an increasingly dominant system of globalization. The controversy over Jameson's intervention into Third-World literature thus becomes a key moment in the critical apprehension of the processes and effects of globalization with respect to literature, politics, and cultural studies more broadly" (4). Erin Graff Zivin, drawing from Paul de Man's position that "allegories are always allegories of metaphor and, as such, they are always allegories of the impossibility of reading" (qtd. in "Beyond Jameson" 162), proposes the following: "If what I have suggested here is that ... 'what we talk about when we talk about' allegory is the question of politics, it is also always to debate over the canon formation and disciplinary authority" (166). I would add that earlier, in *Blindness and Insight*, specifically the essay "The Rhetoric of Temporality," de Man indicts allegory as having been born out of an "act of ontological bad faith" (211). Coupling de Man's characterization with Jameson's model, allegory depends more on the ways in which it is read *as* allegory rather than whether or not it is patently allegorical. In other words, allegory must be read against itself.

2 See Raanan Rein, *Los muchachos peronistas judíos*, and Uki Goñi, *The Real Odessa: How Perón Brought the Nazi War Criminals to Argentina*.

3 An estimated 17 per cent of the desaparecidos during the dictatorship were Jewish, which is clearly disproportionate to the 1–2 per cent of Argentina's total population that Jews comprise. The disproportionate number of Jewish victims of state terror is a well-known fact, yet only in recent years has it begun to receive significant critical attention. The reluctance to discuss Jewish persecution may be attributed to stereotypes and misconceptions about Jewish political tendencies, coupled with the broader tendency – lasting from the dictatorship's end in 1983 into the early twenty-first century – to avoid discussing the political activities of the dictatorship's victims at all. In this regard, Blaustein's *Cazadores de utopías* was unprecedented in its focus on leftist political activism in the years leading up to dictatorship. For many years, to acknowledge an individual's leftist politics was often interpreted as a form of victim blaming, a trend that has subsided over the past decade or so with an increased willingness to revisit the tensions and complexities of militant politics. This point is developed more fully in Marina Franco's *Un enemigo para la nación: Orden interno, violencia y "subversion," 1973–1976*. Similarly, poet Juan Gelman, whom del Barco addresses at the end of his letter "No Matarás," penned a column in *Página/12* in 2000, "Elogio de la culpa,"

addressing this very issue as he lauded his disappeared son, Marcelo. The column begins with Gelman asking, "Did one have to be innocent in order to be a victim? My son wasn't. He wasn't innocent. He was a victim" (Gelman, "Elogio de la culpa"). For more on Jewish persecution during the dictatorship, see Emmanuel Kahan, *Recuerdos que mienten un poco: Vida y memoria de la experiencia judía en la última dictadura militar*, and Federico Finchelstein, *The Ideological Origins of the Dirty War: Fascism, Populism, and Dictatorship in Twentieth-Century Argentina.*

4 In this regard, Blaustein's documentary recalls Albertina Carri's *Los rubios* (2003). *Hacer patria* is much less playful and experimental than Carri's documentary, but the diegetic reflections on the memory politics evoked by the film itself nonetheless share conceptual affinity with *Los rubios.*

5 "Some time later God tested Abraham. He said to him, 'Abraham!' 'Here I am,' he replied" (*NIV* Genesis 22:1). US author Jonathan Safran Foer's recent novel *Here I Am* (2016) also takes its title from this verse of Genesis and focuses on four generations of father-son relationships as disaster breaks out in Israel and the protagonist's marriage falls apart. The protagonist's son has to memorize this part of Genesis for his bar mitzvah, after which his parents plan to divorce. In Foer's novel, "here I am" is bound up in both family and national identities, as the protagonist constantly questions "how Jewish he is" in comparison with his Israeli cousin who is visiting for his son's bar mitzvah. "Here I Am" is presented as both religious and nationalist, akin to its purpose in Chamecki's film.

6 As Hirsch points out, one narrator of *Austerlitz* is a non-Jewish German living in England, whereas the novel's protagonist is a Czech Jew. For Hirsch, "Standing outside the family, the narrator receives the story from Austerlitz and affiliates with it, thus illustrating the relationship between familial and affiliative postmemory. And as a German, he also shows how the lines of affiliation can cross the divide between victim and perpetrator postmemory" ("Generation of Postmemory" 119).

3 *Poner el cuerpo femenino judío*

1 Prell's focus is on US Jewish women. The genealogy that she lays out of Jewish female archetypes in the United States in the twentieth century – namely, the Jewish immigrant mother that precedes the postwar "Jewish Princess" – also maps onto the history of Jewish life in Latin America presented in both *Novia que te vea* and *El amigo alemán*. Again, the similarities in these paradigms of the history of Jewish life throughout the Americas invite further critical inquiries that take this geographical approach. Yet, while in the United States the period after the Second World War ushered in a time of economic prosperity that afforded many Jewish women there

a lifestyle of leisure (the root of the stereotypical Jewish princess that Prell addresses), for the middle classes in Latin American countries this same moment was not a time during which their prosperitywas growing at a rate comparable to that of the United States – largely because of US intervention in the economies of their countries. Nonetheless, for Jews in respective Latin American countries, like in the paradigm that Prell articulates, the postwar years were a time of upward social mobility that saw a generational shift in Jewish female archetypes, as I observe in these films as well. As I discuss in other chapters, circumcision has a central role in considerations of Jewish identity in the case of male protagonists, while there is no similar marker of female Jewishness. Shaye J.D. Cohen addresses this issue in *Why Aren't Jewish Women Circumcised?* One answer that Cohen offers comes from the (faulty, as Cohen himself points out) belief that "women … do not suffer from a surfeit of lust" (174). An assumption of sexual passivity underscores the ways in which society conceptualizes Jewish women's embodiment. Within a context of US postwar films, a complement to these films that also revises this passivity is the 1973 US film *The Way We Were* (dir. Sydney Pollock), in which Barbra Streisand's Katie Morosky, a fervent Marxist Jew, ultimately foregoes her love for the non-Jewish Hubbell Gardiner (Robert Redford) after decades of passionate yet troubled quarrels over her political commitment, which reach a breaking point during the McCarthy years. Morosky does put her body on the line; in fact, the film ends with her on a picket line in the streets of New York City. Yet, like *Novia que te vea* and *El amigo alemán*, Pollock's film (by playwright and screenwriter Arthur Laurents) presents love relationships between Jews and non-Jews in tension with political beliefs. It is also worth noting that this film, written and directed by two Jewish men, does not present Jewish women in the same difficult position of reckoning as do Meerapfel's and Schyfter's films.

2 Sommer's readings of love relationships as "foundational fictions" take root partially in Jameson's reading of national allegories (for a fuller discussion of Jameson, see introduction n8 and chapter 2 n1).

3 See Rebecca Janzen.

4 In the 1980s, Borges was vindicated by the comic strip depicting him, *Perramus*. As Mariana Casale O'Ryan notes, "In the face of the 'friend or foe' way of doing politics in the 1960s and 1970s, [*Perramus'*] Borges can offer a more consensual and diverse mode" (151). In 2011, Ariel Dorfman reflected on the inclusion of Borges in his library despite him having been decorated by Pinochet, suggesting reconciliation with Borges. Borges's politics vis-à-vis Jewish culture should also be noted; Edna Aizenberg presents Borges as a "postcolonial precursor." Graff Zivin posits in *The Wandering Signifier* that, while Borges's work does not constitute

"literatura comprometida," a story such as "Deutsches Requiem" nonetheless contains crucial political implications when one focuses, as Graff Zivin does, on the "rhetoric of Jewishness" therein. Silverstein notes the pro-Israel stance that Borges evinces through two poems penned in response to the 1967 Arab-Israeli War (2014).

5 Anti-Semitism has been studied much more broadly in Argentina than in other Latin American contexts. See Emmanuel Kahan, *Recuerdos que mienten un poco: Vida y memoria de la experiencia judía en la última dictadura militar; El legado del autoritarismo: derechos humanos y antisemitismo en la Argentina contemporánea*; Federico Finchelstein, *The Ideological Origins of the Dirty War: Fascism, Populism, and Dictatorship in Twentieth Century Argentina*.

6 Nicolás Prividera analyses Peronist posters in twenty-first-century Argentine films in *El país del cine*.

4 Lost Embraces

1 Carolina Rocha and Georgia Seminet, for example, begin their volume on children and adolescents in Spanish-language film with a discussion of *Pizza, birra, faso* (*Pizza, Beer, and Smokes*, dir. Israel Adrián Caetano and Bruno Stagnaro, Argentina, 1998). The film ushered in a wave of film-making that has centred on childhood and adolescent experiences so as to engage with issues of history, class, and gender. Not coincidentally, *Pizza, birra, faso* also marks the emergence of New Argentine Cinema, a movement discussed later in this chapter.

2 As mentioned in the introductory chapter, Rozitchner began this essay with the sardonic affirmation that one must sacrifice "lo judío" for the revolution, attempting to reveal and criticize the false dichotomies that many pundits had created between Jewishness and revolutionary commitment. Rozitchner's framing of this issue recalls a previous debate played out in the Zionist periodical *Nueva Sión* in which an anonymous young "non-practicing Jew," critiqued the publication's lack of attention to national politics that directly affected the country's Jewish community. The young man accuses the editor of belonging to a generation of Jews who do not consider themselves *latinoamericanos*, prefiguring debates that will become more pronounced during the 1967 Arab-Israeli War and the 1973 Arab-Israeli (Braustein). The editor ultimately asserted that the younger man's conflict between Zionism and being politically committed to Argentina and/or Latin America's liberation is a "false dilemma." Indeed, the back-and-forth prompted by the "non-practicing" Jew foreshadows a later, more overtly political series of letters that appeared in *Nueva Sión* in 1974 with the title "Carta de un Antisionista." Here, a letter to the editors takes the publication to task for its failure to reference such events

as the 1969 Cordobazo, a notorious incident of repression of revolutionary action. The author asserts that he self-identified as Zionist until he took on "revolutionary tendencies," at which point he ceased to identify himself as such. As Kahan has noted, the Anti-Zionist's letter and the following "Respuesta de un sionista" framed the controversies surrounding youth militancy and political radicalism within the Argentine Jewish community ("Algunos usos del conflicto en Israel-Palestina en Argentina").

3 "See, I will send the prophet Elijah to you before that great and dreadful day of the Lord comes" (*NIV* Malachi 4:5).

4 Amalia Ran notes, too, that Elías's return affords Ariel the opportunity for Israeli citizenship ("From a Dream to Reality").

Epilogue

1 The second issue of the newly inaugurated *Journal of Latin American Jewish Studies* (Winter 2020) will be a special volume dedicated gender, sexuality, and activism among Jewish communities in Latin America.

2 For example, Argentine novelist Silvia Plager's 2006 novel, *La rabina,* tells the story of a woman's journey to become a rabbi in New York and Israel in the years between the 1968 and 1973 Arab-Israeli conflicts in such a way that, I argue, dialogues with Rachel Adler's 1973 essay "The Jew Who Wasn't There: Halacha and the Woman," in which she insists that women be able to "do the things a Jew was meant to do," meaning *mitzvah* and Halachic study. Plager revises women's passivity through her novel.

3 Brechner is known for his earlier critically acclaimed films, *Mal día para pescar* (*Bad Day to Go Fishing,* 2009) and *Mr. Kaplan* (2014), both dark comedies.

4 My essay, "Metamorphoses of 1968: Latin America and the Israel-Palestine Question in Tomás Abraham's *La dificultad* (2015)," argues that Abraham's roman à clef positions its narrator, Nicolás, a Hungarian Jew who immigrated to and grew up in Argentina, in opposition to his European cousins on the issue of Palestine. As the narrator states, he is in solidarity with Palestine because, unlike his cousins, he grew up in a place reaping the effects of colonialism and imperialism.

Works Cited

Films

El abrazo partido. Directed by Daniel Burman, BD Cine, 2004.

El amigo alemán/Der deutsche freund. Directed by Jeanine Meerapfel, Corinth Films, 2012.

Amores perros. Directed by Alejandro González Iñárritu. 2000. Lionsgate, 2004.

O ano em que meus pais saíram de férias. Directed by Cao Hamburger, 2006. City Lights Home Video, 2008.

La bandera argentina. Directed by Eugene Py, 1897.

El barrio de los judíos. Directed by Gonzalo Rodríguez Fábregas, Al Apapacho, 2011.

Botín de guerra: La historia de una búsqueda infatigable. Directed by David Blaustein, SBP, 2006.

El bulto. Directed by Gabriel Retes, Venevision, 1992.

Cazadores de utopías. Directed by David Blaustein, SBP, 1996.

Che: El argentino. Directed by Steven Soderbergh, Twentieth Century Fox, 2008.

Cuando Liberarce se escribe con C. Directed by Gonzalo Rodríguez Fábregas, El Apapacho, 2009.

Danken got/Estamos aqui/Here We Are. Directed by Cintia Chamecki, Chamecki Productions, 2013.

La danza de la realidad. Directed by Alejandro Jodorowsky. 2013. Amazon Prime Video, 2014.

Derecho de familia. Directed by Daniel Burman, IFC Films, 2006.

Deus e o diabo na terra do sol. Directed by Glauber Rocha, Mr. Bongo Films, 1964.

Disobedience. Directed by Sebastián Lelio, Bleeker Street, 2017.

Elefante blanco. Directed by Pablo Trapero, On Screen Films, 2012.

Eles não usam black-tie. Directed by Leon Hirszman, Doriane Video, 1981.

En el aire. Directed by Juan Carlos de Llaca Maldonado, 1995. Cinectu, 2006.

Esperando al mesías. Directed by Daniel Burman, SBP Video, 2000.

Fresa y chocolate. Directed by Tomás Gutiérrez Alea, Buena Vista Home Video, 1994.

Los gauchos judíos. Directed by Juan José Jusid, Videoteca Foco 1975.

I girasoli. Directed by Vittorio De Sica, Lionsgate, 1970.

Hacer patria. Directed by David Blaustein, AVH, 2007.

La hora de los hornos. Directed by Fernando "Pino" Solanas and Octavio Getino, Cinema Tercer Mundo, 1968.

Infancia clandestina. Directed by Benjamín Ávila, Film Movement, 2012.

Kordavision. Directed by Héctor Cruz Sandoval, Starz/Anchor Bay, 2008.

Machuca. Directed by Andrés Wood. 2004. Artificial Eye, 2010.

The Marvelous Mrs. Maisel. Directed by Amy Sherman-Palladino, Amazon Studios, 2017.

Memorias del subdesarrollo. Directed by Tomás Gutiérrez Alea, 1968.

Motorcycle Diaries. Directed by Walter Salles, Focus Features, 2004.

Mr. Kaplan. Directed by Álvaro Brechner, Menemsha Films, 2013.

La noche de doce años. Directed by Álvaro Brechner, Life Films, 2018.

Novia que te vea. Directed by Guita Schyfter.1993 Desert Mountain Media, 2006.

Now! Included in vol. 1 in *Antología de Santiago Álvarez*. Directed by Santiago Álvarez, Video ICAIC, 2008.

On the Basis of Sex. Directed by Mimi Leder, Focus Features, 2018.

O qué é isso, companheiro?/Four Days in September. Directed by Bruno Barreto, Alliance Atlantis, 1997.

Pizza, birra, faso. Directed by Adrián Caetano and Bruno Stagnaro, Líder Films, 1998.

Poesía sin fin/Endless Poetry. Directed by Alejandro Jodorowsky. 2016. Amazon Prime Video, 2017.

El premio. Directed by Paula Markovitch, 2011. Global Lens, 2014.

RBG. Directed by Julie Cohen and Betsy West, CNN Films, 2018.

El rey del Once. Directed by Daniel Burman, Kino Lorber, 2016.

Roma. Directed by Alfonso Cuarón, Netflix, 2018.

Los rubios. Directed by Albertina Carri, Women Make Movies, 2003.

San Ernesto nace en La Higuera. Directed by Isabel Santos and Rafael Solis, Video ICAIC, 2007.

El secreto de sus ojos/The Secreet in Their Eyes. Directed by Juan José Campanella, Tornasol Films, 2009.

Tel Aviv on Fire. Directed by Sameh Zoabi, Samsa Film, 2018.

Terra em transe. Directed by Glauber Rocha, Trigon Film, 1967.

El tigre saltó y mató pero morirá, morirá. 1973. Included in vol. 1 of *Antología de Santiago Álvarez*. Directed by Santiago Álvarez, Video ICAIC, 2008.

Los traidores. Directed by Raymundo Gleyzer, Facets, 1973.

Transparent. Directed by Jill Soloway, Amazon Studios, 2014.

La última cena. Directed by Tomás Gutiérrez Alea, 1976. Zafra Video, 2000.

The Way We Were. Directed by Sydney Pollack, Columbia Pictures, 1973.
The Women's Balcony. Directed by Emil Ben-Shimon, 2016. Menemsha Films, 2017.
Wonder Woman. Directed by Patty Jenkins, Warner Brothers, 2017.

Other Sources

Abraham, Tomás, and Silvia Bleiechmar. "Judío público, judío privado." *Posjudaísmo: Debates sobre lo judío en el siglo XXI*, edited by Tomás Abraham, Sergio Bergman, Silvia Bleichmar, Alicia Dujovne Ortiz, and Dario Sztajnszrajber. Prometeo, 2007, pp. 35–60.
Adler, Rachel. "The Jew Who Wasn't There: Halacha and the Jewish Woman." *Response: A Contemporary Jewish Review* vol. VIII, no. 2, 1973, pp. 77–82.
Aguilar, Gonzalo. "The Documentary: Between Reality and Fiction, between First and Third Person." *New Argentine and Brazilian Cinema*, edited by Jens Andermann and Álvaro Fernández Bravo. Palgrave Macmillan, 2013, pp. 203–16.
Ahmad, Aijaz. "Jameson's Rhetoric of Otherness and the 'National Allegory.'" *Social Text*, vol. 17, 1985, pp. 3–25.
Aizenberg, Edna. *Books and Bombs in Buenos Aires: Borges, Gerchunoff, and Argentine-Jewish Writing*. University of New England Press, 2002.
Alcoba, Laura. *La casa de los conejos*. Edhasa, 2008.
Alfaro-Velcamp, Theresa. "'Reelizing' Arab and Jewish Ethnicity in Mexican Film." *Americas*, vol. 63, no. 2, 2006, pp. 261–80.
Amado, Ana. *La imagen justa: Cine argentina y política, 1970–2007*. Ediciones Colihué, 2009.
Amado, Ana, and Nora Domínguez. *Lazos de familia: Herencias, cuerpos, ficciones*. Paidós, 2004.
Andrews, George Reid. *The Afro-Argentines of Buenos Aires, 1800–1900*. University of Wisconsin Press, 1980.
Anguita, Eduardo, and Martín Caparrós. *La voluntad: Una historia de la militancia revolucionaria en la Argentina*. Norma, 1998.
Arce, Luz. *El infierno*. Planeta, 1993.
Avelar, Idelber. *The Untimely Present: Postdictatorial Latin American Fiction and the Task of Mourning*. Duke University Press, 2009.
Baker, Cynthia. *Jew*. Rutgers University Press, 2015.
Battle, Diego. "La patria, en primera persona." *La Nación*, 9 Aug. 2007. "Espectáculos." Accessed 31 Aug. 2018.
Bauer, Bruno. *The Jewish Question*. www.marxists.org/archive/marx/works/download/pdf/On%20The%20Jewish%20Question.pdf. Accessed 14 June 2019.
Beasley-Murray, Jon. "Life during Wartime: Infrapolitics and Posthegemony." *III Seminario Crítico-Político Transnacional: Pensamiento y terror social: El*

archivo hispano, Cuenca, Spain 2016. jbmurray.sites.olt.ubc.ca/files/2016/07/cuenca_infrapolitics2.pdf. Accessed 14 June 2019.

– *Posthegemony: Political Theory and Latin America*. University of Minnesota Press, 2010.

Bentes, Ivana. "The Sertão and the Favela in Contemporary Brazilian Film." *The New Brazilian Cinema*, edited by Lúcia Nagib. Oxford University Press, 2009, pp. 121–38.

Bergan, Ronald. *Sergei Eisenstein: A Life in Conflict*. Arcade Publishing, 2016.

Birmajer, Marcelo. *Ser judío en el siglo XXI*. Editorial AMIA, 2004.

– *Los tres mosqueteros*. Debate, 2001.

Blanchot, Maurice. *The Infinite Conversation*. Translated by Susan Hanson. University of Minnesota Press, 1962.

Blaustein, David. "La mirada del cine: De la dictadura hasta hoy." *Centro de atención por el derecho a la identidad de Abuelas de la Plaza de Mayo. Psicoanálisis: Identidad y transmisión*, edited by Alicia Lo Giúdice. Abuelas de la Plaza de Mayo, 2008, pp. 153–8.

Blejmar, Jordana. *Playful Memories: The Autofictional Turn in Post-Dictatorship Argentina*. Palgrave Macmillan, 2016.

Bolaño, Roberto. *Amuleto*. Anagrama, 1999.

Bosteels, Bruno. *Marx and Freud in Latin America: Politics, Psychoanalysis, and Religion in Times of Terror*. Verso, 2012. Kindle.

Braustein, N. "Carta de un judío que no ejerce." *Nueva Sión*, June 1961, p. 2.

Broderson, Diego. "Una película sobre los cuerpos: *Desobediencia*, de Sebastián Lelio." *Página/12*, 6 Aug. 2018. Accessed 31 Aug. 2018.

Brodsky, Adriana, Beatrice Gurwitz, and Rachel Kranson. "Editors' Introduction: Jewish Youth in the Global 1960s." *Journal of Jewish Identities*, vol. 8, no. 2, 2015, pp. 1–11.

Brodsky, Roberto. *Bosque quemado*. Mondadori, 2008.

Burton, Julianne. "Toward a History of Social Documentary in Latin America." *The Social Documentary in Latin America*, edited by Julianne Burton. University of Pittsburgh Press, 1990, pp. 3–30.

Butler, Judith. *Parting Ways: Jewishness and the Critique of Zionism*. Columbia University Press, 2012.

Carroll, James. *Constantine's Sword: The Church and the Jews: A History*. Houghton Mifflin, 2001.

"Carta de un antisionista." *Nueva Sión*, 9 Sept. 1974.

Casey, Michael J. *Che's Afterlife: The Legacy of an Image*. Vintage, 2009.

Cohen, Shaye J.D. *Why Aren't Jewish Women Circumcised? Gender and Covenant in Judaism*. University of California Press, 2005.

Cohn, Norman. *The Pursuit of the Millennium: Revolutionary Millenarians and Mystical Anarchists of the Middle Ages*. Oxford University Press, 1970.

Coonrod Martínez, Elizabeth. "Turning the Page on Mexican Women." *Americas*, vol. 57, no. 6, 2005, pp. 48–53.

Cuchetti, Humberto. *Combatientes de Perón, herederos de Cristo: Peronismo, religión secular y organizaciones de cuadros*. Prometeo, 2010.

de Man, Paul. *Blindness and Insight: Essays in the Rhetoric of Contemporary Criticism*. Oxford University Press, 1983.

del Barco, Oscar. "Comments on the Articles by Jorge Jinkis, Juan Ritvo and Eduardo Grüner in *Conjetural*." *Journal of Latin American Cultural Studies*, vol. 16, no. 2, 2007, pp. 155–82.

– "No Matarás." *Journal of Latin American Cultural Studies*, vol. 16, no. 2, 2007, pp. 115–17.

Derrida, Jacques. *Politics of Friendship*. Verso, 2006.

DiGiovanni, Lisa, and Pedro García-Caro. "The Uncertain Territory of Memory: A Conversation with Chilean Writer Roberto Brodsky." *World Literature Today*, Sept. 2012.

Ditmanson, Harold H. "Judaism and Christianity: A Theology of Co-Existence." *Christianity and Judaism: The Deepening Dialogue*, edited by Richard W. Rousseau S.J. Ridge Row Press, 1983, pp. 183–96.

Dorfman, Ariel. "My Lost Library: Books, Exile, and Identity." *Chronicle of Higher Education*, 18 Sept. 2011. Accessed 20 June 2016.

Elkin, Judith Laikin. *The Jews of Latin America*. Holmes and Meier, 1998.

Eltit, Diamela. *Emergencias: Escritos sobre literatura, arte y política*. Planeta, 2000.

Falicov, Tamara. *The Cinematic Tango: Contemporary Argentine Film*. Wallflower Press, 2007.

Fernández Retamar, Roberto. *Calibán and Other Essays*. Translated by Edward Baker. University of Minnesota Press, 1989.

Finchelstein, Federico. *The Ideological Origins of the Dirty War*. Oxford University Press, 2014,

Foer, Jonathan Safran. *Here I Am*. Farrar, Strauss, and Giroux, 2016.

Forster, Ricardo. *El exilio de la palabra: En torno a lo judío*. Eudeba, 1998.

Foster, David William. *Latin American Documentary Filmmaking: Major Works*. University of Arizona Press, 2013.

Foster, David William, ed. *Latin American Jewish Cultural Production*. Vanderbilt University Press, 2009.

Foucault, Michel. "Truth and Power." *Power/Knowledge. Selected Interviews and Other Writings 1972–1977*, edited by Colin Gordon. Pantheon Books, 1980.

Franco, Jean. "The Nation as Imagined Community." *Dangerous Liaisons: Gender, Nation, and Postcolonial Perspectives*, edited by Anne McClintock, Aamir Mufti, and Ella Shohat. University of Minnesota Press, 1997, pp. 130–7.

Franco, Marina. *Un enemigo para la nación: Orden interno, violencia y "subversión," 1973–1976*. Fondo de Cultura Económica, 2012.

Freud, Sigmund. *The 'Uncanny.' The Standard Edition of the Complete Psychological Works of Sigmund Freud, Volume XVII (1917–1919): An Infantile Neurosis and Other Works*. Vintage, 2001, pp. 217–56.

Freyre, Gilberto. *The Masters and the Slaves: Casa-Grande e Senzala: A Study in the Development of Brazilian Civilization*. Trans. by Samuel Putnam. Knopf, 1963.

Gamerro, Carlos. *Un yuppie en la columna del Che Guevara*. Edhasa, 2011.

García Márquez, Gabriel. "El día que Gabo entrevistó a Firmenich." *Perfil*, 31 May 2014. Accessed 26 Jan. 2016.

Garibotto, Verónica. "Private Narratives and Infant Views: Iconizing 1970s Militancy in Contemporary Argentine Cinema." *Hispanic Research Journal*, vol. 16, no. 3, 2015, pp. 257–72.

Gelman, Juan. "Elogio de la culpa." *Página/12*, 3 Jan. 2000, www.pagina12.com.ar/diario/ultimas/subnotas/20-66463-2014-01-14.html. Accessed 11 June 2019.

Gherman, Michel. "Jews, Zionism, and the Left: Echoes of a Relationship." *Analysis of Current Trends in Antisemitism*, vol. 39, no. 2, 2018. www.degruyter.com/view/j/actap.2018.39.issue-2/issue-files/actap.2018.39.issue-2.xml. Accessed 14 June 2019.

Glickman, Nora, and Ariana Huberman. *Evolving Images: Jewish Latin American Cinema*. University of Texas Press, 2018.

Goldfine, Daniela. "Acts of Memory in the Jewish Argentine Cinematic Present." *Jewish Film and New Media: An International Journal*, vol. 2, no. 1, 2014, pp. 89–105.

– "L'dor V'dor in Recent Jewish Argentinean Literature: The Role of Narrative in the Transmission of Memory." *University of Toronto Journal of Jewish Thought*, vol. 4, 2014, https://tjjt.cjs.utoronto.ca/wp-content/uploads/2015/01/Goldfine.pdf. Accessed 17 June 2019.

– "*Hacer patria* de David Blaustein: Reconstrucción colectiva e historia judea-argentina reciente." *Journal of Islamic and Middle Eastern Multidisciplinary Studies*, vol. 1, no. 1, 2011, Article 3.

Goldman, Ilene S. "Mexican Women, Jewish Women: *Novia que te vea* from Book to Screen and Back Again." *Latin American Jewish Cultural Production*, edited by David William Foster Vanderbilt University Press, 2009, loc. 2240–36, Kindle.

Goñi, Uki. *The Real Odessa: How Perón Brought the Nazi War Criminals to Argentina*. Granta, 2002.

Graff Zivin, Erin. "Beyond Jameson: The Metapolitics of Allegory." *Yearbook of Comparative Literature*, vol. 61, 2015, pp. 156–73.

– *The Wandering Signifier: Rhetoric of Jewishness in the Latin American Imaginary*. Duke University Press, 2008.

Gramsci, Antonio. *The Prison Notebooks*. International Publishers, 1971.

Gross, Raphael. *Carl Schmitt and the Jews: The "Jewish Question," the Holocaust, and German Legal Theory*. University of Wisconsin Press, 2007.

Guerra, Lillian. *Visions of Power in Cuba: Revolution, Redemption, and Resistance, 1959–1971*. University of North Carolina Press, 2012.

Gundermann, Christian. *Actos melancólicos: Formas de resistencia en la postdictadura argentina*. Beatriz Viterbo, 2007.

Gurwitz, Beatrice. "Generation and Innovation in the Rise of an *Argentine*-Jewish Community, 1960–1967." *The New Jewish Argentina: Facets of Jewish Experiences in the Southern Cone*, edited by Raanan Rein and Adriana Brodsky. Brill, 2013, pp. 235–62.

Hall, Stuart. Introduction. *Representation: Cultural Representations and Signifying Practices*, edited by Stuart Hall, Sage, 2003, pp. 1–12.

Heker, Liliana. *El fin de la historia*. Alfaguara, 1996.

Hernández Arregui, Juan José. "La imagen colonizada de la Argentina." *Contra Borges*, edited by Juan Fló. Galerna, 1978, pp. 89–111.

Hershfield, Joanne. "Women's Pictures: Identity and Representation in Recent Mexican Cinema." *Canadian Journal of Film Studies / Revue canadienne d'études cinématographiques*, vol. 6, no. 1, 1997, pp. 61–77.

Hirsch, Marianne. *The Generation of Postmemory: Writing and Visual Culture after the Holocaust*. Columbia University Press, 2012.

– "The Generation of Postmemory." *Poetics Today*, vol. 29, 2008, pp. 103–28.

Horowitz, Yael, and Rae Gaines. "We Don't Have to Choose between Dyke and Jewish Identities." *Washington Blade*, 6 June 2019, www.washingtonblade.com/2019/06/06/we-dont-have-to-choose-between-dyke-and-jewish-identities/. Accessed 11 June 2019.

Hortiguera, Hugo. "Políticas del recuerdo y memorias de la política en *El secreto de sus ojos* de Juan José Campanella." *Ciberletras*, vol. 24, 2010.

Huberman, Ariana. "Beyond Exotic: Jewish Mysticism and the Supernatural in the Works of Alejandro Jodorowsky." *Latin American Jewish Cultural Production*, edited by David William Foster. Vanderbilt, 2009, loc. 686–953. Kindle.

Hussar, James. "*Los gauchos judíos* en su centenario." *Hispanófila*, vol. 163, 2011, pp. 39–52.

Hvidt, Niels Christian. *Christian Prophecy: The Post-Biblical Tradition*. Oxford University Press, 2007.

Jameson, Fredric. *The Ideology of Theory: Essays 1971–1986*. University of Minnesota Press, 1988.

Janzen, Rebecca. *The National Body in Mexican Literature: Collective Challenges to Biopolitical Control*. Palgrave Macmillan, 2015.

Jerozolimski, Ana. "Gonzalo Rodríguez Fábregas: Director de *El barrio de los judíos*." *Montevideo Portal*, 27 Sept. 2011, http://columnistas.montevideo.com.uy/uc_487751.html. Accessed 13 June 2019.

Jinkis, Jorge. "A Reply to Oscar del Barco." *Journal of Latin American Cultural Studies*, vol. 16, no. 2, 2007, pp. 119–25.

Jodorowsky, Alejandro. *La danza de la realidad*. Siruela, 2003.

Kahan, Emmanuel. "Algunos usos del conflicto en Israel-Palestina en Argentina: Debates en torno al conflicto árabe-israelí entre el tercer peronismo y la última dictadura militar (1973–1983)." *Nuevos Mundos, Mundos Nuevos*, vol. 2, 2014, pp. 1–20.

– *Recuerdos que mienten un poco: Vida y memoria de la experiencia judía durante la última dictadura militar*. Prometeo, 2014.

King, John. *Magical Reels: A History of Cinema in Latin America*. Verso, 1990.

Kittleson, Roger. *The Country of Football: Soccer and the Making of Modern Brazil*. University of California Press, 2014.

Klein, Misha. *Kosher Feijoada and Other Paradoxes of Jewish Life in São Paolo*. University Press of Florida, 2016.

Kohan, Martín. *Museo de la revolución*. Mondadori, 2006.

Konner, Melvin. *The Jewish Body*. Random House, 2009.

Krauze, Enrique. *Redeemers: Ideas and Power in Latin America*. HarperCollins, 2011. Kindle.

Krupnik, Adrián. "Cuando camino al Kibutz vieron pasar al Che. Radicalización política y juventud judía: Argentina 1966–1976." *Marginados y consagrados. Nuevos estudios sobre la vida judía en Argentina*, edited by Emmanuel Kahan, Laura Schenquer, Damian Setton, and Alicia Dujovne. Lumiére, 2011, pp. 311–27.

Lesser, Jeffrey. "How the Jews Became Japanese and Other Stories of Nation and Identity." *Jewish History*, vol. 18, no. 1, 2004, pp. 7–17.

– *Welcoming the Undesirables: Brazil and the Jewish Question*. University of California Press, 1995.

Levinas, Emmanuel. "Being Jewish." The 1947 essay "Etre juif" translated by Mary Beth Mader. *Contintental Philosophy Review*, vol. 40, 2007, pp. 205–10.

Levinson, Hilary. "Thinking Postmemory through Translation in Roberto Brodsky's *Bosque quemado*." *Revista Canadiense de Estudios Hispánicos*, vol. 39, no. 3, 2015, pp. 589–611.

Levitz, Jacob. "The Jewish Community in Mexico: Its Life and Education, 1900–1954." Ph.D. dissertation, Dropsie College for Hebrew and Cognate Learning, 1954.

Lie, Nadia. "Two Forms of Multidirectional Memory: *Un passaporte Húngaro* and *El abrazo partido*." *European Review*, vol. 22, no. 4, 2014, pp. 575–84.

Lindstrom, Naomi. "La expresión profética y apocalíptica en la producción de Alejandro Jodorowsky." *Chasqui*, vol. 42, no. 2, 2013, pp. 125–133.

Löwy, Michael. "Christianity of Liberation." *Coloniality at Large*, edited by Enrique Dussel, Mabel Moraña, and Carlos Jáuregui. Duke University Press, 2008, pp. 350–9.

Luna, Ilana Dann. *Adapting Gender: Mexican Feminisms from Literature to Film*. State University of New York Press, 2017.

Maguire, Geoffrey. *The Politics of Postmemory: Violence and Victimhood in Contemporary Argentine Culture*. Palgrave Macmillan, 2017.

Mahler, Anne Garland. *From the Tricontinental to the Global South: Race, Radicalism, and Transnational Solidarity*. Duke University Press, 2018.

– "The Global South in the Belly of the Beast: Viewing African American Civil Rights through a Tricontinental Lens." *Latin American Research Review*, vol. 50, no. 1, 2015, pp. 95–116.

Manzano, Valeria. *The Age of Youth in Argentina: Culture, Politics, and Sexuality from Perón to Videla*. University of North Carolina Press, 2014.

Margalit, Elkana. "Social and Intellectual Origins of the Hashomer Hatzair Youth Movement, 1913–1920." *Essential Papers on Jews and the Left*, edited by Ezra Mendelsohn. New York University Press, 1997, pp. 145–65.

Márquez, Francisco. "Nicolás Prividera: 'El horizonte del arte es poder ser cuestionador de todo.'" *La Izquierda Diario*, 27 Jan. 2015, www.laizquierdadiario.com/Nicolas-Prividera-El-horizonte-del-arte-es-poder-ser-cuestionador-de-todo. Accessed 13 June 2019.

Martín-Cabrera, Luis, and Daniel Noemi Voionmaa. "Class Conflict, State of Exception and Radical Justice in *Machuca* by Andrés Wood." *Journal of Latin American Cultural Studies*, vol. 16, no. 1, 2007, pp. 63–80.

Meter, Alejandro. "*The Year My Parents Went on Vacation*: A Jewish Journey in the Land of Soccer." *Evolving Images: Jewish Latin American Cinema*, edited by Nora Glickman and Ariana Huberman. University of Texas Press, 2018, pp. 49–61.

Mignolo, Walter D. *The Idea of Latin America*. Blackwell Publishing, 2005.

Moore, Deborah Dash. Introduction. *American Jewish Identity Politics*, edited by Deborah Dash Moore. University of Michigan Press, 2008, pp. 1–22.

Munck, Ronaldo, and Pablo Pozzi. "Israel, Palestine, and Latin America: Conflictual Relationships." *Latin American Perspectives*, vol. 46, no. 3, 2019, pp. 4–12.

Naficy, Hamid. *An Accented Cinema: Exilic and Diasporic Filmmaking*. Princeton University Press, 2001.

Navarro, Vinicius, and Juan Carlos Rodríguez. Introduction. *New Documentaries in Latin America*, edited by Vinicius Navarro and Juan Carlos Rodríguez. Palgrave, 2014, pp. 1–21.

Navarro-Rosenblatt, Valeria. "The Untold History: Voices of Non-affiliated Jews in Chile, 1940–1990." *The New Ethnic Studies in Latin America*, edited by Raanan Rein, Stefan Rinke, and Nadia Zysman. Brill, 2017, pp. 128–147.

Nouzeilles, Gabriela. "Postmemory Cinema and the Future of the Past in Albertina Carri's *Los rubios*." *Journal of Latin American Cultural Studies*, vol. 14, no. 3, 2005, pp. 263–78.

Nuriel, Patricia. "On Meerapfel's *My German Friend*." *Jewish Film and New Media: An International Journal*, vol. 2, no. 1, 2014, pp. 106–8.

O'Ryan, Mariana Casale. *The Making of Jorge Luis Borges as an Argentine Cultural Icon*. Modern Humanities Research Association, 2014.

Page, Joanna. *Crisis and Capitalism in Contemporary Argentine Cinema*. Duke University Press, 2009.

Peiro, Claudia. "Murió Alejandro Álvarez, mítico fundador de Guardia de Hierro." *Infobae*, 6 June 2016, www.infobae.com/politica/2016/06/06/murio-alejandro-alvarez-mitico-fundador-de-guardia-de-hierro/. Accessed 12 June 2017.

Petruzzi, Liana. "Julia Salazar Is a Cautionary Tale: Question Israel and Your Jewishness Will Be Questioned." *Forward*, 29 Aug. 2018. Accessed 31 Aug. 2018.

Pinázza, Natalia. "Diaspora and National Identity in Daniel Burman's *El abrazo partido*." *Journal of Latin American Cultural Studies*, vol. 21, no. 3, 2012, pp. 437–48.

Plager, Silvia. *La rabina*. Planeta, 2006.

Podalsky, Laura. "Affecting Legacies: Historical Memory and Contemporary Structures of Feeling in *Madagascar* and *Amores perros*." *Screen*, vol. 43, no. 3, 2003, pp. 277–94.

Prell, Riv-Ellen. "Why Jewish Princesses Don't Sweat: Desire and Consumption in Postwar American Jewish Culture." *People of the Body: Jews and Judaism from an Embodied Perspective*, edited by Howard Eilberg-Schwartz. State University of New York Press, 1992, pp. 329–59.

Pridgeon, Stephanie. "Exposing Mechanisms of Truth and Memory in 21st-Century Latin American Documentary Film: Autobiography, Testimonial Language, and the Politics of Production." *alter/nativas: latin american cultural studies journal*, vol. 6, 2016. Web.

– "Metamorphoses of 1968: The Israel-Palestine Question in Tomás Abraham's *La dificultad*." *Latin American Perspectives*, vol. 46, no. 3, 2019, pp. 55–70.

– "Silences between Jewishness and Indigeneity in Eduardo Halfon's *Mañana nunca lo hablamos*." *Revista Canadiense de Estudios Hispánicos*, vol. 42, no. 1, 2017, pp. 99–121.

– "'Yo creo que terminé todas mis guerras': Friendship and Politics Between Jews and Non-Jews in Jeanine Meerapfel's *El amigo alemán*." *Revista de Estudios Hispánicos*, vol. 51, no. 1 2017, pp. 101–25.

Prieto, Adolfo. "Selección de *Borges y la nueva generación*." *Antiborges*, edited by Martín Lafforgue. Vergara, 1999, pp. 55–85.

Prividera, Nicolás. *El país del cine: Para una historia política del nuevo cine argentino*. Los Ríos, 2014.

Pron, Patricio. *El espíritu de mis padres sigue subiendo en la lluvia*. Mondadori, 2011.

Rajca, Andrew. *Dissensual Subjects: Memory, Human Rights, and Postdictatorship in Argentina, Brazil, and Uruguay*. Northwestern University Press, 2018.

Ran, Amalia. "From a Dream to Reality: Representations of Israel in Contemporary Jewish Latin American Film." *Evolving Images: Jewish Latin American Cinema*, edited by Nora Glickman and Ariana Huberman. University of Texas Press, 2018, pp. 164–77.

– "'Israel': An Abstract Concept or Concrete Reality in Recent Judeo-Argentinean Narrative?" *Jewish Latin American Cultural Production*, edited by David William Foster. Vanderbilt University Press, 2009, loc. 441–682. Kindle.

Rashkin, Elissa. *Women Filmmakers in Mexico: The Country of Which We Dream.* University of Texas Press, 2001.

Reati, Fernando. "El Ford Falcon: Un ícono del terror en el imaginario argentino de la posdictadura." *Revista de Estudios Hispánicos*, vol. 43, no. 2, 2009, pp. 385–407.

Reber, Dierdra. *Coming to Our Senses: Affect and an Order of Things for Global Culture.* Columbia University Press, 2016.

– "Love as Politics: *Amores perros* and the Emotional Aesthetics of Neoliberalism." *Journal of Latin American Cultural Studies*, vol. 19, no. 3, 2010, pp. 279–98.

Rein, Raanan. *Argentine Jews or Jewish Argentines? Essays on Ethnicity, Identity, and Diaspora.* Brill, 2010.

– *Los muchachos peronistas judíos: Los argentinos judíos y el apoyo al justicialismo.* Sudamericana, 2015.

Rein, Raanan, and Eliezer Nowordworski. *Argentina, Israel y los judíos: Encuentros y desencuentros, mitos y realidades.* Lumière, 2001.

Rein, Raanan, and Tzvi Tal. "Becoming Part of the Moving Story: Jews on the Latin American Screen." *Jewish Film and New Media: An International Journal*, vol. 2, no. 1, 2014, pp. 1–8.

"Religion in Latin America: Widespread Change in a Historically Catholic Region." PEW Research Center. 13 Nov. 2014. *Religion and Public Life.* Accessed 31 Aug. 2018.

Renov, Michael. *The Subject of Documentary.* University of Minnesota Press, 2004.

Richard, Nelly. *La insubordinación de los signos: Cambio político, transformaciones culturales y poéticas de la crisis.* Cuarto Propio, 1994.

Richards, Keith J. "País de película: El cine boliviano en el siglo XXI." *Nuestra América*, vol. 3, 2007, pp. 147–62.

Rocha, Carolina. "Children's View of State-Sponsored Violence in Latin America." *Representing History, Class, and Gender in Spain and Latin America*, edited by Carolina Rocha and Georgia Seminet. Palgrave Macmillan, 2012, pp. 83–100.

– "Cine despolitizado de principio de siglo: *Bar el chino* y *El abrazo partido.*" *Bulletin of Spanish Studies*, vol. 85, no. 3, 2008, pp. 335–49.

– "Jewish Cinematic Self-Representations in Contemporary Argentine and Brazilian Films." *Journal of Modern Jewish Studies*, vol. 9, no. 1, 2010, pp. 37–48.

– "Judaísmo e identidad masculina en la trilogía de Daniel Burman." *Letras Hispanas*, vol. 4, no. 2, 2007, pp. 26–37.

Rocha, Carolina, and Georgia Seminet. *Screening Minors in Latin American Cinema.* Lexington Books, 2014.

Rocha, Glauber. "Aesthetics of Hunger." 1965. https://www.amherst.edu/media/view/38122/original/ROCHA_Aesth_Hunger.pdf. Accessed 8 April 2020.

Rodríguez Marcos, Javier. "Lo contrario del olvido no es la memoria, sino la verdad: Entrevista a Juan Gelman." *El País*, 16 Oct. 2004.

Rozitchner, León. *Acerca de la derrota y de los vencidos*. Biblioteca Nacional, 2012.

– "Primero hay que saber vivir: Del vivirás materno al no matarás paterno." *No Matar: Sobre la Responsabilidad*. Universidad Nacional de Córdoba, 2014, pp. 367–406.

– *Ser judío*. Ediciones de la Flor, 1967.

Salazkina, Masha. *In Excess: Sergei Eisenstein's Mexico*. University of Chicago Press, 2009.

Sánchez Prado, Ignacio. "*Amores perros*: Exotic Violence and Neoliberal Fear." *Journal of Latin American Cultural Studies*, vol. 15, no. 1, 2006, pp. 39–57.

– *Screening Neoliberalism: Transforming Mexican Cinema, 1988–2012*. Vanderbilt University Press, 2012.

Sanok, Catherine. *Her Life Historical: Exemplarity and Female Saints' Lives in Late Medieval England*. University of Pennsylvania Press, 2007.

Sarlo, Beatriz. *Siete ensayos sobre Walter Benjamin*. Fondo de Cultura Económica, 2000.

– *Tiempo pasado: Cultura de la memoria y giro subjetivo*. Siglo XXI, 2006.

Schmitt, Carl. *The Concept of the Political*. Translation of 1932 German original with introduction by George Schwab. Rutgers University Press, 1976.

Scott. A.O. "A Brazilian Boy, Alone in the Tumult of 1970." *New York Times*, 15 Feb. 2008, www.nytimes.com/2008/02/15/movies/15vaca.html. Accessed 11 June 2019.

Selimoviç, Inela. *Affective Moments in the Films of Martel, Carri, and Puenzo*. Palgrave Macmillan, 2018.

Senderey, Moisés. *Historia de la colectividad israelita de Chile*. Dos Yidische Worst, 1956.

Senkman, Leonardo. *Antisemitismo en la Argentina*. Centro Editor de América Latina, 1989.

Sheinin, David, and Lois Baer Barr. *The Jewish Diaspora in Latin America: New Studies on History and Literature*. Garland, 1996.

Shoji, Kaori. "'Latin America's Woody Allen' on Jewish Life in Argentina." *Japan Times*, 20 Jan. 2006, www.japantimes.co.jp/culture/2006/01/20/films/latin-americas-woody-allenon-jewish-life-in-argentina/#.XP_De5NKgxc. Accessed 11 June 2019.

Silverstein, Stephen. "Jorge Luis Borges's Poetic Response to the Arab-Israeli Six Day War." *Hipertexto*, vol. 19, 2014, pp.29–40.

– *The Merchant of Havana: The Jew in the Abolitionist Archive*. Vanderbilt University Press, 2016.

Skidmore, Thomas. "Gilberto Freyre and the Early Brazilian Republic: Some Notes on Methodology." *Comparative Studies in Society and History*, vol. 6, no. 4, July 1964, pp. 490–505.

Slabodsky, Santiago. *Decolonial Judaism: Triumphal Failures of Barbaric Thinking*. Palgrave Macmillan, 2014.

Slomp, Gabriella. "Carl Schmitt on Friendship: Polemics and Diagnostics." *Critical Review of International Social and Political Philosophy*, vol. 10, no. 2, 2007, pp. 199–213.

Solanas, Fernando "Pino," and Octavio Getino. "Towards a Third Cinema." *Documentary Is Never Neutral*, http://documentaryisneverneutral.com/words/camasgun.html. Accessed 16 June 2019.

Sommer, Doris. *Foundational Fictions: The National Romances of Latin America*. University of California Press, 1993.

Stavans, Ilan. "Think Julia Salazar 'Isn't Jewish Enough'? You're Writing Off All Latin American Jews." *Forward*, 28 Aug. 2018. "Opinion." Accessed 31 Aug. 2018.

– Introduction. *Tropical Synagogues: Short Stories by Jewish-Latin American Writers*, edited by Ilan Stavans. Holmes and Meier, 1994, pp. 1–38.

Stein, Rebecca. "Performative Zion: Butler's *Parting Ways*." *Studies in American Jewish Literature*, vol. 33, no. 2, 2014, pp. 259–63.

Stein, Shawn. "*O ano em que meus pais saíram de férias* de Cao Hamburger: Desmitifição ou propagação de democracia racial?" *Hispania*, vol. 97, no. 2, 2014, pp. 256–63.

Stockton, Kathryn Bond. *The Queer Child, or Growing Sideways in the Twentieth Century*. Duke University Press, 2009.

Strong, Tracy B. Foreword. "Dimensions of the New Debate around Carl Schmitt." *The Concept of the Political, Expanded Edition*, by Carl Schmitt, translation and introduction by George Schwab, notes by Leo Strauss. University of Chicago Press, 1995, pp. ix–xxxi.

Suárez, Pablo. "The Burman Identity." *Film Comment*, vol. 42, no. 3, 2006, pp. 54–9.

Sutton, Barbara. *Bodies in Crisis: Culture, Violence, and Women's Resistance in Neoliberal Argentina*. Rutgers University Press, 2010.

Tal, Tzvi. "Jewish Puberty in Contemporary Latin American Cinema: Constructing Judeo-Latinidad." *Returning to Babel: Jewish Latin American Experiences, Representations, and Identity*, edited by Jean Axelrad Cahan and Amalia Ran. Brill, 2011, pp. 143–58.

– "The Other Becomes Mainstream: Jews in Contemporary Argentine Cinema." *The New Jewish Argentina: Facets of Jewish Experiences in the Southern Cone*, edited by Raanan Rein and Adriana Brodsky. Brill, 2013, pp. 365–91.

Tally, Robert. "Fredric Jameson and the Controversy over 'Third-World Literature in the Era of Multinational Capitalism.'" *Global South Studies: A Collective Publication with the Global South*. Web. Accessed 30 Aug. 2018.

Tompkins, Cynthia. *Experimental Cinema in Latin America: History and Aesthetics*. University of Texas Press, 2014.

Torres Gutiérrez, Osvaldo. "Las 'ratas' del Movimiento de Izquierda Revolucionaria (MIR) de Chile." *Revista de Estudios sobre Genocidio*, vol. 2, 2008, pp. 56–68.

Traverso, Antonio. "Contemporary Chilean Cinema and Traumatic Memory: Andrés Wood's *Machuca* and Raúl Ruiz's *Le domaine perdu*." *IM Interactive Media: E-Journal of the National Academy of Screen and Sound*, vol. 4, 2008, pp. 1–26.

Vasconcelos, José. "La raza cósmica." *Biblioteca Virtual*, http://www.biblioteca.org.ar/libros/1289.pdf. Accessed 30 Aug. 2018.

Verbitsky, Horacio. *El silencio: De Paulo VI a Bergoglio. Las relaciones secretas de la iglesia con la ESMA*. Sudamericana, 2005.

Vezzetti, Hugo. "Archivo y memorias del presente: *Elefante blanco* de Pablo Trapero: El padre Mugica, los pobres y la violencia." *A Contracorriente: A Journal on Social History and Literature in Latin America*, vol. 12, no. 1, 2014, pp. 179–90.

– *Sobre la violencia revolucionaria: Memorias y olvidos*. Siglo XXI, 2009.

Vidal, Hernán. "Ariel Dorfman: The Residue of Hope after Public Personae Construction." *Hispanic Issues Series*, 5, 2012, pp. 4–24.

Viñas, David. "Borges y la nueva generación." *Antiborges*, edited by Martín Lafforgue. Vergara, 1999, pp. 77–85.

Visacovsky, Nerina. *Argentinos, judíos y camaradas: Tras la utopía socialista*. Editorial Biblos, 2015. Kindle.

Vohnsen, Mirna. *Portrayals of Jews in Contemporary Argentine Cinema: Rethinking Argentinidad*. Támesis, 2019.

Wade, Peter. *Race and Ethnicity in Latin America*. Pluto Press, 1997.

Wamba Gaviña, Graciela. "La recepción de Walter Benjamin en la Argentina." *Sobre Walter Benjamin: Vanguardias, historia, estética y literature: Una visión latinoamericana*, edited by Gabriela Massuh and Silvia Fehrmann. Alianza Editorial and Goethe-Institut, 1993.

Waugh, Thomas. *The Right to Play Oneself: Looking Back on Documentary*. University of Minnesota Press, 2011.

Williams, Raymond. *Marxism and Literature*. Oxford University Press, 1977.

Xavier, Ismail. *Allegories of Underdevelopment: Aesthetics and Politics in Modern Brazilian Cinema*. University of Minnesota Press, 1997.

Yim, Ho-Joon. "La infancia como mito e historia en *La lengua de las mariposas* (1999) y *Machuca* (2004)." *Bulletin of Hispanic Studies*, vol. 94, no. 2, 2017, pp. 199–214.

Žižek, Slavoj. *For They Know Not What They Do: Enjoyment as a Political Factor*. Verso, 2008.

Index

www.ingramcontent.com/pod-product-compliance
Lightning Source LLC
LaVergne TN
LVHW090159080826
844660LV00013B/872/J
9781487508142